THE CRIMINAL MIND

ISAAC RAY AWARD BOOKS
CHOSEN BY THE
AMERICAN PSYCHIATRIC ASSOCIATION

1953	THE PSYCHIATRIST AND THE LAW	*Winfred Overholser*
1954	THE PSYCHOLOGY OF THE CRIMINAL ACT AND PUNISHMENT	*Gregory Zilboorg*
1955	THE GUILTY MIND	*John Biggs, Jr.*
1956	THE URGE TO PUNISH	*Henry Weihofen*
1957	THE CRIMINAL MIND	*Philip Q. Roche*
1958	Work in progress	*Manfred Guttmacher*

THE CRIMINAL MIND . . . A STUDY OF COMMUNICATION BETWEEN THE CRIMINAL LAW AND PSYCHIATRY

By PHILIP Q. ROCHE, M.D.

GREENWOOD PRESS, PUBLISHERS
WESTPORT, CONNECTICUT

70742

Library of Congress Cataloging in Publication Data

Roche, Philip Q
    The criminal mind.

    Reprint of the 1958 ed. published by Farrar, Straus
and Cudahy, New York.
    Includes bibliographical references and index.
    1. Insanity--Jurisprudence--United States.
2. Criminal liability--United States. 3. Forensic
psychiatry. 4. Insane, Criminal and dangerous. I. Title.
[KF9242.R6 1976]   345'.73'04   76-28524
ISBN 0-8371-9056-8

Copyright © 1958 by Philip Q. Roche

All rights reserved

Originally published in 1958 by Farrar, Straus and Cudahy,
New York

Reprinted with the permission of Farrar, Straus & Giroux, Inc.

Reprinted in 1976 by Greenwood Press,
a division of Williamhouse-Regency Inc.

Library of Congress Catalog Card Number 76-28524

ISBN 0-8371-9056-8

Printed in the United States of America

TO
JOCELYN AND ROBIN

CONTENTS

	Introduction	ix
I	THE MID-20TH CENTURY SETTING OF AMERICAN CRIMINAL LAW AND PSYCHIATRY	1
II	WHAT IS MENTAL ILLNESS?	14
III	THE CRIMINAL LAW AND PSYCHIATRY IN ACTION: THE PRE-TRIAL PHASE	30
IV	THE CRIMINAL LAW AND PSYCHIATRY IN ACTION: THE CRIMINAL TRIAL	64
V	THE CRIMINAL LAW AND PSYCHIATRY IN ACTION: THE POST-TRIAL PHASE	196
VI	SUMMARY	244
	Notes	275
	Index	293

INTRODUCTION

This book is an expanded statement of the Fifth Annual Isaac Ray Award Lectures which were delivered at the University of Michigan in the spring of 1957.

In 1952 the American Psychiatric Association established the Isaac Ray Award, to be conferred annually upon a person deemed "most worthy by reason of his contribution to the improvement of the relations of law and psychiatry." Four awardees have prepared the way to an understanding and agreement between criminal law and psychiatry: Dr. Winfred Overholser, past President of the American Psychiatric Association; Dr. Gregory Zilboorg, distinguished historian of medical psychology; Judge John Biggs, Jr., Chief Judge, Third Judicial Circuit Court of the United States; and Henry Weihofen, Professor of Law, University of New Mexico. Their contributions have indeed imposed upon those who follow a high standard of scholarship and expression.

In this book the reader will find less of a description of the "criminal mind" in the clinical conventions of psychiatry, and more of a point of view and invitation to both lawyer and psychiatrist to re-examine the premises upon which we structure our concepts of mental illness and the *subjective element* of crime.

The major implication of this point of view is that conflict cannot be resolved until the lawyer and the psychiatrist join in an acceptance that the "real world" is unconsciously shaped and colored by our language habits which predispose certain interpretations; that the verbal world of abstraction is illusory and detached from the facts of life. A further implication of this point of view is that as long as traditional criminal justice continues as an autonomous system of supernatural concepts, which cannot be defined in terms of experience, the positive sciences will continue outside of its operations and the relations of criminal law and psychiatry will remain tensional.

A concluding implication in this point of view invites a reassessment of the psychiatrist's function in criminal justice. A realignment of psychiatry will limit it in the public (adversary) phase of criminal justice and enlarge its function in the pre- and post-trial phases.

In the creation of these lectures, I have accumulated a large debt to others. I am mindful of my debt to several thousand inmates I came to know at the Eastern State Penitentiary, Philadelphia, in the years of 1934 to 1945. The late William Conquest and the young cleric assented to my use of their life stories. I had brief contact with the late James Ernest Monroe. I never met the late Edward Lester Gibbs, but I came to know him through Richard Gehman who kindly consented to my free use of his sympathetic delineation of Gibbs' tragic life in *A Murder in Paradise*. I have not met James Colbert Smith, Monte Durham, or the college student except through the pages of legal documents. I had extended contact with Francis X. Ballem, whose fate may have been determined by the time these pages come to print.

I am grateful to Judge John Biggs, Jr., Professor Samuel Polsky of the Temple University Law School, and David and Jean Burrell for their unstinting diligence in reading the manuscript and for their criticisms, suggestions, and guidance in matters of law. Parts of the manuscript were read and criticized by Judge Joseph C. Sloane, Dr. Leo H. Bartemeier, Dr. Edward A. Strecker, Dr. Albert M. Biele, Dr. Andrew S. Watson and Jacquelyn Fay. William Turner, Albert Blum-

INTRODUCTION xi

berg, William J. Woolston and other members of the Bar gave valuable assistance in the analysis of the cases, particularly those of Ballem and the college boy. I can only hope that this book will vindicate the confidence conveyed in the decision of my fellow colleagues of the American Psychiatric Association to designate me as the fifth Isaac Ray awardee.

An expression of appreciation goes to President Harlan Hatcher and Deans E. Blythe Stason and A. C. Furstenburg respectively of the Law and Medical Schools and Dr. Raymond W. Waggoner, Director, Neuropsychiatric Institute and Chairman of the Department of Psychiatry, University of Michigan, for their hospitality and their facilities for the presentation of these lectures to a discriminating audience.

I am in inestimable debt to Mrs. Jennie M. Harmer for her patient, unflagging diligence in typing and proofing the manuscript, and in verifying references.

P. Q. R.

Miquon
Pennsylvania

I THE MID-20TH CENTURY SETTING OF AMERICAN CRIMINAL LAW AND PSYCHIATRY

> The Nile Valley is for us therefore the earliest social arena, where we may observe man victoriously emerging from an age-long struggle with nature, and entering this new arena of social forces, to begin the baffling struggle of mankind with himself—a struggle which has hardly passed beyond its beginning at the present day.
>
> JAMES H. BREASTED [1]

"The movement of highest thought has been from magic through religion to science," wrote Sir James G. Frazer in *The Golden Bough*. The recorded history of man's intellectual achievement in Frazer's imagery is compared to a long rope woven of three colored threads, the black thread of magic, the red thread of religion, and the white thread of science. History begins with the black, then moves to black and red, and in time shows a white thread or two. In modern times the white thread imparts a dominance, but the black is still discernible and the red exists in large measure. In this metaphor one could identify the highly advanced knowledge of the outer, physical world as an attribute of science, but our knowledge of the inner world of man himself has yet to attain a growth, through which can be achieved a means of exerting a rational control of his social life. Frazer's lifeline is now showing a few golden strands of man's self-knowledge.

Our century worships science. In everyday talk of science there is a confusion of what it actually is with what passes for it in the notions of those who are daily assailed in mass communication with "scientific" pronouncements and science for sale. Max Otto laments the false notion which is durable in the noun "science" and says that if the word had never come into use and "a verb like *sciencing* or *scienced*" were used instead, the popular mind would not have come to regard "that a thing must exist corresponding to every noun in the language." [2]

People think of science not in terms of how scientists think but

of something above and beyond all this, a huge *entity* which has an independent existence of its own. Science is a kind of metaphysical mother wooed by men of science and giving birth to a mighty progeny of atoms, molecules, chemical elements and laws of nature not to speak of vitamins, electric light bulbs, radio tubes, yeast cakes, breakfast foods and cosmetics. . . . A good deal of magical belief hovers over science as a kind of superstition which surrounds its sacred buildings, its mysteries, its esoteric language, its priests, and acolytes, even its incantations and mummeries.[3]

We do not regard science as a method of thinking, of viewpoints, attitudes that lead to a successful solution of social problems. We know more of what scientists *make* than we do of what they *know*. This same science is used today more to exploit man in a consumer economy rather than to develop his creativity and higher capacity for orderly social life. From the foregoing there might arise the conclusion that sanity implies the universal mastery of science in the entirety of its technical aspects. This is not intended. What is implied is that science as a working method in orientation insures the largest measure of foresight and behavioral adaptability. The scientific way of life implies the attainment and maintenance of sanity. The prescientific orientation which has held dominance for so many centuries implies the high incidence of social maladaptations in its full range. Ideally, a scientific projection system is one in which self-awareness of projection is an incessant, austere discipline. Even the most dedicated scientist must be eternally watchful that his wishes are not projected into his findings. This is difficult since the larger part of the projection process goes on unconsciously, both in waking life and in sleep, and since it is emotionally rooted in the earliest pre-logical projection system of the child. A scientist must live in his culture and he can examine it only from within. A professional scientist may be almost a true one in his laboratory or a philosopher almost a true one in his study, and yet in his fellowship with colleagues or in his domestic life a prescientific orientation may show itself.

Like anyone else the scientist has a cultural heritage of the black and red threads; hence he cannot be of one piece and is probably least so when he enters into the area of social tensions uncovered in moral problems. Judges and lawyers are sometimes scientific in their outlook and yet can view only from within the formalism of the law which is derived largely from the black thread of magic with the red thread of religion as an overlay. That the scientist can communicate at all with the law arises from the fact that judges and lawyers are not entirely committed to the magic of social forms. Perhaps in the unconscious of both scientist and lawyer there exists a half-belief in the magic which characterizes our culture's method of evaluation. In this the scientist falters; only the arbiters of culture have a sense of certainty.

The relationship of criminal law to medical psychology has been a kind of symbiosis of two systems of evaluating reality and as well a relationship of men. The history of the relationship is long and in it, from its dim beginnings to the present, can be discerned the lineaments of man's developing scientific orientation to the outer physical world and the persistence of his inner primal ties with his magical religious past. Criminal law has remained relatively unchanged, while the rise of medical psychology has been recent and rapid. When viewed side by side the metaphor of symbiosis still holds, although less firmly. Law and psychology do not stand apart in clear antithesis: only the methods employed by men who profess them. Perhaps a more pertinent distinction resides in Vaihinger's statement that "jurisprudence is not really a science of objective reality but a science of arbitrary human relations." [4] Both law and psychiatry retain vestiges common to man's limitations as he relates himself to his surrounding reality. One cannot say that the psychiatrist is scientific and the lawyer unscientific. Edward S. Robinson states in his book, *Law and the Lawyers*, "The world is not divided into scientific people and unscientific people, rather into groups of problems for which the general culture provides us with a scientific or an unscientific approach." [5] The practice of psychiatry and that of the law in action comes to the relationship of men. This relationship, as in all other human concerns, is that of communication.

Law and psychiatry are today overlapped and extended, and some confusion results from the fact that each reaches for the responsibility for the management, prevention and control of antisocial behavior. There remains to be developed a means of common endeavor within the frame of scientific method. It seems unlikely that much can be achieved by quarreling about responsibility—it is everyone's. The problem is a philosophic one touching upon our basic assumptions, our orientation to the universe and upon the nature of human communication.

The conflict between a "psychiatric" and a "legal" approach to wrong-doing probably goes back to the dawn of conscience. The ancient Greeks distinguished between the so-called paranoias, dementias, hypochondrias and other mental disorders but never managed to get these concepts into a legal system. On the other hand, the Romans lumped mental disorder under the term *insaniens* which provided the medium for judicial decision. Some are content with a dismissal of this conflict between lawyer and psychiatrist as a continuing reluctance of the psychiatrist to "submit to the demands of the 'Roman' legalism just as the lawyers are reluctant to submit to the vagaries of 'Greek' science." [6] However, this is descriptive of the reluctance of men, of their lack of common approach and effective communication. Neither Roman "legalism" nor Greek "vagaries" defines the issue.

Actually the chronicle of conflicts between lawmen and psychiatrists has not so clearly aligned them into opposing camps. Psychiatry as we know it today has come into its own only within a short span of a little more than a century. What before passed for medical psychology could scarcely be regarded as a science, even Greek science; lawmen and doctors were then joined in the common work of exorcising an incarnate Devil. As one turns back to these older times, one is struck by the fact that the conflict between lawyer and physician was more on the issue of humanitarian and economic motives consonant with an awakening skepticism which was to eventually temper the barbarity of the times.[7] Certain physicians are identified with this social change in keeping with the medical man's focus on the alleviation of individual suffering. Zilboorg has illuminated these extraordinary figures in his *The Medical Man and the Witch During the Renaissance*. Outstanding was Johann Weyer (1515-1588), whom Zilboorg regards as the father of modern psychiatry. Weyer combined in his character a compassion for human suffering with a courage to quarrel with his culture which made little if any differentiation between mentally sick people, criminals, witches and heretics. He regarded the "demoniacal world about him as an enormous clinic teeming with sick people." [8] Perhaps this view is pertinent when applied to modern, urban, industrialized society, a society teeming with "mentally sick" persons and maladapted personalities who could be regarded as the modern counterparts of the witch and heretic.[9]

The creation of the Devil was a projection of evil on a grand scale like a dream in which a hidden part of man's self was externalized onto a vast screen of delusion. The

Devil is still with us but he no longer has the wide range abroad as in Weyer's time. Today he lurks in the interstices of the unconscious and the Inquisition and the rack have given place to modern analysis and therapy.[10] Weyer made the simple observation that the Devil had an existence only in the imagination; we owe to his patron and protector that Weyer personally survived this observation.

Only in the past fifty years have we possessed a beginning approach to mental health and illness which can be regarded as scientifically oriented. But magical and superstitious orientations to both mental and physical disease exist side by side with the highest developed techniques of medical science." The primitive mind with its magical thinking is by no means confined to savages and to the early mental life of the infant and child or to the insane. Frazer's black strand of magic obtrudes in all walks of life, including the highly educated. The reader of Bergen Evans' *The Natural History of Nonsense* may find amusement not unmixed with injured pride in the following discovery:

We may be through with the past but the past is not through with us. Ideas of the Stone Age exist side by side with the latest scientific thought. Only a fraction of mankind has emerged from the dark ages, and in the most lucid brains as Logan Pearsall Smith has said, "We come upon nests of woolly caterpillars." Seemingly sane men entrust their wealth to star-gazers and their health to witch-doctors, giant planes throb through the stratosphere but half their passengers are wearing magic amulets. . . . Hotels boast of express elevators and a telephone in every room, but omit thirteen from all floor and room numbers lest their guests be ill at ease. . . . The discoveries of the telescope, the spectroscope and the interferometer are daily news but the paper that carries them probably has an astrologer on its staff. . . .[12]

It would be well to review the characteristics of the black thread of magical thinking and to observe their occurrences in contemporary life. Karin Stephen gives a good summary of them in her book, *Psychoanalysis and Medicine*:

The first and perhaps most striking characteristic of primitive thinking is that it is not hampered *by any need for consistency*. While disbelieving and denying it can also in the same breath believe or it can believe contradictory things simultaneously. Logicians of the unconscious might call this the law of unconscious thought, but it is the exact opposite of the first law of thought in conscious logical mental operations. The second distinguishing characteristic of primitive thinking is the belief in the *omnipotence of thoughts and wishes*. The third is the *confusion of fact with fantasy, thinking with doing*. The fourth is the *small importance attached to knowing and the all importance of wishing*. The fifth is the *complete failure to distinguish from one another things which are somehow emotionally identified*.[13]

A moment's reflection may bring us to a realization how much this baggage of magic persists in variable measure and at different times in our own communications with our surrounding reality. Perhaps it has a singular exertion in our operation of a moral order, in the balancing of criminal behavior on the one hand with law enforcement on the other. When we move into the area of mental illness, our concepts yet carry latent vestiges of magical thinking. We no longer speak of the criminal or lunatic as really possessed by an alien spirit or demon, and lycanthropy has no official accreditation, but we have retained the old vocabulary unmistakably linked to such notions. Not long ago the press gave wide dissemination to an utterance of one of Philadelphia's prominent psychiatrists who came to the conclusion that prowling sex offenders were Cat People. Thus, in this city of several great institutions of learning Galeanthropy and Incubus came to life behind every lamp post, and for all I know these revenants may yet linger in many good Philadelphians who likewise ponder and act upon the notion that cats "bring bad luck" and "suck babies' breath." [14]

As we consider primitive thinking, it is understandable that by association it is regarded as peculiar to the mentality of savage peoples in far-off lands so different from ourselves. Yet there is a far-off land within ourselves wherein the same mentality is at work. This is the far-off land of the unconscious which has by no means in us the insular remoteness of our contemporary Stone Age brothers, who have not yet devised a symbolic environment like ours to replace their own.[15] The savage has an unconscious also but its boundaries are blurred so that it shapes and animates the world in which he lives. In ourselves the unconscious shapes and animates our world in the degree that we achieve repression and control of it, established in early life by conscious effort implemented by our educators. In ourselves primitive mentality yet colors all conscious life. We get glimpses of it in the psychopathology of everyday life to which Freud dedicated an entire monograph,[16] in dreams, neurotic symptoms, slips of the tongue, the forgetting of names, fantasies, in criminality and in mental illness in general. These observations come to our attention in much of adult life, and are not found wanting in the courtroom. Piaget identifies them with the "adherences," fragments of internal reference which cling to the external world.[17]

In the progression from magical thinking through religion to science, the primitive first nature has been gradually replaced by a new and different world of symbols and with them new values to form a second nature. In this metamorphosis of the symbolic environment the primitive first nature has receded into the unconscious levels of mental life. But like the phenomenon of entropy spoken of by engineers and cyberneticists, the unconscious still exerts a tendency to break down order and structure. How spectacular is this process in human thought as we watch the breakdown of the mind in psychosis. Take a common example of a person who contracts an infection the toxic effects of which temporarily change his chemistry. Before our eyes the mind of a wakeful, rational man becomes flooded with the unconscious, communication with his surrounding reality becomes incomprehensible, and therefore frightening, his actions are unpredictable and even sometimes dangerous to himself and others.

The delirium passes and we observe a rapid kaleidoscopic return from the magical primitive man to our rational man. In a matter of hours the evolution of higher thought in man unfolds before us. More commonplace is the transformation observed in acute alcoholic intoxication which dissolves the outer shell and exposes the inside man. Or take recent experiments in which young, normal subjects are placed in an environment in which sensory stimulation is practically removed. After a lapse of variable time, the subjects reported a loss of reality-orientation with unconscious intrusions filling in the awareness vacated by the usual environment.[18]

Indeed, psychiatry itself has yet to distill away its magical contaminants. Reider has examined some of our projections and personifications which linger in our nosological and theoretical concepts in psychiatry. He points out that "symptoms are fought in many a psychotherapy by the magical device of mentioning a name ... If a patient is told he is hostile, immature, abnormal, anxious and so on, he will forthwith give up the demon." [19] In our efforts to change the criminal do we not *fight* his criminality by name-calling and exhortations, and failing these, *beat* the Devil out of him? The psychiatrist can be reminded that in a more benign application, the reification of such terms as id, ego and super-ego can in uncritical hands be a sophisticated form of magical projection and exorcism of good and bad demons in modern guise. Freud warned against taking such representations literally.[20]

Among his concluding remarks Reider makes this statement: "Magic is our heritage. We cannot divest ourselves of it completely, for even if we deny it in ourselves, our patients still see us as performers of magic in our acts, gestures and words—and above all in our words." [21]

I have made reference to the characteristics of the thinking observed in primitives, children, the insane and in ourselves which have been widespread in Western society until only recent times. The work of the great men of the 17th and

18th Centuries brought to the world a new outlook which replaced the belief in portents, demoniacal possession, witchcraft and sorcery. Lord Russell has reduced the work of these men to three important ingredients of scientific outlook: "1. Statements of fact should be based on observation and not on unsupported authority. 2. The inanimate world is a self-acting, self-perpetuating system in which all changes conform to natural laws. 3. The earth is not the center of the universe and probably man is not its purpose (if it has any); moreover, 'purpose' is a concept which is scientifically useless." [22, 23]

This third ingredient is of particular interest to the lawyer and the psychiatrist, for the notion of "purpose" and causation finds a large place in our concept of motivation. Our thinking of causation comes from Aristotle who maintained that there are four kinds of causes. Two of these (the *matter* or *material* cause of the thing, and the law according to which it has grown or developed—that is, the form or *formal cause*) need not concern us here. The two that do are the *efficient cause* and the *final cause*. The former is simply "the cause"; the latter is actually the "purpose." We are more prone to the asking of the "why" of events rather than the efficient causes for them. The answer by "final causes" has meaning in events involving human centered values.

The difference of the *how* and the *why* can be viewed in terms of causality. For our purposes we can regard causes as of two kinds: those which imply *deterministic necessity* and those which imply *purpose*. Science is mainly concerned with how things come about; less with why they should be. The psychiatrist as a citizen is as much moved as the lawyer by the large question of purposeful causality, but as scientist he must regard this with its ethical implications, irrelevant to his inquiry.

The criminal trial is a forum for the determination of the fact of the wrong-doing and the question of "why" is implicit in the process of making a moral judgment and of attaching a condemnation and penalty on the convicted wrong doer. In the mind of the public the demand for the "why" (purposeful causality) of the criminal act is satisfied with the determination that the doer had "intent," in which case the doer is punished, or that the doer lacked "intent" for any reason, in which case he is not punished. In either case there is conveyed a pseudo-understanding. The psychiatrist as expert in a criminal case can do no more than catalogue data of behavior; correlate them with some scale to an arbitrary norm, and give the whole of his data a name. In the field of morals, this does not say *why* the crime was committed, only *how* it came about; in this sense his statements impart only a limited "understanding." [24]

A moral judgment is mediated on the appearances of things and not on the "how" of them. In law, this implicit "why" is conveyed in the legal terms which qualify behavior. Thus, did the wrong-doer have "intent"; did he act out of "malice aforethought, willfulness with premeditation," etc.? These qualifications are imposed on those who are to make judgment. They answer the question, "Why did the accused do it?" and the answer joins the arc to make a circle; he did it because he had "intent," "malice aforethought, premeditation," etc. Here one is reminded of Moliere's physician who explained that opium puts people to sleep because it contains a dormitive principle.

The psychiatrist's language of the "how" of behavior does not meet the requirement of law which employs moral language of the "why." Indeed the testimony of some psychiatrists in criminal cases sounds strange and even weird to those who are seeking the "why" of the unlawful act. I suspect that often the psychiatrist is not clear in his own perception of the levels of communication he employs and what he says that meets with ridicule is matched by his own confusion and chagrin. I will touch more fully on these matters later.

The language of the criminal law explains unlawful conduct in terms of willfulness, malice, intent with a *dressage* of "free will" and of "knowledge." Thus, a person commits an unlawful act and somehow he does so because he is willful, malicious and so forth. It should be clear that these abstractions explain nothing, have no independent existence and their usefulness is limited as a kind of paraphernalia in the rituals of guilt fastening. They provide no view of the "how" of anti-social behavior.

J. Z. Young observes that man thinks in terms of models, in thinking of himself man has used various models: before Descartes he peopled himself with possessing spirits (entities), after Descartes man became a clock with mechanical parts. Using current models (computing machines, the wave patterns of cerebral electroencephalography) Young suggests that life is the maintenance of pattern. When man is temporarily able to fit stimuli into some pattern he has what Young calls certainty. When new stimuli disturb the pattern, it is the period of doubt. And the method of science has been a process whereby ". . . as man uses new physical tools, his brain acquires new models or symbols. Then, fitting its input to its new symbols, the brain makes new observations possible, and produces a fresh output of further tools. The cycle of doubt and certainty continues, in science, as it did before." [25]

When we speak of the modern climate of doubt and certainty, we speak of the method of acquiring knowledge through the description and classification of facts and of subjecting such facts to theoretical analysis and experiment with the view of making reliable predictions. The ancients were impelled as we are by the same incentives of personal survival through prediction. Today our science has increased our personal stake in survival and our hope lies in the method of science to insure better odds. The past few decades mark the beginnings of a systematized dynamic model of mental operations and the shift of psychology from the field of morals into the discipline of science.

The psychiatry of the mid-20th Century has seen a beginning change from its former occupation with class-theoretical concepts of human behavior, which stress etiology, single lineal causation, the invention of types and an elaborate taxonomy, to a field-theoretical approach to behavior with concepts of process, multiple and reticular causality and with circular systems of social interaction. In the past, the psychiatrist focused on the individual as a specimen in isolation from the social situation. Today such isolation is practically gone in a technological environment of inescapable mass communication. Psychiatry itself is no longer in isolation but joined with other disciplines, including law, as a social science. Just as the individual psychiatrist reckons himself as an interactional part of a system he is describing and analyzing, so is the body of psychiatric theory being placed in the community of other disciplines. Psychiatric theories are implicitly theories of communication and the conventional groupings of psychopathology are so regarded as disturbances of communication, in part defined by the culture in which they occur. And there are several disciplines employing their own concepts and technical languages, all in need of attaining a unified theory of behavior. This goal is envisioned in the use of communication as a model which can explain physical, intrapersonal, interpersonal and cultural aspects of events within one system. Such a model has been elaborated by Ruesch and Bateson.[26] This would be indeed a much desired goal for criminal law and psychiatry.

II WHAT IS MENTAL ILLNESS?

> Every isolated passion is, in isolation, insane; sanity may be defined as a synthesis of insanities. Every dominant passion generates a dominant fear, the fear of its non-fulfillment. Every dominant fear generates a nightmare, sometimes in the form of an explicit and conscious fanaticism, sometimes in a paralyzing timidity, sometimes in an unconscious or subconscious terror which finds expression only in dreams. The man who wishes to preserve sanity in a dangerous world should summon in his own mind a parliament of fears, in which each in turn is voted absurd by all the others.
>
> BERTRAND RUSSELL [27]

What agreement can be reached on the meaning of the terms "insanity" and "mental illness"? Goodwin expressed the despair of those who pursue the circle of verbal definitions. He wrote, "Neither the lawyers nor the doctors have been able to evolve, either separately or conjointly, any rigid definition of insanity for the simple reason that there is none." [28]

Insofar as verbal definitions apply, this statement is equally applicable to "mental illness." This probable truth does not deter either lawyers or psychiatrists from acting as if the terms themselves have a "natural" and "proper" meaning, and one hears the recurrent complaint by lawyers that psychiatrists adhere too stubbornly to the old Roman practice of regarding all forms of mental illness as *insaniens*. In turn, the psychiatrists find lawyers troublesome in their insistence that "mental illness" is not invariably "insanity." Beyond this, some psychiatrists are given to calling mental illness insanity (which is not a medical term); and occasionally one hears the term "medical insanity," which is surely a bad marriage.

If lawyers and psychiatrists will agree to regard "mental illness" and "insanity" less as they are verbally defined and more as what we do to people to whom we attach such terms, we will be nearer the sharing of behavioral reality not only that of others but of ourselves. Law in words remains in the abstract; in action it is something affecting people in their social relationships. Bridgman says "The true meaning of a term is to be found by observing what a man *does* with it, not by what he *says* about it." [29]

Law is what it does and if law does what it says, what it says has meaning. In this view it is clear that the term "insanity" is meaningful if defined beyond words. "Insanity" designates that a civil status is alterable by consensual authority and force. The term "mental illness" merely designates behavior which, in a given society, is regarded as maladaptive; it designates an altered internal status of the individual vis á vis his external world as interpreted by others. The alteration of interpersonal status *seems* to come from within the person. When this alteration reaches a point regarded as intolerable, the culture provides expedients of alleviating the social tensions attending it. Behavior so designated as "mental illness" merely becomes changed in name to "insanity." The name carries with it a susceptibility to externally applied force which alters civil status. Marriage changes a girl's name and alters her civil status; it does not change her. The term "mental illness" can mean any degree of symptomatic maladaption, but it can mean "insanity" only if a legal manipulation makes it so.[30]

Both lawyer and psychiatrist can view the same set of facts of behavior. But at least two persons do the viewing and to different viewers the same behavior acquires in its naming different meanings. The meaning does not really alter the set of facts itself, but it enables each viewer to make different *use* of it. Thus, the set of facts remains intact, but the names erect different operations contemplated by the viewers. The legal operation is that of effecting, through external conclusive actions, an immediate alteration of the relationship of the individual with his fellow community; the psychiatric operation is that of effecting an internal alteration of the individual.

We may restate our operational approach to mental illness. The signs displayed and the symptoms reported by the patient are his illness, his "sickness" as he experiences and expresses it. The sickness can exist in psychiatry only as an abstraction which is given a name, i.e. *mental illness*. The patient's sickness can have a meaning to the doctor and others only in the sense of what in the future will be done to or with the patient to relieve him and those around him. Before the doctor can name the sickness and relieve the patient, the signs and symptoms must fall within a model of science accepted by other doctors. Within this model the sickness can be named and a design of relief can be made and carried out. The same signs and symptoms, within a model of a legal system, are called by a different name, *insanity,* which designates a different order of abstraction and a different design of relief. In civil matters the patient's sickness exists in the doctor and lawyer as different abstractions having different names, but the designs of relief generally achieve a unitary goal; the common design of relief is a therapeutic manipulation of the sick individual. However, in criminal matters the design of relief is a therapeutic adjustment of the law-abiding. When "mental illness" enters into criminal matters the design of relief becomes ambivalent.

It is said that the giving of a name to a set of facts enables the viewer of them to erect an operation within himself and to take some action affecting another. There must, however, exist some previous model for his intended action. The lawyer has his model in the penal code, ordinances and procedures; the psychiatrist in his science and art. The lawyer's model is *public-centered,* relatively fixed and authoritative, whereas the psychiatrist's is *individual-centered,* moving and susceptible to the discipline of constant reassessment and alteration with new discoveries. Even so, the models employed by both lawyer and doctor are subjective frames of orientation to social reality; they exist by necessity even should they be false. Whether false or not, each must rationalize his actions which flow from his models. The lawyer and the psychiatrist may thus act unreasonably or in ignorance, but it is unthinkable for either not to give his actions the appearance of rational motivation. At a given moment these rationalizations give us an assurance that all is well with the actions we take affecting our fellow men. However, the world around us is not static. Our surrounding reality is a process of an unceasing change. Futhermore, no identities can be found in the universe, no two situations or behavior are identical. There is no better demonstration of this than in the legal process itself which operates in terms of fixed models of precedence applied to repeating life situations which are never the same. Perhaps the essential similarity of our nervous systems gives us the illusion of similarity in the outside world. However, we can be comforted by Wendell Johnson's apt reminder that a "similarity is comprised of differences that don't make any difference." [31]

If we are moving in a world of ever changing process and no two events are identical, if we must be content only with similarities, where can we find a point of reference for deciding what is "insanity" and what isn't? This poses the problem of what is "normal." If some individuals are found to be insane or mentally ill, it is implied that in such finding we select others who are not so, that the remainder of the given group are sane. At this point arise questions the first of which concerns the manner in which we structure our concept of normality. If we draw a fictional "normal distribution" curve to demonstrate degrees of "sanity," the distribution suggests that only a small few can be considered "sane" from the standpoint of their self awareness, of how their unconscious belief systems affect their relationships with their surrounding reality. The other foot of the curve is occupied by the "insane." The large average, the statistically "normal" group (the hump of the bell curve), is made of ourselves, the unsane, the partially sane or the part-time sane. The so-called neurotics are those who appear to be suspended in the middle of unresolved conflict between the magical and scientific orientation to their surrounding reality. They maintain a "cold war" between the ancient black and the recent white, co-existent and unreconciled. In Frazer's metaphor each individual, through the manifest factors of heredity and environment, is a woven rope unique in its pattern of colored strands, which in varying combination impart the hues of personality. Everyone's beginning orientation to the world is magical in the sense that it is a primitive projection system. In the course of one's maturation the white threads of science begin to make some show. Each recapitulates individually the experiences of the race from magic, to science. In some few the white may show and a few golden threads may impart a luster, but the black and the red are not entirely effaced. A number of persons at some point in their lives revert and cling to the earlier black and red orientations and for them the world becomes filled once more with animated magic, both benign and malignant. These are the people who return to the prelogical projection system of our neolithic forebears. These the psychiatrist calls *psychotic,* and the lawyer calls *insane.* Again there are many others who live in both the ancient black world of magic and the modern white world of science, and often succeed in concealing their double existence. To some extent we all lead double lives; most of us succeed in confining our magic to our dream life; in others the magic comes to wakeful symbolic expression in atavistic sexual and aggressive behavior

WHAT IS MENTAL ILLNESS?

and we have not yet made up our minds whether such people are insane or plain wicked.

In terms of sociological relativism, a society is "normal" if it is a going concern, and mental illness is defined in terms of the individual's failure to maintain "adjustment" to it. The pattern of a given society may contain contradictory elements which a minority of its members cannot absorb or find satisfactory remedies. These are the persons who do not maintain an "adjustment" to it. This is a social concept which finds its ultimate expression in either custom or law. The Pennsylvania Mental Health Act of 1951 conveys this idea of "adjustment" in its definition of mental illness. Article I, Section 11, provides:

> Mental illness shall mean an illness which so lessens the capacity of a person to use his customary self-control, judgment and discretion in the conduct of his affairs and social relations as to make it necessary or advisable for him to be under care. The term shall include insanity, unsoundness of mind, lunacy, mental disease, mental disorder and all other types of mental cases, but the term shall not include mental deficiency, epilepsy, inebriety, or senility unless mental illness is superimposed.

Here the Act uses the term "mental illness" as a lessened capacity in relationships between the individual and his community, and it does not attempt to specify clinical types of mental disease. The exclusion of mental deficiency, epilepsy, inebriety and senility is administrative. The Act provides for these elsewhere. The first part of the Act provides that certain persons can be so regarded as incapacitated by other persons designated by the act as competent to make diagnoses of mental illness. This operation is implicit; in the second part of the Act which provides "care", the operational meaning of the Act is explicit. A force can be applied to the person; he can be involuntarily removed from his community. This is an excellent working definition of something which is not mental illness, but of something we would regard as the social reaction to what is called mental illness. It is of passing interest that persons committed as insane under this Act would not be held responsible for illegal acts carried out while so committed; of greater interest is the suggestion that the definition of mental illness as incapacity for social "adjustment" and as a need for "care," is equally applicable to persons whose criminal behavior is a lessened capacity for social "adjustment," requiring "care." By analogy criminal behavior is lessened capacity for social "adjustment," and the criminal requires "care," i.e. removal from the community. This analogy motivates the psychiatrist in his individual-centered approach to the "mind" and person of the wrong doer. But if we recognize "justice" as an arbitrary social convention and as a public-centered operation, the analogy becomes a wishful sentiment.

Our society, as we think we know it, contains patterns which enable many persons "to live with a defect without becoming mentally ill," provided, it seems, so long as the culture maintains continuous remedies which balance out the socially patterned defect. Here in point is the probable consequence of the cessation of mass communication, television, newspapers, radio, etc. on individuals who would otherwise be "thrown upon their own resources." [32] There is good reason to believe that many persons would suffer acute anxiety and that a large scale form of "mental illness" would follow. In like reference, our society maintains a kind of remedy in the existence of a police force which, in untroubled times, serves to keep antisocial activity to a tolerable level. But such a force may be inadequate if on short notice a large scale civil disruption takes place. With catastrophe many persons lose their "sanity" and instinctively revert to violence, looting and panic which are in regressive substitution their own remedies. In a given culture a portion of its group will not find the social remedies sufficient to prevent mental illness. They regress to an ancestral projection system of magic and if they do so while awake, they lose communication with others. Such are regarded as mentally ill. However, it is not enough to define mental illness as a regression and retreat from the social environment. Regression is not uniphasic. Regression applies a process in which the progressive forces have merely lessened. Thus, in the development of mental illness of any clinical variety, we observe the workings of forces in conflict and, in the behavior of mental illness, symptoms have in themselves a meaning of attempts of restitution. Recovery is the reversal of the conflict and return to the level at which the remedies can be used in the service of "adjustment" to the prevailing social patterns. In this sense, psychiatric therapy is applied to persuade the mentally ill person to come back to the fold, even if it isn't "the best of all possible worlds." [33]

Wilson speaks of the growing concept that regards the culture, not the individual, as sick:

> The disease lies not in people, but between people in their relations one to the other. It is thought by some that the mentally ill, in their own peculiar way, are pointing out the culture disease, the focus of infection in interpersonal relations, and finally to show what to do about it.

Wilson makes a suggestive comment that if the culture is the source of mental disease, the psychoses as we know them should be redefined.[34]

Wilson's novel approach to one meaning of mental illness is not to be taken lightly. Mental health is not merely the "adjustment" of the individual to the pattern of his culture. It is more than this. It is also the adjustment of society to the needs of man. Fromm points out that mental health cannot be defined in terms limited to man's adjustment to his group and emphasizes that a healthy society

> furthers man's capacity to love his fellow men, to work creatively, to develop his reason and objectivity, to have a sense of self which is based on the experience of his own productive powers. An unhealthy society is one which creates mutual hostility, distrust which transforms man into an instrument of use and exploitation

for others, which deprives him of a sense of self, except inasmuch as he submits to others or becomes an automaton. Society can have both functions; it can further man's healthy development and it can hinder it; in fact, most societies do both and the question is only to what degree and to what directions their positive and negative influence is exercised.[35]

In sum, Fromm would define "normality" as

characterized by the ability to love and to create, by the emergence from incestuous ties to clan and soil, by a sense of identity based on one's experience of self as the subject and agent of one's powers, by the grasp of reality inside and outside of ourselves, that is, by the development of objectivity and reason.[36]

The terms of Fromm's definition of mental health are dependent and related to a central element which is the awareness of the inner self, the golden strand of Frazer's life line upon which a concept of relative normality can be erected. From this view of mental health, one cannot be content with a statistical definition representing what most individuals do feel and think. And as emphasized by Fromm, mere conformity or "adjustment" to a given culture does not constitute normality, nor does the effect of a given behavior on the society either as a contribution to its welfare or to its destruction determine the difference between normal and neurotic.

At this place it would be proper to state that the currently employed legal distinction between sane and insane contributes little to the definition of normality. The knowledge of right and wrong in the legal sense or the knowledge of what one is doing and of its wrongfulness may serve legal expediency but it is an obstacle to the quest for a definition of normality.

We have viewed the public-centered aspects of "normality" and of what we choose to call "mental illness" and "insanity." Let us turn to the individual-centered examination of "normality" and view it in the idiom of psychiatry. Currently in our hypothetical model "normality" is implied and can be talked about to the extent that one's behavior is governed by conscious choices. By corollary a government by conscious direction implies a relative self awareness of unconscious forces which energize our primitive, magical wish thinking. Self-awareness implies a discipline of constant appraisal of the rationalizations we employ in vindicating our decisions. In this frame, one regards self-awareness as a kind of insight whereby one senses the extent that unconscious drives color and distort perceptions and conceptions of surrounding reality, and also makes corrections. Conscious control of behavior implies that one can be influenced through communication with others by appeal, argument, by experience with rewards and punishments, achievement and frustration; in short, by learning. Conscious control of behavior enables one to learn, predict and to adapt. The extent to which by means of such learning predictive capacity and adaptation are acquired is a measure of a relative freedom of will. Such freedom is an essential criterion of normality, of mental health. Money-Kyrle expresses that ideal of normality, of mental health, embraced in Frazer's figure, the level marked by the white and golden threads of science and self-awareness in the woven rope of higher thought:

In the ordinary and wider sense, a healthy person is anyone who has a good capacity for work and pleasure, or who is well-adjusted to his social environment. This concept is useful enough as a practical guide; but it is inevitably a little vague and also relative to the prevailing cultural standards. *In contrast to it, the concept of an integrated person—of a person whose mind has nothing permanently hidden from itself, and who is rational in the sense that the belief-systems governing his behavior are true within the range of his experience because they have been consciously tested—is at least precise.* And although this is the concept of a limit not attainable in practice, it has the great advantage of being independent of all arbitrarily chosen cultural standards and linked with the absolute criterion of truth. It thus itself provides us with the kind of standard needed if we are to get beyond the relativist position in either politics or morals.[37, 38]

The individual whose unconscious forces govern his behavior is, to the extent of his self-awareness, in sharp contrast to the man of self-awareness and freedom of will. Unconscious forces tend to bind and fix the personality in a frame of archaic patterns, inflexible and repetitive. Unconscious forces are uninfluenced in communication through appeal, argument, rewards and punishments and are exceptionally alterable only through the arduous work of analysis. One bound to unconscious dominance is bound to the magical orientation of one's Stone Age ancestors.

The psychic forces which we postulate as conscious and unconscious do not operate separately but seem to make their exertions together in relative proportions like those in the parallelogram of forces which conjoin in unitary resultants of behavior. If this be the case, we can view conscious mentation as a surface manifestation of a process which has extensions in depth to atomic levels. This process is one of living energy exchange and distribution in continuous balance, infinitely varied in a time-space continuum. As we observe it in an infinitely small segment of this ever changing conscious-unconscious spectrum, there can be discerned in gross outline patterns of repetitive behavior never identical but having sufficient "similarity" to enable us to classify them. In our culture a certain number of such patterns are regarded as pathological and a number of them have come into public currency. The psychiatrist speaks of the so-called adaptive reactions as neuroses, psychoses and character disorders. But we should bear in mind that such typing has limited usefulness.

Two of the most frequently encountered terms in psychiatry are "psychosis" and "psychoneurosis" ("neurosis") and it might appear that in such currency their meaning should be settled in universal agreement. This is not the case. Not only is there confusion, theoretically and practically, as to the precise meaning of each term, but also is there often as much confusion as to the existence of a pathological process to which either or both terms can be applied. The practical need for some administrative sorting based on crude descriptive categories of symptoms and to some extent for teaching purposes impels the psychiatrist to retain such terms. Even so, the traditional classification of mental illness is no longer adequate.[39] The terms refer to distinctions which more often have greater legal and social implication, not uncommonly associated with economic and social circumstance.

Psychiatric nomenclature is undergoing revision and there is considered the possibility of discarding the terms "psychosis" and "neurosis" altogether in favor of a more flexible framework in keeping with our present knowledge and operational methods. At the moment psychiatric disorders are distinguished under two groupings: (1) those associated with organic brain changes and (2) those without demonstrable brain changes. It may be noted that this distinction does not go beyond that of a differentiation of probable physical and organic changes co-existent with symptoms which may be more or less the same in either case and manifest as reactions to which may be applied the discriminative adjectives psychotic, neurotic and behaviorial. It would be of interest to the legal profession that the term "psychopathic personality" is no longer regarded by psychiatry as meaningful, yet it will probably remain embalmed for some time to come in the statutes of several States where the pursuit of demons disguised as sexual psychopaths affords a glimpse of a 16th Century approach to mental illness.

Thus we have the terms which we apply to the surface patterns of behavior for which we postulate co-existent forces of mentation. If we think of such forces simply within a concept of energy distribution and exchange, we are limited and there is the need of a concept of the operation of stress in such a system which results in what we observe as psychological illness.

Allusion can be made to the conscious and unconscious as polarities, the conscious in sensate contact with the outside environment, the unconscious nearer to the chemical, physiological, living process. There is a transition in both directions; the bulk of sensate experience passing unnoticed from the external world into unconscious registration, and a counter-flow of unconscious stirrings moving to the periphery and acquiring at successively higher levels more and more logically structured and refined symbolization in final pathway communicated to others in conventional actions and in formal language. We observe that in the newborn there exists no psychic energy which we could call an ego, that the behavior of the child is unmodified and in the service of biological survival. And certainly, there is in the infant no psychic agency which we could call a conscience or super ego. The ego appears to be an internalized accretion of values imposed from without by the child's educators who are the carriers of the culture. The ego could be regarded as a built-in feed-back system which within the intentions of the educators serves as a modulator of the elemental strivings of the child. The remarkable fact is that the prolonged biologic dependence of the human child makes such ego function attainable. It appears that the totality of interpersonal communication with the growing child in the first few years of his helplessness endows him with the internalized self-operating means of exerting conscious control of his unconscious strivings.

The process of growing up appears to be a renunciation of gratifications of the moment bartered in terms of higher rewards that come with postponed demands. Not only is the gratification delayed but it is offered in modified form acceptable to the current social values. How the child's eventual acceptance of delayed substitute gratification is achieved by ego operations enforced by the vigilance of educators is yet to be completely understood. This is tantamount to forgetting and we observe much of such forgetting to be the case specifically in the first five or six years of life. Forgetting is more one of a forgetting of feelings than of articulate memories since the verbal world of the child is scant. Everyone intuitively senses that mental conflicts are tied to the earliest infantile experiences and it is perhaps this intuition which enables us to identify ourselves with others afflicted with neurotic suffering and to some extent with the criminal. This was expressed so eloquently in the comment of the British judge John Bradford who, in passing condemnation upon one, remarked, "There but for the grace of God go I."

So far we have structured a crude dynamic model in which we hypothecate the exchange of energy and the movement of vectors towards behavioral end products. Yet this model of mental life carries with it some of the old symbols. It is a slanted projection of a concept of the world expressed in paired values such as pleasure-pain, good-evil, God-Devil, heaven-hell, and love-hate. In this operation we act as if the bad unconscious contends against the good conscious, "as if" within the mind there is a perpetual struggle between the cave man within us and the socially domesticated gentleman. The psychiatrist views behavior in terms of the measure that it can be determined by conscious and unconscious forces and he attempts to do this viewing with a minimum of evaluative bias. The same behavior can stem from both conscious and unconscious forces but there is a formidable difference. Consciously determined behavior is correctable through communication with others and by simple common sense devices such as punishment for wrong-doing. If the same behavior is determined predominately by unconscious forces, it is not correctable by such means. Unconsciously determined behavior tends to be repeating and unmodified and the individual is correspondingly less free in making decisions. He is less an agent of free will. When such repeating patterns fail to gratify, a cycle of repetitive impulse and frustration is set in motion attended by what we call anxiety, hostility, confusion and resultant social failure. Now in this connection mention can be made of the appearances noted in the working out of conflict and resolution of conscious and unconscious forces of mental life. Two avenues of resolution are open: one a *living* out, the other an *acting* out. Living out implies behavior reflecting the resolution of conflict absorbed within the organism, manifest in some modality of internal change.

The alienation of mentally ill people implies the need for a stronger force outside to take over that which has lapsed in them. This stronger control is supplied by hospital custody. Elsewhere I have referred to an arbitrary model of normality in terms of the degree that the conscious part of the personality has control and that the illness is a measure of the extent to which unconscious forces dominate behavior. In this light, it would appear that hospital custody is a substitute for conscious control applied from without until such time as conscious control from within is regained. One cannot properly insist that in mental illness the process is exclusively the self-changing living out. Acting out is in the picture, but under the spell of the self-transformation more often it appears as a mere token accompaniment of the inner magical process.

The bulk of psychiatric literature is devoted to hypothecating the factors that account for social failure. We have many explanations for antisocial behavior whether lawful or unlawful, but there is little to explain why people conform. We take this for granted. However, from our investigations, even if slanted to the pathological, we have general agreement that social behavior, adapting to given norms, is a derivative of the earliest experiences of the infant and child and that the reactive patterns then established exert a large force in day by day adaptation.

We may speak of overcompensated living and acting out. Both are adaptive survival gestures and both are aspects of what is properly mental illness; both are a retreat to the magical orientation to surrounding reality. In criminality one observes rebellion with destructive action directed outwardly; in mental illness rebellion with destructive reaction absorbed inwardly. Actually all behavior contains both elements in varying proportions. When the acting out predominates, the impact on our fellow men is greater than when the conflict is absorbed within the individual who alone suffers. In psychiatric parlance these are referred to respectively as the *alloplastic* and the *autoplastic* resolutions of conflict. From the standpoint that the individual reverts to a magical orientation in social adaptation, the distinction between the criminal and the mentally ill is arbitrary. Every criminal is such by reason of unconscious forces within him just as every mentally ill person is so dominated by unconscious forces, and the so-called "normal" people operate in their lives with margins not far from either.[40] Commonly one observes criminality and mental illness in the same person, sometimes alternating, and the legal attitude towards him may come out of chance. Those who are given to acting out as a mode of adaptation by corollary tend to less living out of conflict. At least they tend to do so less in the appearance to others. Since there are in them no gross appearances of living out, we tend to assume there are none; in fact, from the standpoint of appearances, there is little to distinguish those who act out from ourselves. And then there is the formidable obstacle in our realistic appraisal of them. This may come in part out of traditional insistence that the criminal must be basically different from mentally ill persons. This is a theological concept and has no basis in fact—criminals differ from mentally ill people only in the manner we choose to deal with them.

III THE CRIMINAL LAW AND PSYCHIATRY IN ACTION: THE PRE-TRIAL PHASE

> Empirically, the concepts of justice which men have maintained throughout history are as varied as the religions of the world, or the cultures recognized by anthropologists. I doubt if it is possible to justify them by any higher sanction than our moral code itself, which is indeed only another name for our conception of justice.
>
> NORBERT WIENER [41]

The entirety of criminal law has not remained anchored in its magical religious footings. The constabulary aspect of it employs the latest scientific equipment and methods and that part of it occupied by legal scholarship has taken on some coloration and a vocabulary of a science discipline. If we should phase out criminal justice into operational functions, we could more readily appraise it in terms of how much magical religious vestige is yet contained in each. The operational functions of criminal law can be fitted into a temporal order; the interval from the event of the crime to apprehension, the interval between apprehension and the trial, the trial process and the penological aftermath. In these phases the magical religious contaminants loom large relative to the degree that the manipulation of the wrong-doer has public-centered dramatic communication.

The report of the crime alerts public attention to a play

by way of a prologue. The search for the unknown perpetrator is set in motion and a detective mystery is unraveled and culminates in his apprehension. The intimate work of detection itself does not reach the public. In it is an extensive magical lore which goes on off stage. Theodore Reik has treated these arcana comprehensively in *The Unknown Murderer*.[42] He touches upon the interest we take in crime, the peculiar psychological requirements of those who adumbrate clues and track the evil doer, the unconscious meanings of the return to the scene of the crime, the contrivances of the criminal in providing self-incriminating clues and the criminal's inner psychic structure of superstition. The final work of detection and arrest comes to the public as a reassuring notice of the omnipotence of law enforcement and the stage is set for the play itself. Psychiatry can and does enter into the phases between apprehension and the trial. The employment of psychiatry in this phase has an increasing frequence, having had an earlier acceptance in juvenile jurisdictions in time to be called upon in criminal courts which utilize psychiatric data not only in pre-trial but also in the pre-sentence phases of disposition.

Although the psychiatrist works in a setting surrounded by legal apparatus and symbol, never completely free of an adversary spirit, his communication with lawyers can be relatively unimpeded. In these phases peripheral to the guilt fastening phase itself, the operation of the law is more individual-centered and clinical in its approach to asocial behavior. In these phases the psychiatrist's work and service to the law can be as free as in civil matters. In these, he has less difficulty in communicating with the law. In civil matters of competence, testamentary capacity, or commitments to a mental hospital there does not enter the occult element of legal guilt. His evidence is based upon data of experience which he assembles and interprets and a practical result can be obtained. To be sure, psychiatrists can and do make conflicting interpretations but the communication with the law is on a fairly satisfactory level. Likewise the level in the criminal case is his communication to the law in issues of mental illness in bar of trial and after conviction. The pre- and post-trial phases are off stage so to speak. In either station of the process the psychiatrist works in his shirt sleeves. The accused or convicted prisoner is viewed in the same light as any person thought to be mentally ill. The psychiatrist reports what he finds and the courts generally accept the findings. With a plea in bar of trial, the mentally disordered accused is manipulated accordingly; he is committed to a hospital for treatment. However, the psychiatrist is required to translate his clinical findings also into a judgment of capacity of the accused to confer with counsel in his defense and to understand the proceedings against him. This test from the Anglo-American common law plea in bar of trial can be met in some cases of advanced psychotic dilapidation but it does not apply to many other mentally ill persons accused of crime. Many psychotic persons both in and out of institutions are quite capable of aiding their defense and of understanding the charges and the procedures against them. The ideal pre-trial procedure has been developed in Scotland and in one American State.[43, 44] In the pre- and post-trial phases of criminal justice, the lawyer and psychiatrist can and do find a closer collaboration. Those critics of the law who find in it an irksomeness to psychiatry may overlook the fact in these phases the psychiatrist himself may be a larger contributor to his own hardship. This comes out of a lack of defined functions and limitations of psychiatry in these phases. I will supply illustrations which move me to make a *caveat* on common practices of psychiatrists who take part in pre-trial examinations.

The communication of psychiatrist with lawyer has a minimum encumbrance so long as the element of culpability is not contained in it. In the case of homicide in which the accused appears before trial to be mentally disordered, there is a fair acceptance of psychiatry on its own terms. Even so, there lingers among some psychiatrists the unclear definition of their function. In the pre-trial inquiry some carry into it the notion that the aim of a psychiatric examination is the determination of the defendant's capacity for meeting the test rules of responsibility. In effect, a psychiatric inquiry with such direction and finding is tantamount to an informal trial conducted by doctors. That some psychiatrists should center their examinations on the legal tests of criminal responsibility does not come from instructions of the court, but from an assumption that such tests as imposed in the trial itself can be equated with clinical behavioral findings in a phase of pre-trial examination. Perhaps more basically this assumption obscures their own unconscious positive or negative identification with the defendant.[45]

The College Student

In the early part of 1955 a young college student shot and killed a fellow student.[46] The killing was a culminating event of a psychotic process the significance of which had become apparent only by hindsight. In his history there had been three hospitalizations for mental disorder. In due course, a Sanity Commission was appointed by the Court consisting of two psychiatrists and a lawyer. In the examination of the prisoner, the lawyer, a member of the Commission, indicated that the two physicians had been appointed by the State to act as examining psychiatrists for the State and that counsel for the defendant and also a representative of the District Attorney's office should be present at the examination. He indicated that he did not intend to take part in the examination but to act only in the interest of the prisoner's rights in case the defense "should feel any improper questions were being asked that they could object to protect the defendant's rights." It was clear that with these remarks and with the proposal that the Commonwealth and the defense attorneys be present at a Sanity Commission hearing, it would take on the character of an adversary proceeding, the lawyer acting as a referee or judge. In this spirit one of the examining physicians did express his view that the attorney for the defendant should not have a right to object to questions that might be asked by the physicians. The attorney for the defense expressed the view that the presence of the District Attorney could be challenged as a legal matter but as a courtesy objection would be waived. A question was raised as to the capacities of the examining physicians. As if in realistic anticipation, the attorney for the defense reminded the members of the Commission that they were bound to be "impartial" but at the same time expressed the view that since they were appointed by the Commonwealth and acted as witnesses for the District Attorney they might well be protagonistic. Here was a kind of adversary apparatus and court setting for the determination of clinical matters. The Commission made its examination of the defendant and took statements of witnesses. In its final conclusions, the Commission reported that the defendant had some evidence of organic disease of the nervous system, that he was insane and suffered with paranoid schizophrenia. The Commission volunteered that the defendant could not distinguish right from wrong, that he was not able to comprehend his position with relation to the crime of which he stood accused and unable to confer with his counsel in an intelligent manner to prepare his defense. The Commission further stated that the defendant was unable to make a rational defense to the crime for which he stood accused, that he was of *criminal tendency* and that he should be committed to a hospital for the criminal insane to be confined for the remainder of his life. The Commission's report was accepted by the court, no trial was held, and the defendant was committed to a hospital for the criminal insane.

From an operational standpoint this procedure effected the removal of a socially disabled person to a hospital and with this end achieved we might let the matter stand. But an appeal was entered based upon exceptions to the report of the Commission. Let us look at these exceptions and see if they relate to our attempted survey of the territorial boundaries within which the psychiatrist can properly function in the pre-trial phase. The Commission had recommended that the defendant be sent to a hospital for the criminal insane and for the remainder of his life. The exceptions pointed out that the Commission was limited in scope to a mental examination of the accused at the time the Commission met. The Commission went beyond its function to either designate the kind of hospital or to set the length of the commitment. In effect, the Commission had attempted to settle both the present and future disposition of the case. It was pointed out that even a Court cannot specify the duration of confinement of one committed to a mental hospital; that duration of a confinement cannot exceed the duration of the mental illness. The duration of the mental illness is determined in good measure by the person who suffers with it. The Commission made a prediction of the ultimate course of the mental illness and in effect said that even if the defendant should be *cured* he would be prone to relapse despite temporary benefit. Such a prediction was a nihilistic one indeed attached as a kind of identification tag to the defendant consigned to a place which is dedicated to the restoration of mentally sick persons. Such a prediction pushed into infinity the defendant's contingent right to a jury trial. These recommendations of the Commission were accepted and acted upon by the Court. Translated into the formal actions of a conviction, in effect the defendant was sentenced to life imprisonment. Some will say my remarks here are mere juggling, but the fact remains that the defendant is behind locked doors, labeled incurable. In civil commitments psychiatrists do not presume such omniscience; rather the commitment is made in the same spirit with which people are sent to regular hospitals; we expect them to leave. At any rate, the business of prediction is more properly left to those who have had more than a few hours of contact with a mentally disturbed person in an adversary setting.

It may be that the medical findings of the two psychiatrists were articulated by the lawyer member of the Commission. The language of the final report of the Commission had an unmistakable legal accent. But in this writer's opinion the psychiatry in this case, although sound in its medical findings, was wayward in the use to which it was put. This Commission found that the accused was insane, which is a legal concept, and by way of support of this opinion declared that the defendant could not distinguish right from wrong. This opinion anticipates the test questions for responsibility which are employed in the formal trial which is not a medical but a moral inquisition. This was a proceeding in the phase *before* trial and the opinion accepted by the Court had the effect of a finding by a jury. How the psychiatrists determined the defendant's incapacity to know right from wrong was undisclosed in the Commission's report. In a strict sense the finding of insanity is not a medical function; it is a legal function even in civil matters. The psychiatrist is responsible only for the finding of mental illness by medical criteria. Burr stated this clearly a half century ago:

> The physician's duty in court cases is simply to discover the mental condition of the patient. That having been done, the question of responsibility or irresponsibility, competency or incompetency of a man in his mental state is a matter of law and to be decided by judge and jury.[47]

It remains for some legal authority to pass upon such medical findings and to adjudicate insanity which is not a medical condition but an altered civil status, which sets an individual apart from his fellows. The Commission's findings which anticipated the test questions of right and wrong, implied that the accused was mentally ill at the time of the killing. To limit the findings to the time of the examination would leave the question open of his capacity at the time of the killing. The Commission had the killing in mind at the time of the examination; the entire business was laid before them in a manner not unlike that which would have been narrated in the formal trial. Indeed, there would have been little else to talk about. The answer to the right and wrong question was a matter that the psychiatrists would have faced if and when the accused was formally tried in court. In effect, this individual was tried by a Commission and the Court endorsed its "adjudication" of insanity. The Court abided by the Commission's bestowal of the stigma of criminality on a person who in the same breath the Commission declared was incapable of committing a crime. The accused was sent to a hospital for the criminal insane.

The Mental Health Act of Pennsylvania (1951) contains a definition (Article I, Section 102, Paragraph 4) of "criminal tendency" which *"shall mean a tendency to repeat offenses against the law or to perpetrate new offenses as shown by repeated convictions for such offenses or tendency to habitual delinquency."*

In Pennsylvania when a Commission examines a person either accused of crime or a prisoner convicted of one, it is formally required to determine if the subject has "criminal tendency." The repetition of offenses certainly implies criminal tendency; so far the definition defines itself. "The perpetration of *new* offenses" seems to imply a prediction of something the prisoner would do tomorrow if given the chance, but the law qualifies this prediction by stating that perpetration of new offenses "as shown by repeated convictions for such offenses, etc." This qualification refers to past events. Old offenses are not cancelled out by imposed penalties but with renewed vitality become extensions into the future—the perpetration of new offenses. The only relief to this ambiguity of the word "new" is that it may mean "other." It is remarkable that so many psychiatrists can know criminal tendency when they see it within the scope of this definition. But even more remarkable is the fact that a Commission can discover criminal tendency in "one who is so insane as to be incapable of entertaining the criminal intent, which is one of the essential ingredients of a crime." [48] Even more remarkable that a Commission should find "criminal tendency" in a mentally ill person accused of a killing who had no record of previous offenses and who could not perpetrate new offenses because he had not shown repeated convictions or tendency to habitual delinquency. Yet our college student who suffered with a psychosis and with the "incapacity to distinguish right from wrong" and therefore with the incapacity to commit a crime, was nevertheless filled with "criminal tendency." Upon delivery he became an innocent criminal, who was thenceforth called a patient.[49] Such legal requirements affecting the disposition of psychotic offenders have been accepted in the faith that since they are a part of our legal institutions they must be answerable. In the reflection of what has been written here by way of an analysis of the magical revenants of criminal law "criminal tendency" may have at best a collateral lineage out of demonological possession.

With one member dissenting the Supreme Court of Pennsylvania observed that one of the two major reasons of the Mental Health Act was to protect society from those who are mentally ill and have "criminal tendency" and ruled that the accused "came squarely within these provisions."

The procedure of this Commission was not an exclusive medical inquiry but a quasi-judicial collateral inquiry in an adversary setting. In Pennsylvania the law sets forth that petitioning for a Commission is not a criminal prosecution, but an inquiry made before trial or after conviction and before sentence "to inform the conscience of the judge." The petitioning for a Commission is not a criminal prosecution, yet the procedures of this Commission and the legal criteria it attempted to meet in this instance have a taint of criminal prosecution. The Commission made a legal finding of insanity by a legal criterion (the M'Naghten formula), and of "criminal tendency" which automatically consigned the unconvicted accused to a hospital for the criminal insane, and declared that the accused should be confined in this specific hospital for life and framed his future in the following language:

> In our opinion therefore this man is insane at the present time and unable to stand trial and he should be committed to Farview State Hospital for the rest of his life. His prognosis is extremely bad in view of the long history and he will remain a potentially dangerous person. If some new treatment should become available in the future to effect a cure in this patient it will require a number of years to evaluate what might appear to be a recovery, as patients of this sort are very prone to relapse even though they benefit temporarily from one or another kind of treatment. Relapse moreover might appear in a sudden or explosive form the damage being done almost before it is recognized.

The findings of the Commission went beyond the psychiatrist's individual-centered orientation and crossed the boundary into the public-centered function of the trial. This is not the psychiatry of the clinic. In charity one could say that the psychiatrists framed their findings the way they did because of their desire to comply with what they have come to believe is expected of them. The Commission's findings responsive to the M'Naghten Rule were gratuitous; its findings on the question of "criminal tendency" were required and created a fatal hardship. If we follow the maxim, "a thing is what it does," it becomes clear that "criminal tendency" is something that sends people to a hospital for the criminal insane, but what it tells us about them as people is fugitive.

This case is instructive, and warrants a restatement of analysis. It is clear that when psychiatrists are engaged by a court to examine a person accused of crime or convicted of one they bring a clinical, individual-centered attitude into a relationship with the law which is essentially public-centered. In this meeting boundaries become blurred. As expert, the psychiatrist tends to extend his data of observation into the realm of moral judgment and this he must resist. In such an extension he becomes more than a reporter of facts—he becomes a judge of them. If the psychiatrist is not fully aware that his findings carry an impact of moral judgment, it is then clear that he has not defined his role and limitations in his communication with the law. When he speaks he will not know whether he is talking as a psychiatrist advising on the *how* of human behavior or talking as a judge about the public disapproval of it. If the psychiatrist has not yet defined his relationship with the law it may be that he has yet to clearly define the relationship of mental illness to criminal behavior which in historical reflection not long ago was one and the same.

An offender may meet the psychiatrist in any one of the three phases of his processing in criminal justice. His relationship with the psychiatrist may have variable degrees of ambivalence and distance. If the psychiatrist is identified with the defense he is at once a support; if with the prosecution, he may be the District Attorney in disguise. I will mention in brief a case in which the employment of a psychiatrist came to the attention of the Supreme Court of the United States.

That the employment of psychiatry in criminal justice is not yet fully defined and its limitations accepted is illustrated in the case of Leyra v. Denno. Camilo Leyra, age 75, and his wife, age 80, were found dead in their Brooklyn apartment. Several days later their son, age 50, was arrested and charged with having murdered them with a hammer. He was convicted and sentenced to death chiefly on several alleged confessions of guilt. It appears that following the killings, the accused was interrogated by the police for some three and a half days without securing from him a confession of the crime. The accused at this time was suffering with a sinusitis for which the police had promised him that they would secure a physician. During the police interrogation, the accused was permitted a respite of several hours of sleep

THE PRE-TRIAL PHASE 41

and in this interval a concealed microphone was installed with wire connections to another room in which the State prosecutor, the police and possibly some others were stationed to overhear what the accused might say. In due course, Leyra was introduced to a physician supposedly to render medical relief. The doctor, however, was not a practitioner but a psychiatrist with considerable knowledge of hypnosis. The opinion relates:

> Instead of giving the petitioner the medical advice and treatment he expected, the psychiatrist by subtle and suggestive questions simply continued the police effort of the past days and nights to induce the petitioner to admit his guilt. For an hour and a half or more the techniques of a highly trained psychiatrist were used to break the petitioner's will in order to get him to say he had murdered his parents. Time and time and time again the psychiatrist told the petitioner how much he wanted to and could help him, how bad it would be for the petitioner if he did not confess, and how much better he would feel, and how much lighter and easier it would be on him if he would just unbosom himself to the doctor. Yet, the doctor was at the very time the paid representative of the State while prosecuting officials were listening in on every threat made and every promise of leniency given.

A tape recording of the psychiatric examination was made and a transcription of the tape was read into the record of the case. The court commented:

> First, an already physically and emotionally exhausted suspect's ability to resist interrogation was broken to almost trancelike submission by the use of the arts of a highly skilled psychiatrist. Then the confession the petitioner began making to the psychiatrist was filled in and perfected by additional statements given in rapid succession to a police officer, a trusted friend, and two State prosecutors.[50]

A transcript of this "psychiatric examination" was affixed as an appendix to the opinion of the Court and it reads like Trilby.

Yet most offenders convey a surprising amount of confidence, the burden of which is often more onerous to the psychiatrist than to the defense attorney who may know his client is culpable but his pledge is to abstractions called the client's "rights." The psychiatrist is pledged to the person of the accused. Generally, however, the accused has made little effort to conceal the fact of his offense. More often it is either his indifference to it or his own failure to supply an explanation for his actions; sometimes it is the denial of the fact in the face of unequivocal evidence. The accused somehow communicates to those around him that something is wrong. Let us suppose that the psychiatrist examines the accused before trial. The psychiatrist will have two aims in mind. First, from his data he will give an opinion whether the accused is so incommunicable (mentally disordered) as to be untriable. If such be the case he will advise counsel who will act accordingly. The court will likely wish to appoint experts of its choosing to confirm or dispute the opinion or it may accept the findings. Second, if the accused appears to be triable then the psychiatrist will ponder his data in view of its introduction into the trial. To the first application of triability the data are considered in their clinical significance; to a second application in public they have to be reduced to a different level of abstraction—they must be brought to a focus the point of which must be on the dead center of a legal test of responsibility.

The Cleric

I will relate a case in which psychiatry was used in the individual-centered pre-trial phase of criminal justice. In this case the court-appointed Sanity Commission acted properly within the limitations of psychiatry. A clinical recommendation free of any implication of a moral evaluation was accepted by the Court.

A thirty-year-old man was arrested on fraudulent conversion and false pretenses. In default of $25,000 bail he was de-

THE PRE-TRIAL PHASE

tained in the County Prison by a Magistrate. Two complainants at first reported that they had given the accused certain advances in payment for new automobiles for which he had failed delivery. In turn, six similar complaints were pending involving a sum in the neighborhood of $14,000.

This case was not ordinary in the calendar of crime in a large metropolitan center. Two conditions gave it a unique character; first, the accused was a clergyman, and second, the money manipulations were not governed by the usual motivation associated with fraudulent conversion and false pretenses. Those who carried the onus of official judgment likely sensed incongruity in both, and shared the element of surprise that a cleric should find himself so accused. Incongruity and surprise do not combine easily for ready-made answers. The accused did not readily fit the formula. The committing magistrate made the following public statement:

> This unfortunate young man was suspended by the Archbishop and deprived of his priestly facilities many months ago when his derelictions were reported to the church authorities. He received the utmost consideration and the church authorities endeavored vainly with no cooperation from him to assist him both financially and otherwise to extract himself from the transactions he committed and entered into. Meanwhile, he engaged in many similar and other transactions on a fantastic scale all involving the acquisition of large sums of money in violation of civil and church laws. He was finally induced to go to Chancery office last week, where he was turned over to the police and had a hearing on only a few of the charges.
>
> There are six additional charges here today and many other complaints which he must face. He has caused much distress and loss to innocent persons. To protect others as well as himself he was placed under protective security. It may very well be that he is mentally ill for undoubtedly he is under delusions of grandeur, admits no wrong and will not cooperate with church or civil authorities. Whether he is mentally capable of distinguishing right from wrong is a medical problem and a competent Commission to inquire into his sanity and make this determination will be appointed. In the meantime, he should be retained in protective

security where all his rights will be amply protected and his person respected.[51]

A Sanity Commission composed of two psychiatrists and a lawyer was appointed. When a Commission undertakes an examination of an accused, a number of forces can come into play. Three persons set out to find out something about the subjective world of the accused and by their findings to reconcile the anxiety born of incongruity and surprise. The three came from different backgrounds of experience and ideology; two had had similar technical indoctrination. The lawyer occupied yet another orbit closer to the court. None had found himself in the situation of the accused and thus any identification either with him or with his accusers, could be bridged only by language. The Commission's task was first to establish and sustain a communication among its own members and second between the Commission and the accused himself. When the Commission met there was a tacit agreement that the method of examination would consist of collecting information from the accused and from those about him. Information would be secured in response to questions framed as direct inquiry intended to elicit facts of the biographical environment and as indirect inquiry designed to stimulate spontaneous responses from levels below surface consciousness by means of associations and metaphor arising from any point in the subject's time table and reconstructions of the past. Once the collection of information was obtained there remained the problem of how to extract meaning out of it which could be communicated to others and to the court.

The Commission met in the prison and was supplied initially with a record of the institutional observations. This was unrevealing. The accused was brought to the examining room and when he entered, he did not manifest unusual behavior nor outward indications of mental illness. He was cooperative and seemingly willing to convey to the best of his ability information desired by the Commissioners. There was no order in the interrogation and for the most part the Commission waited upon him to relate himself spontaneously.

The accused was an only child brought up in parochial schools in Philadelphia with eventual study and ordination as a priest in 1950. The Commission was given its first hint of some inner movement within the accused when a request was made that he supply some data in regard to his family. At this request, a slight change of mood with troubled reflection came over him and in this signal the Commission was given tacit notice of what would be the likely center of his inner disturbance. With visible agitation his first utterance referred to the death of his father in 1952. The circumstance was shocking. This occurred on a Sunday. The patient and his father had agreed that the latter would join him at the rectory and they would take dinner at the home of a cousin. The father was to meet him around noon. When his father did not arrive, the patient telephoned his apartment but there was no answer. He thought his father might have been arrested for speeding. His father had frequently driven too rapidly. He drove to his father's apartment and observing his father's car parked in its usual location, it occurred to him *that his father had died.* He had not found him at first and only after some search discovered his father lying dead between two beds. The patient was greatly disturbed the next day when he read in the papers the statement that he had had a key to his father's apartment. This, he thought, might have given the impression that he was implicated in his father's death. He followed this report with an account of his mother's death in 1949 which terminated a long invalidism of some thirteen years. To him it was significant that the mother's death took place the day before he was to receive his "collar." He recalled a year later at ordination:

I will never forget the loneliness and heartbreak that I felt when I was waiting on the Seminary grounds for the limousine to take me to the Cathedral—I saw the car turn into the grounds, saw that my relatives were in it—all except the one that I had wanted most, my Mother. It is difficult to explain how I could go through the ceremonies of Ordination. I fully realized what was taking place, but I had no emotional thrill about it. This feeling of emptiness—this lack of enthusiasm—has always been with me since my Mother's death. There is nothing that seems to penetrate this inner gloom that rests upon me.

His thoughts then turned to the surviving relatives some of whom had had nervous breakdowns. The Commission's attention was directed to his references to the female relatives, one of whom he described as possessive and dominating, and to his reflection that none of his relatives had made an appearance on his behalf. Up to this moment the accused had made no spontaneous references to his legal predicament. In this alignment of his thoughts and feelings the Commission could already sense that beyond the verbal statements of the accused there was a deeper communication of an only child reacting to the actual loss of ties with supporting figures and in this his isolation and inner anxiety. It is significant that first spontaneous statements often convey the nuclear problem and in the telling of it the patient is communicating material that has the character of a dream. It has meaning, but the meaning is not known either to him or to others. Like the dream it has no apparent immediate connection with the objective problem. What could fraudulent conversion and false pretenses have to do with the lonely figure who had suffered the loss of his parents and who had felt the abandonment of near parental figures? Here were two worlds. His communication was centered on past events but they are related as if he were living them again in the present. But another world was in the present; the criminal charges and confinement in a prison. Between these two worlds there had to be some connection. It is in some language beyond the grammar of common sense; future analysis may reveal its symbols. Even in this introductory stage of communication the Commission was aware of these two worlds; the one occupied by the accused, the other by the Commission. The Commission could not easily evaluate his in its own terms, it could only enter his.

His life was recalled in the interval following his mother's death. He prefaced his account: "I had no feeling for anything—no emotion for anything—even when I was ordained in 1950. Since then, even now, I am not affected. I felt no security after mother's death. I was never close to father. Father and I leaned on mother." In further exchange it developed that since the mother's death, he had had no one with whom he could share his experiences. Ordination and assignment to a parish accentuated his sense of separation. The fellowship of the Seminary was dispersed. At this point, he referred again to a relative in whom he sensed a threatening possessiveness and domination of him which became particularly evident if he showed any tendency to have interest in others. If he did not find in another woman a figure to replace his mother, he must turn elsewhere in order to fill the hiatus. He referred to the fact that after his mother's death, his father began to drink and "both of us got flashy—big cars —went to Florida." During the stay in Florida on several occasions, he and his father went to the races. "On the surface, my father and I had both settled into stride—both of us were seriously upset. My father began to drink, which he had never done before, and he looked very bad."

In this connection the Commission learned that the father began drinking at the son's suggestion, with the latter aware that his father had previous difficulty with alcohol and that such a suggestion released the father from the mother's prohibition. He also suggested that his father needed to socialize more; that his father was an "easy touch" for women. Eventually in the course of his socialization with women, the father did spend a great deal of money.

I, for my part, began to spend money freely and foolishly. The money, about another $2,000 that I had received as gifts at my ordination was soon consumed. My father and I went to Florida in the winter, something we were to do every year until he died. My father went for a month and I for a week. While in Florida, I noticed that the change seemed to make a new man of my father—so I came to the conclusion that living alone in our house with so many memories was what had been making it difficult for him to get back on his feet. I then suggested to my father that he sell our house and move to an apartment. Later on, I always regretted this fact. It was a good step for my father; but with the breaking up of my mother's home, I lost all feeling of security. Security to me has never meant money—security to me means that some one loves me, and will stand by me, and that I have someplace to call "home"—from this time on, all that has left my life.

Apparently this was the beginning of a substitutive activity which persisted until the time of his father's death. The accused spoke of the only residual interest in life as that of going to the races. Following his father's death he continued to do so as it was somewhere to go, particularly on his days off when his sense of loneliness was accentuated. The races filled the whole day and in the meantime, he carried out his functions as a clergyman. The father's death marked the renewal of his loneliness and imposed upon him further adjustment. Further detail filled out the picture of the family relationships. The mother was characterized as a dominant force felt by both male members. Father was kept in line. The dominance came not only out of the mother's own position in the arbiter's role but also out of the powerful effect of her invalidism, in the course of which disability there was notice of an unremitting demand and appeal. The design of daily life was keyed to her needs. This was particularly the case of the father who for many years was at his trade at night and at her side as attendant nurse by day. The death of the mother brought release. At his mother's funeral an aside came to him. "At last I'm free—no longer do I have to be a *good boy*." Father set upon a course of excessive drinking and the son turned to him. Both found a larger range together and the previous lack of closeness between them seemed to be filled in by companionship of the trips, a big car and a day at the races. A change had taken place in both of them but not a similar change. The accused once asked his father what had come over him. Drinking was replacing something in the past and also releasing something in substitute long held in abeyance. The two were drawn together in a bond of mourning. Something had come over father. Our concern was for what had come over the accused. He related as best he could in words his reactions to mother's death and to the subsequent loss of father. There remained a further telling of his reactions in the language of actions and events. The Commission turned to a chronicle of them.

About the time of the mother's death, a maternal uncle had developed mental illness. Another uncle gave the accused a sum of money to administer for medical expenses. This was the first time he had ever handled a sizable sum of money. Following the uncle's death the accused became one of the executors of the estate from which he received a fee as well as a small legacy. Here was the beginning of some interest in the handling of money for others. A thread of it was to follow throughout subsequent events. The accused placed two sentiments in apposition; one, his sense of acute loss of interest in living in which he went through the motions even at the time of his ordination. He was "spiritually dry." The other, an avowed indifference to the value of money. Perhaps these were isomers; neither living nor spending gave him meaning or satisfaction. He said, "I have no value of money; five dollars, fifty, or five hundred mean the same or nothing to me." Yet he found momentary relief from tedium. Living and spending were revivified at the race track. Here he felt a return of enthusiasm in the excitement of the crowd, in the betting and in the races. A day at the races became an antidote against depression, first shared with his father and continued alone after his death. In time the antidote became an addiction. In the meantime, his betting grew in size and at times his luck ran with him. The dim outline of a magical compulsion was beginning to show through on this side of the narrative; on the other side, something of a complementary order was making its way into view. The attendance at the races brought a kind of intoxication; with it money came at times as if by magic—on two occasions he took home some $6,000. To some the acquisition of money means security which on the unconscious level means being loved. But in our accused the sense of security was not seemingly the getting but the giving of money.

The Commission noted that with the onset of the race track addiction there was also the beginning of an undoing of it. Here in the chronicle is a spending of money that is almost a parody of charity. He became generous. He gave with mere asking, he gave because he couldn't refuse, he gave anonymously and he gave in the sense that in giving one accumulates virtue which seems to transcend the means of getting. The Commission attempted to follow a long and intricate series of transactions of getting and giving, the records of which were beyond audit and in keeping with Gertrude Stein's remark about money: "As a cousin of mine once said about money, money is always there, but the pockets change; it is not in the same pocket after the change, and that is all there is to say about money."

Let us follow his account.

It was about this time when I started to go to the races. In the beginning I went only occasionally but gradually I went more and more. My father too enjoyed the races. We went together every Wednesday when the races would be in New Jersey, Delaware, Maryland and West Virginia. Father was always a moderate player but I bet pretty heavily. About this time too father made me a gift of $5,000. When I did go to the races and would win, always $1,000 or $2,000, I rarely spent any of the winnings on myself. I would give it away freely and I started about this time to buy expensive gifts for my relatives and various friends. It has been remarked that it was strange that none of these recipients of my expensive gifts ever questioned where I got the money; a fact which is literally true, but I suppose all my life those close to me have just naturally assumed that I was well oiled. Wherever I went, I always picked up the tab with very few exceptions although there were a few friends who would not let me do this for them.

From that time on, I was more and more lonely. The only enjoyment or relaxation that I experienced was at the races and I attended them much more frequently from this time on. I also spent money much more liberally from this time . . . I gave hundreds of dollars to charity, and also to friends, and anyone who asked me. I gave and loaned several thousands of dollars to people who came to me in the rectory; and had standing orders with several local merchants, whereby I would send people to them for food and clothing and the storekeeper would bill me at the end of the month. I also took several people on trips to Florida at this time, and covered all bills; and bought my cousin and my Aunt diamond rings, diamond watches, fur coats, etc. From about this time on too, there were several families to whom I slipped ten or fifteen dollars every week.

Up until about two years ago, I always kept my bills in good order. After my father's death, I became very careless—and can't even remember when I first got myself into debt. Through the influence of a wealthy cousin, I borrowed large sums of money from the bank; and since I always paid them before they were due, later I was able to get loans on my own signature. I also began to borrow from loan sharks, and paid them back when due with large additions of interest. Although I must admit that I think in general the loan sharks are pretty nice fellows. If you need money—they give it to you, and no questions asked. The banks on the other hand charge interest too, but make you go through a lot of red tape.

One day almost by accident I met a boy who told me that he wanted to go to the Seminary. He was not from my parish; but I always assumed that it was a matter of conscience that God had sent him to me for a purpose. His own people wouldn't give him any money to do this. I told him that I would get someone to help him—and it was only later that he found out that I was helping him myself. His tuition was about $750 a year and train fare and spending money—so that as an estimate, I suppose that I have given him about $4,000. However, of all the people that I have helped I think that this fellow appreciates it most. I normally wouldn't say anything about this, but it seems to be generally known that I did help this boy when he needed it.

More and more, I had to do some juggling to have money when I needed it. I borrowed and was always worried about paying it back—and luckily most of the time, I could spend as freely as before and still win enough on the races to cover what I had borrowed. Very few people, I think, ever realized that I was in financial trouble.

About January of this year, my cousin told me he was thinking of getting a new car. Because I was able to get a car at great savings through the Institutional Procurement Service, I suggested that he let me get his car for him. He gave me the money, and I got him his car. I think that I lost even on this car, but I was glad to see that he got a nice car out of it. I had no intention of getting any more cars after I had gotten this one for him. Later on, this same fellow called and asked me if I would get a car for a friend of his. I agreed. I suppose that I needed money at this time, and I figured that getting the fellow a car for more than he paid me was just like borrowing money and paying the interest on the money. Once again I got this car, and thought that this would be the end of it. After that, my cousin kept asking me to get cars for various friends, and then he started making some money on the deal himself. However, in all truth, my cousin never knew that there was anything fishy about these deals, especially since he saw that the cars were delivered and that the people received their titles to the car. I think that there were about seven or eight cars that I delivered in this way, and I must have lost about $400 to $600 on each car. At times, when I would receive some of this money I would gamble at the track, and my winnings at least got me through several months of this. It is interesting too that I never had to sales-talk people about the cars. I met very few of the people concerned, and the things seemed to be pyramiding. There were other people too who would talk up the cars, expecting to get a cut on them.

The Commission had difficulty in following these financial manipulations beyond perceiving that in time the accused had reached a point of constant state of arrears and renewed efforts to recoup by gambling his chance assets. This is an old formula that we associate with bank tellers who use money of others. The bank teller usually spends his embezzlements on himself. Our accused spent it on others. He was asked: "Why do you need to lose money?" He replied, "I really don't know . . . I went wild and gave it away." Later he reflected: "I behaved as if I were asking to be caught. I wanted to be

THE PRE-TRIAL PHASE 53

caught." He also expressed the belief that his arrest, confinement and hospitalization had a great deal to do with his aunt's attempt at suicide.

The accused had no developed system of horse betting. "I looked at the names of the horses." This statement was connected with his next thought. "I have no interest in life . . . in my conscience I do not feel I did a moral wrong. I gave the money away, I never planned this and I never intended to cheat them."

In the appearances of things here is a person of good education and moral training who had turned to fraudulent conversion and false pretenses. The accused made no effort to deny the charges; in fact, he was moved to some resentment for the inaccuracies and condemnatory tone in them. It was as if he were demanding that others make sure of the truth of his guilt. Something had come over him in time to bring him to an undoing. From the viewpoint of law there was no question that he carried out a long series of illicit acts for which a penalty would be attached. Yet his actions and the absence of defensive rationalizations of them could not be easily accounted for. Was the Commission dealing with an internal process which governed the accused, independently of the external reality spelled out in a moral code? The accused was a person equipped by long training and rigid self-discipline to guide and instruct others in moral matters and yet he felt within himself that he had not committed a moral wrong. From outward appearances alone, little could be elicited to reconcile this paradox.

We may reflect that child-rearing is an individual experience in the development of higher thought from magic, through religion to science. There is scarcely any doubt that gambling is a behavior reflecting an archaic magical orientation to reality and that it leaves to chance the determination of survival. In our accused there came to light another aspect of magic. His giving of money was seemingly to maintain a magical connection with his dead mother in whose name he associated the giving. In general, his behavior was diametrically opposed to his mother's desires. In this destructive behavior he was attempting to emancipate himself from the "internalized" mother. When behaving in this manner he felt "a sense of freedom" as though he were himself possessed. This, however, was short-lived and quickly followed by feelings of loneliness, despair and obsessional suicidal thoughts. Our interest became centered on these magical elements in the mental life of the accused and on the possible correlation between them and his child rearing.

We are dealing here with an only child who was "spoiled." As a child he always had more pocket money than others of his age group and this indulgence continued with him throughout his later years of the Seminary. At the age of twelve, in the 7th grade, at the onset of his mother's invalidism, there was discontinuance of developed relationships with his school contemporaries. Each day after school, he would dutifully return home in order to care for mother. Nursing care was shared with father who in turn adjusted his life to supply in attendance in daytime. The accused himself sensed that his emotional growth was unhealthy. "I was not trained for growing up . . . never had any real disciplined life . . . I had never been *treated*." The Commission made note of this lapse of speech. He corrected this to be "trained." And the Commission pondered the significance of this slip and the ambiguity in the word "treated." The accused did excellent work in school but soon learned that his high performance alienated him from his classmates. Later in high school he deliberately did inferior work in order that "I could become a regular guy." He epitomized the parental attitude towards him as a growing boy as one "treated like he couldn't make a mistake." The accused entered the Seminary from high school. His choice of life work was seemingly his own. Yet there was in the background the mother's uncommon displeasure when in high school he had shown a tentative interest in girls and an unequivocal approval when he announced his intention to become a priest.

We sense in this revelation the strength of the ties between the accused and his mother and the tacit dominance of the supporting figure. The accused accounted his first memory as a dream in which "father and mother left me in the house by myself," and his spontaneous next utterance was, "from the age eleven to the present, I never had a break, I am a peaceful man." This statement compressed a world of meaning. The hope for a "break" again spoke for some magical element of his orientation and the declaration that he is a peaceful man can have no other meaning than its contrary; he is filled with long repressed resentment which comes to eventual assertion in the devious path of a magical self-destructive enterprise. With the dénouement the accused felt a sense of ineffable relief and for the first time could sleep well. The connection between his undoing and the mother figure was hinted in his own words: "If mother were alive things would not have happened. She would have managed my affairs. I know I have hurt myself, mother's death affected me but *it is not the cause.*" Indeed mother's death was not the cause, but the denial of it can also convey the affirmation of it expressed in the forepart of his statement. He verbally contradicts himself; one part of his statement comes from the unconscious, the other comes from the conscious correction of the moment. How often do we note in our patients the dual train of communication in which an inner truth is revealed only to be denied in the next breath; how much does such communication link the present with the past.

The Commission requested the accused to make freehand drawings of a man and a woman. He complied. On inspection an immediate and conspicuous feature was of his having drawn the woman considerably larger than the man. This feature also appeared in perspective so that the woman stood in a more forward position. It was noted that in the outline of the man there were no details of the hands or feet; the woman's hands were in detail but not the feet. In the drawing of the man there was an avoidance of completion of the genital area; in both figures there was a close resemblance in facial features, notably in the woman a conspicuous outline of very broad shoulders. Here, at least superficially, the Commission could get a glimpse of the relationships of the accused with men and women figures. They are not complete and neither are his actual connections with them. Certainly within his inner perceptions of the world the woman holds a more forward and manipulating relationship. Perhaps within the inner earliest images imprinted in childhood there is an unclear differentiation between the sexes.

In the course of the Commission's interview there did not appear in the accused any features of impaired orientation with time, place or person, or defects of memory or any distortion of affect beyond the appearance of a subdued, quiet, rather passive individual. There was a hint of effeminancy in his mannerisms. The Commission could elicit no delusional material nor any evidence from the history of an active psychotic process. And there certainly was no psychotic process at the time of the examination. To make a diagnosis of psychosis in the sense of conventional symptoms would be to account only for the grosser features of mental pathology. Yet the Commission could not dismiss the accused as a normal person.

In the view of his community the accused had made a satisfactory adaptation in the first twenty-five years of his life. The loss of supporting figures had been an abiding fear since earliest recollection. The inner integrity of the mind is maintained by the earliest imprints of child rearing and exerts a controlling influence on our decisions in life as if our course and balance are fixed by an internal gyroscope. Our maturation is the attainment first of physical independence and later of emotional independence. But the latter is relative and perhaps the measure of it can be expressed in terms of one's capacity to make decisions, less determined by old unconscious bindings and more by objective reality values. It would appear that in our accused the maturation was apparent but not real; that as long as the parental figures existed and there continued a love, support, protection and affirmation that he could not make mistakes, our accused had purpose and direction in his life. The loss of such supporting figures was the loss of something within him and what remained was a child filled with fear and loneliness. The perception of the inner deficit came to him acutely at the time of the mother's death.

From that moment on, I seemed to lose all interest in life and a melancholy came upon me that was to increase as the years went on.... This feeling of emptiness, this lack of enthusiasm, has always been with me since my mother's death. There is nothing that seems to penetrate this inner gloom that rests upon me.

The accused referred to his recurrent thought: "I didn't care whether I lived or died." These thoughts were a persistent undertone of unformed suicidal fantasy that filled in the moments when he was alone. He complained that since mother died he lacked feeling. In his religious life he regarded himself as spiritually dry: "I can go through the motions, perform my religious duties and feel no emotion. It means nothing. I cry without reason. I do not know why." Following the father's death, the accused found that his vocation and parish duties could not absorb his sense of loneliness. He had never found confidence with others and could not establish a fellowship with his colleagues. From time to time he would be drawn to a railroad station where he would eat, read the news, watch the passing crowd and then go to the movies. He went to the races as if joined in memory of pleasant times with father. He struck up acquaintances, but never cultivated them. In relating his experience at the races he spoke of a sense of excitement of the great thrill of watching the race at the home stretch, especially if his horse were winning. He averred, "I never got a thrill like this even before mother died. I was never happy except at the races." At the races his money worries evaporated. "After the races the happiness left and was replaced with gloom." The winning of money was not essential to this happiness—there was some other occult attraction. All practical concerns and tedium of every day life were held in abeyance for the excitement of the race track.

It is to be recounted that the accused knew that he was eventually to come by substantial legacies. This knowledge became more and more a preoccupation with him as his gambling and money manipulations became more involved and as he became more and more enmeshed in them. There remained two avenues of eventual reckoning; either his relatives would die or he would make a "big killing at the races." The Commission sensed that for the accused the thrill of the race had meaning beyond the surface reach of the Commission; that with other unconscious determinants it combined several elements to make a common pathway of expression. Several needs of the accused found an economy of expression and release at the races. He spoke of "something holding and binding me in deep conviction at the same time with the wish to do something and the wish not to."

The accused returned again and again to his inner feelings that had persisted since the death of his mother. "I lost all meaning of life. I *know the difference between right and wrong,* but I am inclined to help or condone wrong in others." The Commission found difficulty in interpreting this statement. He pointed out that before mother's death in his own way the knowledge of sinning and evil in others would have indeed shocked him. Afterwards he sensed an indifference in himself; in his parish work he gained much knowledge of various activities of his parishioners which would be considered both antisocial and evil. "Few know and can accept people now as I do. I turned against God not to become an agency of evil, but to have an acceptance of it." The Commission remarked that this was a reminder of his inability to reconcile himself to the death of his mother at the very threshold of his ordination and that he could not quite feel that

God had been just and that there had come into his inner feelings something of a compliance and acceptance of evil in others and in this there was a hint of latent revenge. He did not turn against God in the sense "especially when I think of others and their mothers and fathers and families," but rather in the reference to his great feeling of utter sense of loss and the lack of any personal ties. Again he appealed, "Why couldn't I have had a break?"

We reflect on the turn of events affecting the career of this young man who communicates meaning to us so little in words and much in actions. If we will refer to Frazer's metaphor of the development of higher thought and to the phases of it in the growth of the child and set the accused in the light of it we discern the outlines of the phenomenon only too commonplace in modern times. In the accused as in many there is behind the facade of apparent adaptation a different world of magical orientation to reality. This apparent adaptation is not self-sustained; in the accused it is undermined with the loss of those around him who were his support during the earliest years of dependency. There remained a shell of apparent normality by which, in psychiatric idiom, he was able to maintain a minimum contact with reality. Behind this we find the insidious growth of a private system of magical manipulations which in symbolism link them with the remote past and with primal figures, particularly the mother. It remains for future analysis to work out this symbolism.

The Commission was impressed with the apparent absence of anxiety in this young man. This was in keeping with the mood which he conveyed verbally and with what seemed to be a kind of relief and resignation. Some inner "need" had been satisfied, but the Commission was yet to learn the "secret" of it. This was a profile of an apparent normality associated with a loss of interest with a depression of mood and with a kind of ill-concealed gratification which set off the individual. He is alienated from the objective reality of his circumstance in which he finds himself. There are a great many such persons to be found in our penal institutions. In our view of them we seldom get beyond the appearances of their normality into their inner psychopathology. The inner tribunal of these persons exacts a toll of private suffering. Such persons appear to be driven by an inner necessity to dramatize their inner conflicts on an external theater. They seldom come to self-awareness, to the determined necessity of their behavior and to the meaning of their suffering. They have many counterparts among the law-abiding who likewise are driven to self-destructive ends.

The Commission returned to its purpose in scope which posed the following questions: Was the accused psychotic? Did he have the capacity to appreciate the significance of his charge and to cooperate in the preparation of his defense? Such are the questions to be answered in a pre-trial examination of a person about whom there is a question of mental illness. The Commission was mindful that the court which appointed the Commission had posed to it the question whether the accused was sane or could distinguish between right and wrong.

In the previous remarks I have expressed the view that the psychiatrist is not concerned with the determination of insanity which is to be regarded as a legal matter, determined by legal authority. The Commission could not answer the question of the accused's capacity to distinguish right from wrong. He had himself spoken of the issue and his answers could not be disputed. He clearly acknowledged that his actions were legally and morally wrong and he spoke as one eminently qualified to discriminate them. Having settled this matter as a judgment upon himself, the accused shared with the Commission an ignorance of his inner motivations. He sensed the symbolic linkage between his wrongful acts with past events of his life, but he lacked that self-awareness that would have given him control of the emotional forces at work in him in shaping his behavior.

The Commission made its report to the court. The accused

was not psychotic, which was to say that he was triable, but he did have a "mental illness." To state that he had a mental illness was in effect to say that the accused lacked a self-awareness which in the past would have contravened his self-destructive tendencies which brought him to law breaking, and that the accused had the capacity to acquire a self-awareness, to effect a change within himself and restore him to a social usefulness.

The court accepted the Commission's report which gave emphasis to the operational aims of the law. It suggested that the court, acting as parent in the interest of the correction of the child, should take such measures to that end. It was pointed out that a moralistic, punitive rejection would do little more than exacerbate the defendant's "mental illness." The defendant had already provoked the moral order and brought punishment upon himself. He had orphaned himself from a secure livelihood and vocation. The Commission's recommendation made it clear that the defendant did not have an awareness of his own inner motivations, his private cult, working within him on a level of fugitive memory traces. It would take some time to reach this part of the defendant and it could be done only with a non-moralistic approach requiring the skill of experienced hands. The Commission was clear in its own view of the defendant that he represented one of many persons so "criminally" motivated, who is "mentally ill" yet triable, and for whom the participation in a moral adjudication of his own behavior could have a salutary effect. The adjudication would say that his defection and guilt are real in the eyes of the community, that no amount of word manipulation could exculpate him. The problem now was shifted from a guilt fastening procedure in which there would have been much talk about him to a procedure of what to do with him or to him. The court shifted the issue from the penal code to the Mental Health Act and in the latter was found means of attaining the aim of best bringing our defendant back into the fold. The court acted upon the provisions of the Pennsylvania Mental Health Act of 1951, Section 342, (Amended January 14, 1952, P.L. 2053.) which reads as follows:

Section 342. Commitment of Person Charged with Crime.—Whenever any person charged with crime, upon production or appearance before the court, appears to be mentally ill or in need of care in a mental hospital, the court shall designate a responsible person to apply for his commitment, or for his commitment for observation, treatment and diagnosis, by order of such court, in accordance with the provisions of this act for the commitment of persons who are not convicted of crime or who have not been charged with crime.

The defendant was committed to a state hospital for further study and the court sanctioned his subsequent placement in another psychiatric institution for more intensive study and treatment.

In a later chapter I will offer some comments upon the question of the causal connection between mental illness and unlawful behavior. In these I will attempt to show that a causal connection always exists between a given mental state and the unlawful act. It is superficial and single only in the appearances of things. We must go deeper to discover that the outward behavior is determined by antecedent events usually multiple and additive, experienced in the earliest of the formative years, centered around significant traumatic events or sustained tensions and that the outward behavior will have a linkage in symbol with the historical conflict. In our case of the clergyman, the symbol which speaks simultaneously both for the present and the past associates money with secure ties with a family figure. After some months of work with the defendant the memory traces, like primitive embryonic cells, slowly arranged themselves into symmetrical forms of experience relived in the present. In this inner metamorphosis such restructured experiences gradually surfaced as the traumatic events linked with the outward behavior in the present. It was significant to the Commission that in the defendant's later account of his early formative setting he did not reveal one vital dimension of his experience. He did not do so either because it had been securely repressed or if remembered some inner assessment dismissed the matter as having little to do with his problem. Sometimes the things that people do not speak of are more significant. Some months later we came to learn that the defendant's father by former marriage had a son eleven years older than the defendant. At some point in his adolescence the stepbrother got himself in trouble with the police, either because of involvement with automobiles or for loitering on the streets. The defendant's mother prevailed in her demand that the stepson be removed from home. This banishment occurred when the defendant was seven years old. The following year the stepbrother made weekly visits but was not taken back into the family. The defendant now recalls that at the age of eight he witnessed an argument between the stepbrother and the mother, from whom the stepbrother had requested money for a better car. After this experience the stepbrother never visited again. In the defendant's feeling life there is much of it centered on this fugitive stepbrother and we can regard these events as having meaning of an unmastered traumatic tension. It is now more clear to us and to the defendant himself that his outward behavior had some linkage in the symbol of money and with a vital relationship with the mother figure and even in its barest outline we can discern a repetitive undoing of the earlier banishment of the stepbrother. Now we cannot ignore the defendant's acting out of this ancient moral problem. He uses money for others as if to undo what mother failed to do for his brother. This, despite his realization that mother was not wealthy and that the stepbrother's demand was unjustified. His brother came in time to be those whom the defendant indemnified with money and with whom the defendant became reunited. In this identification the defendant is in his brother's place. In this context in his outward acts he has repeated the old "crime" of the brother and come to similar end. At the same time in this private theater he has emancipated himself from the mother never to return.

IV THE CRIMINAL LAW AND PSYCHIATRY IN ACTION: THE CRIMINAL TRIAL

> So important is the criminal trial to the whole ideological structure of government that its disappearance in favor of an efficient and speedy way of accomplishing the incarceration of persons supposed to be dangerous to the social order, is always a sign of psychological instability of a people.
>
> THURMAN ARNOLD [52]

The Inner Side of Crime

In earlier times lawyer and doctor were joined in a common endeavor and method of dealing with psychological problems; in successive phases of doubt and certainty they came to some parting of the ways. In our so-called scientific civilization, only recently has man begun to achieve self-awareness through the method of science. In a prescientific orientation, man's inner world, closer to nature, was projected in symbol onto the external world as visible and invisible forces which enabled him to invent and maintain bindings of a social order. As man has turned to his inner world, he has found an increasingly larger part of his former outer world in it and has come to the discovery that this outer world was already in it behind a curtain of symbols. This penetralia is his unconscious and the systematic exploratory chartings and soundings of it have been the work of psychiatry and psychology. In our exploration of the unconscious, we come upon no new world but a very old one and we have a prescient sense of treading well-worn ancestral paths. The old, magical, union with nature again comes into stark view as in mental illness and in criminality. Benignly we view it in our own fantasies and dreams, in fact, in the entire range of normal mental life and communication. In this communication with the unconscious, the psychiatrist has abandoned some of the old symbols of social binding and he has done so because his patients had either never reached them or had retreated from them to earlier stations of reality orientation. The psychiatrist has had to learn the grammar of the unconscious which speaks and acts in ways that seem strange. He has had to devise a key to their inner meaning, not *why* they should come about but *how* they do. I have emphasized that the psychiatrist as scientist attempts to minimize the ethical aspects of his findings lest he find himself floundering in his search for the *how* of human behavior. Finally, as psychiatry as a method attains a larger measure of scientific validation, more should come of it as a means of promoting the movement of higher thought through self-awareness. In time, through self-awareness, a higher order of self actuated social order may be achieved.

In reflecting on what has been developed as a viewpoint and as a meaning of criminal justice in action, other perspectives come out to invite further commentary and to define the place of psychiatry in it. The criminal trial can be regarded as a social event which dramatizes the never ending conflict between that part of man closer to nature, his first amoral nature, the child in him, and that part of the symbolic environment, his moral second nature expressed in a religious ideal. In this view, it is of small importance that in its present day operation the vocabulary of the trial is no longer mystical or that its secularized ritual has lost some of its former awesomeness. Its essential meaning as a ligating religious force is unchanged.[53] That the trial is laid bare of its former panoply does not erase the deeper ties with the magical past.[54] Criminal justice is an institutionalized exteriorization and extension of the child rearing operation and its existence implies realistically that child rearing must be continuously applied beyond the conventional age when a person reaches his majority. The existence of criminal justice implies the fact of differences observed in a sizable number of persons who grow up physically and become adults but actually in emotional aging remain anchored to the infantile. Child rearing does not stop when the individual ceases to be a child. The law takes over where the parent leaves off. The law continues as an externalized regulatory arm in group life implementing in symbol its archtype, the internal tribunal of the individual conscience.[55, 56] In our day, the enormous amount of energy needed to maintain a stable community household is allocated to the task of dealing with only a relative few. Our child rearing is a perpetual uphill labor of promoting the movement of higher thought from magic to science.

On further inspection criminal justice in action will bear similarity to the unconscious operations within ourselves and will reveal the same contradictions and ambivalence. Now there is a difference between the internal tribunal of the individual and the externalized tribunal symbolized as justice and dramatized in the criminal trial. In the latter we find a system with more or less uniformity insofar as law can be made so in language, and in procedure. In this respect law posits the ideal of invariance. But in real life we come upon a range of variance. From clinically established observations it can be shown that; first,

> the internal tribunal of "conscience is widely variable and not standard as fictionalized in the law as the average and reasonable man; second, that some individuals are unresponsive to punishment; and third, that forbidden wishes are universal, the wrong doer acting out what the law abiding successfully repress or live out in dreams, fantasies, neuroses and in vicarious festive participation in fantasy with the wrong doer." [57]

The struggle between good and evil is carried out in two arenas of life; one within the private world with its adjudications derived from all levels, some conscious and a larger part unconscious which impart to actions and decisions a deterministic necessity; the other is the outer tribunal derived from rigidly structured models designed to minimize the taint of unconscious operations. The deterministic necessity flowing from unconscious operations has the meaning of the obsessive compulsive forces behind the symptomatic acting out of the criminal and in the living out of the mentally ill, and in the compulsive conformity of the law abiding.

To turn to the criminal trial itself. When law is put into action it publicly dramatizes the conflict between good and evil with triumph over evil. The persons who pass over its stage form an endless procession. They come out of anonymity, have a moment in their role, and pass on. The community reaction to the criminal as a person is rejecting; to him as a symbol it is all absorbing. Thus around the person of the criminal is the taboo of avoidance; even science shares this. The person of the criminal arouses anxiety in the generality of the law abiding, not so much for the fact that he has committed a specific crime but for the fact that any crime is a materialization of what the law abiding wish to deny; namely, the latent criminal wish common to all. But the criminal as symbol has a high value in the trial drama. When the trial is over, the criminal as a person is quickly put out of sight and given a number. This avoidance of the criminal is suggestive of the avoidance of contagion as if the law abiding have some uncertainty of their immunity. This avoidance with anxiety pertains as well after the criminal has "paid his debt" in penitence in a place called a penitentiary—he still has his symbolic value of contagion. He may be reformed but he has no way to reform the irrational beliefs of the law abiding who cannot relinquish the symbol.

A moment of reflection and we can discern the magical workings of projection onto the criminal which set him off from others as different and as "dangerous." A further reflection and we are back to demoniacal possession which was reported to have gone underground long ago. Now, one can easily accept the idea that the criminal is different and dangerous but the demon in him comes to life in our own invocation. In exorcizing the demon we cannot avoid rejecting, humiliating and injuring the person in whom the demon resides. The person naturally reacts to insult and hostility with like responses, consistent with his prior conditioning in his child rearing. In this circle of projection and interaction there is contained predictive self fulfillment which is so common in our child rearing. In a sense, the criminal, like the child, is duped into repeating his crime, since it is expected of him and in the rejection and injury to him there is an implied invitation.

In the view of such events our task is to clearly distinguish those parts of the operation of justice which exist purely in theory and systematization, which enable us to avoid coming face to face with the criminal himself, in the like fashion that we avoid confrontation with our inner selves. This we succeed in doing so long as we remain in a verbal world of self reflexive "as if" fictions; in a vast amount of talk about abstract criminals, crime, mens rea, motivation, deterrence, retribution, responsibility, reformation, etc.[58] Actual contact with the concrete criminal as a person is avoided. Only rarely do a few judges visit jails or penitentiaries; and the walls of such institutions are said to serve as large a purpose of keeping the outside world from looking in as of keeping evil inside. The avoidance of the person of the criminal has firm foundation in clinical psychiatry. This has a parallel in the defense of displacement in the obsessive compulsive pattern. The compulsive person does not succeed in the complete repression of his urges, sexual or aggressive. The overt expression of them would bring him into open conflict with both his inner tribunal of conscience and the outer tribunal of the group conscience. He can find neither direct expression of such urges nor does he completely succeed in sublimating them into substitute activity which is socially acceptable. He is too close to his urges and they are too close to him. Hence his persistent anxiety. His alternative is to displace the forbidden urge to an object which in distance now becomes simultaneously the symbol for the forbidden urge and the object of repulsion. His aggression can now find a scapegoat effigy. A commonplace example of this is in the case of the person who has intense unconscious death wishes against another. Such wishes cannot be admitted into consciousness but they can find indirect expression in the individual's fear of knives, guns and other objects of possible harmful use. He may forbid another to touch such objects which in his fantasy could be employed in doing harm. Such defenses tend to spread beyond the original object through many avenues sometimes remotely, but in symbol the line to the wish remains intact. In this process the fear of contact with the symbol of the wish pervades the obsessive pattern. In the public fear of contact, the criminal is the instrumentality of the forbidden wish and he is shunned and lost in society in person and displaced and lost in symbol in the abstractions of jurisprudence.

This will sound like nonsense to many and it will seem strange if not unseemly talk to those who conduct criminal trials. Judges and prosecutors will remonstrate that such projection and displacement of secret unlawful wishes are encountered only in abnormal people and that in their own exposure to the criminal they do not experience unlawful desires to commit crimes. The avoidance of the criminal is a practical matter of "protecting" society, like the avoidance of our obsessive compulsive who fears knives. His concern is for the "protection" of intended victims, yet it is also a protection of himself. But here the judges and prosecutors are speaking of the appearances of things; and when we look at the appearances of things the unconscious is out of focus. Reiwald emphasizes that the trial ceremony has the design of isolating the accused. He writes:

> Today, the protective screen between the judge and the criminal is constructed by means of stereotyped patterns of speech used during the proceedings, by the majestic formalities of the court and by the solemnity of the well conducted criminal court . . . here again the comparison with the compulsive ceremony of the neurotic can be seen. The energy which would be consumed in understanding the deed from its psychological and sociological standpoint, is displaced. It is used in the careful protection of the recognized institutions, in the avoidance of formal errors and in the need to base the judgment upon statutes, and the sections contained in them (the judgment must be made 'safe against revision'). An extraordinary dexterity and precision in the technical legal formalities and at the same time a fearful care for the proper regard of all form become apparent.[59]

Reiwald further comments that

> This is no peculiarity to criminal justice; it is the way of all dogmas which constantly lead away . . . from the human content in the case. Dogmas always tend to make the means the final end and place upon them the emotional value which in truth should be reserved for the main purpose.[60]

When we lead away from the heart of the case, we lead away from the individual-centered aspect of it—from its psychiatry, and when a case reaches the appellate courts the remoteness from the criminal in person supplants the ceremonial of the trial courts to screen him from view. The judges of the appellate courts do not see the accused. He is contained in the briefs.

The Criminal Trial as a Game

There is another aspect of the criminal trial as a public drama in which the "play is the thing,"—the actors are incidental—drawn from an apparently never-ending supply. In child-rearing social values held by the group are eventually worked out by the child in successive levels of intense fantasy play life which are but the shadows of what might be substance in action. In these successive levels we again discern Frazer's life line of the development of higher thought. The basic themes of the child's fantasies are already supplied by the culture in the form of folklore, fairy tales, standard myths and in the crime novel. In all ages children have been nourished upon them. Mother Goose, Jack the Giant Killer have their modern counterparts in commercially manufactured crime stories and Westerns. The themes have the same motifs and are filled with the entire repertory of implied crimes, but generally constricted to manslaying. The blanks are filled in by the child out of his own native resources. Of particular significance is repetition which is almost as imperative as the hunger cycle. At this point, one can draw the public drama of the criminal trial, in which crime is repeated in its recital, into the same context as the crime repeated in commercial fantasy. What fantasy from artifice is for the emotional growth phases and balance in the child, the real criminal from the stream of life is for the adult. This analogy holds only to a point. It is probable in our day, in reckoning the appetite and volume of current commercial product, that many adults may be in as great a need of this kind of fantasy pablum as are children. The criminal court is yet the central symbol of power in unifying community life, but in recent times it has lost the function as the principal theater of crime drama.

We exist in a world of external things created by the methods of science, but in the maintenance of secure social existence we are still anchored to a prescientific orientation. We have yet to achieve through the method of science a knowledge and control of our inner world through self awareness. Our social institutions are exteriorized aspects of the inner world and in them we can discover indirectly something of the unconscious operations in ourselves which remain fixed to earlier historical levels in our development of higher thought. In this thesis is the suggestion that criminal justice is a religious operation derived from traditional child rearing, and a continuation of it, in modern times divested of its former outward supernaturalism. In this view, criminal justice today is an operation moved by mortals, but as symbol and as ligating moral force, it articulates a religious meaning—it mediates an inner conviction of divine intervention in earthly affairs, *ex ore Dei*. In the inner belief of divine intervention are the latent elements of divine will, destiny and chance. On archaic levels of thought such concepts are tied to the idea of "fate." We have commonplace expressions of "having a lucky break, or an unlucky one," of being "jinxed," etc. Such ideas dominate the criminal mentality and have large currency in litigation. Even lawyers speak of law suits as a kind of gamble the results of which often come out of imponderable elements beyond visible evidence. A good lawyer is one who has an intuitive sense of them. In the criminal trial such elements play a large role. If we inquire into these elements we may come to a better appreciation of the impediments to the functioning of psychiatry in the public-centered phase of criminal justice. Here I am referring to the play or ludic element.

Huizinga writes:

> At first sight few things would seem to be further apart than the domain of law, justice and jurisprudence and play. High seriousness, deadly earnestness and the vital interest of the individual and society reign supreme in everything that pertains to the law. The etymological foundation of most of the words which express the ideas of law and justice lies in the sphere of setting, fixing, establishing, stating, appointing, holding, ordering, choosing, dividing, binding, etc. All these ideas would seem to have little or no connection with, indeed to be opposed to, the semantic sphere which gives rise to the words for play. However, as we have observed all along the sacredness and seriousness of an action by no means preclude its play quality." He adds, "That an affinity may exist between law and play becomes obvious to us as soon as we realize how much the actual practice of the law, in other words a

law suit, properly resembles a contest whatever the ideal foundations of the law may be.[61]

We think of the criminal trial in which two sides are aligned in opposition and we call it an adversary proceeding. The concept of a contest and struggle is conveyed both linguistically and in the actions of the trial. It is initiated by an *accusation* and challenge thrown by the *prosecution*; the accused responds in *defense*; sides are chosen in such terms, and the actions have a character of regulated attacks and counterattacks performed according to set rules. In Greece, litigation was considered as an *agon*. It was a contest sacred in form, contended before an arbiter. This agonal aspect persists today and there is in it an abiding solemnity which covers a latent sense of sacredness. Even the word "court" is derived from a "sacred circle," a place set off from the ordinary world. When a judge dons his robes he becomes another "being," to whom a rigid deference is made. He conducts the trial within a system of restrictive rules which set it into a domain of antithetical play. In modern trials the concept of abstract justice is invoked as the single aim of the proceedings, but the proceedings themselves can be no other than a cover of the desire to win the contest. Disputes about right and wrong are primary, but they remain in the realm of abstraction; winning or losing are secondary, but they are concrete. The desire to win the contest is the archaic, agonistic element for which in academic circles the term "adversary" is a mere euphemism. In the evolution of criminal law this agonal element as well as that of *chance* energizes the entire trial. The emblem of blind justice, the scales, conveys a metaphor of divine will, fate and chance which are "in the balance." But chance determines the winner; not the abstract, moral concept. Sometimes the two are conjoined. The criminal trial in our time retains the play elements of the game of chance, the contest and the verbal battle, the contest and the verbal battle overshadowing the more archaic game of chance.[62] In some cases the contending lawyers resurrect the more archaic elements of the verbal battle in which the agonistic factor is strongest and the ideal of justice is at its weakest. In such cases we are reminded of the slanging matches in which justice is worked out by the magical device of excoriating invective. Our verbal habits seemingly impel us to approach most of our personal problems by aggressively *acting upon* others, to *make* them understand, i.e. agree with us. Our techniques of refutation are highly developed and nowhere more than in the courtroom. Except for the nominal acceptance of the rules of the game, the techniques for agreement, i.e. action not *upon* but *between* ourselves and others, are practically nonexistent in criminal courtrooms.[63]

The play element of the criminal trial would not be unfolded without the audience. In our times through mass communication this audience is unlimited either in size or in distance. The contest is followed play by play and the courtroom is as large as the audience. The audience of the public trial is the same as that which works through life tensions displaced to any arena of contest. This has been so since ancient times. The trial is not far away from the sporting event the outcome of which is restricted to the rules of the game. In a capital case, particularly in that which dramatizes the age-old oedipal conflicts of parricide and incest, the ludic element attains a high level and extends beyond the actors of the courtroom. The discerning spectator of the criminal trial will not fail to note its festive character, the atmosphere of excitement, the shifts of interest and the scoring of the opposing sides. The accused is in prime focus. Everything said is about him and as the trial proceeds there is often noted that he attains a stature and image that set him beyond the measure of a malefactor. In a recent murder trial which I attended, no ingredient was missing for the emotionally satisfactory case. The principals were young and good-looking, the plot was as old as Homer; the triangle of the fickle wife who eloped with an older man, the scorned and injured husband who followed in frantic pursuit and killed the usurper. This trial took place in a small community and lasted several days during which the press seemed to be a preferential group and photographers were omnipresent. Only the judge was spared the intrusions of the press which seemed to have the prerogative to impose on anyone questions and to engage answers. One sensed a caution lest one offend the press which was trying the case. In the courtroom there was talk about elemental rights; outside the courtroom the concern was for "readers' interest." One observed in the entourage of the principals a furtive concern and maneuver for the chance inclusion in photographs and in news accounts. Everyone was having a holiday. Leads leaked out with much astir. Press reporters interviewed, information was exchanged, new angles discussed and wagers laid on the outcome. After the jury returned a verdict of acquittal at a late hour, the courtroom became a scene of indescribable uproar and rejoicing, compared perhaps to that exuberance that comes with the winning of a hard-fought game.

I have drawn this description with an over-emphasis on the emotional aspects of this case perhaps to the neglect of the intrinsic human social values. Justice was served. Psychiatry had a part in this case. It was a difficult but legitimate one. My emphasis on the emotional and ludic elements of the public-centered phase of criminal justice is submitted in the interest of my thesis that within the present restrictions imposed by legal procedure only a psychiatry of a kind could be introduced. It is a "legal" psychiatry founded on the static, elementalistic class theoretical concept of human behavior couched in terms of the M'Naghten Rule of right and wrong. A dynamic psychiatry of field-theoretical concepts purporting deterministic necessity could not be articulated in this medium. In this case, I suppose a little of it did get in through the interstices of the expert testimony. Maybe some of it reached the intuition of the jury. But the legal formula was not interested in the player who breaks a rule; it was concerned that the rule was broken. In the formal testimony the facts of human motivation in terms of the *how* of it and the psychological forces at work in the parties to this tragedy, never reached those who made the verdict. The psychiatric "truths" were inadmissible and it is probably better that they were. They would have been as readily misunderstood and resented as surely as our patients are moved to disdain insight and to withdraw from the window of the unconscious.

The journalist, Charles Fisher, supplies us with a moving portrait of a criminal lawyer and from it we have a telling account of the ludic element in the criminal trial. He wrote:

We aren't qualified to judge whether John R. K. Scott stood among the masters of the law in Philadelphia, but we know that according to the easy judgment of newspapermen he was about the most *satisfactory* attorney in town to have associated with a murder case. [Emphasis added.]

The moment it was announced that Mr. Scott was acting for the defense a murder story acquired a certain *cachet*. You knew that the news would make the District Attorney's office doubly canny. You could anticipate the most expert maneuvering during the long spadework of preparing the case and in the thrust and parry of the trial. The weeks between the arrest of the suspect and the verdict of the jury might be confused, but they weren't going to be dull.

Did his duty. When he was retained in a criminal action it was his duty to get his client off. To that end it was sometimes useful to see that facts were presented to the public in a certain sequence. If Mr. Scott was clever and adroit enough to arrange an advantageous presentation, we could see no reason for sharing the prosecution's anger and cries of outrage. We just sat back and admired the skill involved.

Nor was there anything cynical about the attitude. In homicide cases the law doesn't operate in a vacuum. We've never known one of any large public interest where each side didn't try and foster its cause by public statement long before the trial. "I won't try this case in the newspapers!" an attorney would thunder. Then, dropping his voice, he would add: "But, off the record . . ."

Mr. Scott was undeniably smarter at the game than most. We remember one fatal shooting which simmered for a whole day, seeming more cold-blooded and capricious with every hour the

THE CRIMINAL TRIAL 77

assailant was questioned. Then Mr. Scott strolled into the suburban police station where the defendant was housed and announced that he would be delighted to meet the reporters in his office in an hour. The time, we might add, was happily selected so that it might catch the last editions of the evening papers and still leave the news fresh for the morning bulldogs.

He didn't fake. We all trooped along to the office, deserting the side of law and justice in the interest of novelty. It must be pointed out here that Mr. Scott didn't fake. If he said he had something of interest to disclose, he did it. On this occasion we journalists listened to an affecting tale of a betrayed maiden and gallant vengeance. Relayed to a bug-eyed public, it set the whole mood of the case and drove the prosecution crazy. The DA never had a chance to catch up. The verdict was acquittal. (From the beginning of the trial there had never been so much as a nickel bet on anything else.)

The world has been so grim and full of death lately that it seems strange to remember a time when a single murder could take on an epic quality. A pretty good argument could be developed for a return to that perspective—to a belief that the taking of one life and justice for the accused involve questions of immense importance.

We shall probably get back to it one day or another, and new and increasingly dexterous attorneys will attain great celebrity in the practice of criminal law. But we had rather hoped to see Mr. Scott in action again in the great trials of the future, quick-footed and sardonic, tense and abstracted and vastly stirring. We don't, indeed, see how the courts can do without him, for it occurs to us, from our rather specialized viewpoint, that it didn't matter much who else there was in the cast, so long as he was playing the lead.[64]

In the movement from magic to higher thought we have reached a level of a moral order which is maintained only with an enormous drain upon our material and emotional resources, matched only by an outlay money-wise for national defense. Our lives are filled with crime in two forms, crime in fantasy and crime in reality and in them we carry on an incessant obsessive compulsive warfare. It is a universal warfare which cannot come to a decisive ending; we cannot afford to win it and we must keep the Adversary alive.

In the hero myth it is necessary to create a never ending supply of celluloid villains. Likewise a bad conscience finds its projection onto real criminals who form a continuous procession of pawns moved across the stage of criminal justice. This preoccupation with crime must serve some social purpose. Crime in fantasy is a working through of unresolved inner conflicts in the law abiding who require a continuous dramatization of their moral notions. Such dramatization has its prototype in the moralistic exercises of child-rearing continued into later life as a public tax supported enterprise which is called law enforcement. This function is entirely separate as a routine administrative maintenance of order in the community which is necessary. The dramatic function of law enforcement has been always experienced as *entertainment* which literally means to "hold together." In view of our theme of communication between lawyer and psychiatrist, I believe it is important to keep apart those functions of law enforcement. No one will deny the realism of maintaining order and of bringing malefactors to book. Communication here carries no ambiguity. It is in the idealistic side of law enforcement, dramatized in the trial, tied to ancient magical formulas, closer to the inner contradictions and ambiguities of unconscious operations, that we find non-communication between the lawyer and psychiatrist. The failure to keep these functions of law enforcement separate leads to a confusion out of which I suspect there is a widespread belief that psychiatrists are a class of soft eggheads who in explaining the *how* of criminal behavior are undermining the very foundations of our moral order. In this fear there is the shadow of truth. In bringing into view the *how* of criminal behavior, the psychiatrist is also bringing our own unconscious into focus, inviting examination and self-awareness. To this we are resistant and it is easy to understand why the introduction of psychologic science into the public drama of criminal justice meets with anxiety and awe mixed with mistrust of psychiatry as a disturber of the faith. In truth, in the trial the psychiatrist as scientist should not be concerned with the moral order, but with the individual whose behavior happens to be amoral. The psychiatrist is in the same position as those earlier physicians who did not learn anything of the *how* of venereal diseases until they were able to divest themselves of their own moral prejudices. And the same physicians in discovering the how of venereal diseases found a way to cure them; in turn they were condemned as undermining morality.[65] Until the psychiatrist's role in the public drama of criminal justice is clearly defined and acknowledged, he will continue to be suspect.

Every criminal trial conveys a moral lesson just as every crime in fantasy has a happy ending with evil once more vanquished. We can see that this function of the criminal trial is vital to the maintenance of a moral order; the actual events of a particular crime are important only to the extent that they set again in motion a process of realignment of moral values. The parties to the actual crime pass into obscurity; the moral remains. Arnold speaks of the judicial trial as a "series of object lessons and examples. It is the way in which society is trained in the right ways of thinking and action, not by compulsion but by parables which it interprets and follows voluntarily." [66] This is unmistakably our child-rearing within a secularized religious formula. It is important for us to maintain a clear separation of the practical law enforcement of public order from the ritual process as it pertains to the need and demand of the public for an ever repeated reaffirmation of a faith that the forces of virtue do prevail. A hundred years ago this function was shared by the church. Without this faith the bindings of social order would be less firm.

Within the trial communication breaks down and I think it does so because the trial, separate from the individual-centered problem, is a public-centered administrative problem dealing with ideals and symbols worked out in ceremonial with its own vocabulary which renders visible the deepseated popular morality. Popular moral ideals have no necessary correspondence with what detached observers report of the data of experience. Thus, in the criminal trial the psychiatrist must fit this data of experience into an institution in which the "truth or falsity or even the content of the fundamental principles to which the institution clings for moral support is completely immaterial." [67] The psychiatrist's data of experience must be reconciled with the faith that the principles and assumptions of the institution are logically consistent. In the trial, the individual-centered aspect loses its psychiatric significance and is absorbed into the public-centered part simply out of the fact that the interest is more in the crime than in the particular individual who did it. The individual is in the picture and it is he who will feel personally the consequences of the crime, but in the ritual ordeal itself there will be less of him as a person and a great deal more of him as a "mind" containing "intent," "premeditations," "malice," "knowledge of right and wrong," etc., finally to form in the same mind an amalgam of collective images called "guilt." A taboo will settle upon him from without. The psychiatrist is called upon to support the triers in their determination of the composition of this amalgam. His assay, however, is based upon his data of experience and derived from a conceptual model which purports to relate the *how* of the behavior. The concept of legal guilt is derived from a different frame of reference. It is a metaphysical concept which enables the triers to inflict a punishment on the wrong doer in the name of an abstract ideal. In so doing the agonal process eventually returns to the original rational and concrete law enforcement function, namely, the removal of the obnoxious individual from further opportunity for wrong doing. But in the public-centered part of law enforcement we observe the results reflecting contradictory social ideals. In one for example, there is the notion that an insane person is not responsible for his criminal actions. This is to say that he is not liable to punishment prescribed by law for a sane person convicted of the same offense. Consonant with this principle is the idea that an insane person would not know what he was being punished for, and also that the punishment of an insane person would not provide a deterrent example to potential offenders.[68] This idea rests upon another which has its foundation in one of the magical religious patterns of traditional child rearing. It is the two-valued right and wrong rule of conduct. In this, the child has theoretically the same immunity as the lunatic.

As defender of inherited tradition the parent finds that the misbehavior of the child who "knows" better is a willful attack. The child is responsible and a counter attack is aimed at correcting the vicious will. This can be said in any reference to God and man, to father and child, to Judge and criminal. If a child doesn't "know" better there is no attack; the child is not responsible. All of this ignores the unconscious emotional forces that work in both parent and child. The parent's struggle with his own antisocial impulses is shifted to the arena of the child's; his counter attack upon the malicious will is not perceived as antisocial but as an altruistic offense. This is the rationalization of those who believe they correct crime by duplicating it. The parent's counter attack is both the first and the last resort. In the meantime, the malicious will is elusively unchanged and the child has some bruises. Now in recent times, we have lost our confidence in the traditional child rearing system limited to attack and counterattack. Anxious parents nowadays consult medical men but the enlightened ones do not demand that the doctors confine their examinations to the sole matter of whether the child "knows" better.[69]

This technique was expressed by the Duchess to Alice:

> "Speak roughly to your little boy,
> And beat him when he sneezes:
> He only does it to annoy,
> Because he knows it teases." [70]

A variant of the "know better" theme is noted in some educators who subscribe to the belief that even when the child does not "know better," the application of punishment will have a salutary effect of inducing the child to "know better." This is consonant with what was once a principle of therapy of lunatics upon whom corporal punishment was calculated to bring them to their senses. When the child grows up into a man he is still held to account by his "knowing right from wrong," but should he develop a mental disorder he will find that even then he will be held to account if he "knows" better. Behind this concept of "knowledge" and "knowing better" we can discern its germinal antecedents in the concept of the witch. The word "witch" comes from *wit,* to know. Witches' knowledge has always been especially foretelling. "When this is done in the name of the deity of one of the established religions it is called prophecy; when, however, the divination is in the name of a pagan god it is mere witchcraft." [71] In a paraphrase applied to our child-rearing, what the child "knows" in the name of the prevailing morality is prophetic of its rewards; however, what the child "knows" in the name of that which adheres to his first infantile morality is anathema.

Mens Rea and Modern Psychology

> Do you imagine that Orestes grew mad after the parricide, and was not distracted and haunted by execrable Furies before he warmed the pointed dagger in his mother's blood? *Nay, from the time that you supposed him out of his senses, he really did nothing that you can blame.*
>
> HORACE [72]

Our Anglo-American system of jurisprudence declares as fundamental that to establish a crime in the legal sense two elements must concur, namely, a prohibited physical act (e.g. an action, participation in the act itself or an omission to act), and a non-physical or subjective element. We note this lineal order of observation; first the act itself and then the after inquiry into the state of mind of the actor. The first element is a relatively easy matter to establish in terms of the objective identity of the actor and of the clues and the chain of evidence woven around him. In our times all of the material techniques of science are brought into play in the process of identifying the doer. So far this inquiry has a similarity to the method of medicine whereby the physician employs the technique of science in identifying material body changes in the patient and follows the clues that lead him to the identity and removal of the offending agent.

When we venture to assess the second element, the subjective, non-material, mental ingredient, required by the law to establish a crime we enter into a different world of operation. This world does not lend itself so readily to the apparatus of empirical science. It is a world of a different order of thinking which is consonant with the prevailing group notions and which has its roots in magical religious foundations.

The idea that a person afflicted with madness is not to be held culpable for his unlawful acts has had a development and application in Anglo-American criminal law since the 13th Century. The subjective element of unlawful acts has been the property of legal philosophy which has had its groundings derived largely from scholastic theology. There is hardly a trace of medical psychology in it. The subjective element is defined in terms of *mens rea,* the mind of the doer. Criminal intent partakes of deliberation, design, knowledge, object, resolve, and determination; its absence is more or less indicated by ideas of mistake, reasonable belief, good faith, etc. The idea of intent is inherent in the concept of free choice from which responsibility flows and which is explicit of the "vicious will." In private law torts can be intentional or involve negligence. In such matters economic damage is primary, moral culpability secondary. Intentions are considered in divorce actions, in criminal attempts, in omissions, breaches of contract, etc. They have a common ground in intent, but in civil matters the intent *per se* is not punished.[73]

Intent constitutes half of the definition of crime; the outward act being the other half. From this the law has a twofold task; one, to establish the identity of the doer, and second, to determine his mental content. The latter move calls for some model of psychology. The law does have such a model which is a class type theoretical construct after St. Thomas Aquinas: "Now man, the framer of human law, is competent to judge only the outward acts; because 'man seeth those things that appear,' (1 Sam. xvi-7); God alone, the framer of the divine law, is competent to judge the inward movements of wills."

Legal psychology posits the existence of *intent* as a property of the mind, with such qualifiers as malice, willfulness, wantonness, etc. Intent is quantified in an infinite range calibrated to a moral scale very much as is sin. Intent is identified as some elementalistic, separate entity within the wrong doer which articulates free will.[74] In this concept one cannot escape the implications of obsession and possession, of something within the person which turns itself on or off. These are attenuated demonological concepts which have no consonance with modern individual-centered psychology and everything to do with a psychology of a public-centered ritual of condemnation, sacrifice and redemption. This is a psychology that remains within the conscious range of outward things. It is a psychology that reveals little of the mind of the evil doer, but a good deal of what is going on in the minds of the law abiding joined by those who perform the ritual. Moreover, it is a psychology in which the competence to judge "the inward movements of wills," once a facile competence of qualified theologians, is today a dubious distinction imposed upon certified psychiatrists.

The concept of *mens rea* in the criminal case with insanity as a defense is difficult to reconcile with modern, dynamic psychiatry, or better stated, psychiatry has difficulty in reconciling its model of psychology with it. The hardship comes to the psychiatrist when he is required to bring his data of observation into the legal concept of intent. To the psychiatrist intent has the meaning of a behavioral event, the precursors of which operate within the accused in a structured manner having an instinctual source and having a flow into final pathways of action. To the psychiatrist all behavior whether called "sane" or "insane" has psychic prefabrication within the mental apparatus manifest in both conscious and unconscious levels. Mental life is a continuous processing of behavioral events in part distributed in *alloplastic* actions upon the environment combined with a variable part absorbed *autoplastically*. The psychiatrist could think of legal intent as a psychic prefabrication, and both psychiatrist and lawyer would agree that they can observe only its effects. The psychiatrist can think of intent as an internal process incipient in unconscious levels, perhaps at first as inchoate visceral impulses which in process become more structured in graphic fantasy, like dream work, and upon reaching more conscious levels closer to the modifying factors of the outside world, come to eventual expression in motor acts. Such acts may be verbal or directly manipulative of the environment. The internal movement and structuring of the psychic ingredients of outward behavior are again conveyed in our metaphor of the movement of higher thought from magic to science. Every psychiatrist is familiar with this movement in daily experience with his patients who unfold before him the inner psychic life filled with magic, wishes, feelings, tensions and a vivid fantasy world of "crimes" which languish aborning. To the psychiatrist the inner private world is filled with "intentions"; without them in incessant creation and dissipation the psyche would be a void. The legal model of psychology posits intention as an actuator of outward behavior. This is a mental process on a conscious level and can be easily adjudicated in terms of right and wrong choices. In this model unconscious emotive elements are not formally reckoned. Needless to say they operate in the triers on the periphery and reach into the center of the judging process and form linkage with their deeper identifications with the accused. In this, intentions and motivations become inseparable; lawyers sense this, and sometimes the verdict is no surprise to those whose ear is close to these *sub rosa* motivational connections. It is also no surprise that these connections are at work in the case of the accused who pleads a defense of insanity. Here in legal psychology the lunatic is exculpated if he *does not know* what his intentions are; in fact, he cannot know them because mental illness dissolves them. This is so because the Judges of England said so. Knowledge of the nature and quality of an act and of its wrongfulness opens the door to the house wherein dwells intent. In final analysis the term *intent* actually refers to how the triers feel about the wrong doing; it is a vehicle of description and a means of fastening guilt upon the accused. Sir James Stephen declared that "The only possible way of discovering a man's intentions is by looking at what he actually did and by considering what must have appeared to him at the time of the natural consequence of his conduct." [75]

Here Stephen externalizes intent and makes it visible in the act and leaves to others the conjecture of what the act must have been as an inner perception to the actor. This is plainly a projection of the triers and has its existence only in the abstract. Intent has little meaning beyond that which probably refers to the rationalizations that take place *after* a crime; the attempt of the doer to reckon with both his inner guilt and the likely legal consequences, and the attempts of the triers to balance their impulses of direct revenge with the weight of their humanistic sentiments. There remains, however, the question why the law should insist that intent is dissipated by mental disease and that a lunatic cannot be judged guilty of a crime. A possible explanation is that in the extravagances of the lunatic, in Lord Erskine's vivid phrase, ". . . the mind is stormed in its citadel, and laid prostrate under the stroke of frenzy," and with the mind goes "intent." In the same appearances, if the mentally ill person cannot communicate reason it would seem likely that he is unable to form intent. If this be so, how can we account for the everyday observation that psychotic people do carry out criminal actions with plan, design and studied execution like the case of a schizophrenic who killed little girls and practiced cannibalism.[76] We are left with the conclusion that the concept of intent in cases of mental disease is useful only as a device of legal semantics, having no correspondence with the facts of life. If the lunatic commits crimes without criminal intent we place a high premium on sanity. This idea is close to the attitudes of some primitive people who confer special impunity and privilege on psychotics who are regarded as having about them an aura of sacredness.

When the law says that the absence of intent renders one incapable of committing a crime, it really means that the triers are incapable of attaching guilt upon the offender, i.e., of inflicting punishment on one who actually committed a harm which if done by a sane person would be punishable. The incapacity afflicts the triers who cannot identify with the psychotic offender.

Let us turn to the mentally ill person and to a psychiatric view of the workings of intent. In the model of dynamic psychology intent refers to all structural, instinctual impulses which are carried with a centrifugal force to the conscious periphery with or without verbal counterpart. In this view, the essential elements that shape behavior are not only the primary instinctual drive or the formed intent alone which defines the goal of behavior, but also the secondary elements acquired from the conditionings of child rearing. These are referred to as the patterns of control which are interposed between the stimulus and response. In psychiatry we speak of them as the ego and super ego; the former, the executor of behavior, the latter, the evaluator. In health and maturity the ego and super ego stand in the way of intent, to stay it, if it is not in conformity with moral and realistic standards. We think of the ego and super ego not as personifications, but as neutral patterns of feedback responses built into the nervous system and acting in a large degree automatically and beyond conscious awareness. Mental life is a continuous flow of psychic forces arising from the organic matrix of the body, directed as adaptive responses to the outside world, and modified more or less in conformity with the symbols of the environment. In a sense, we equate criminal intent with unmodified instinctual behavioral expression. This is the "intent" which normal people succeed in repressing directly. In them criminality is confined to token expressions, slips and mistakes of everyday life, and as Plato remarked, to their dreams.

Clinical observations establish clearly that mental illness is a compensatory, behavioral expression of adaptive failure. In psychiatric shorthand it is spoken of as the impairment of the ego. Ego impairment is relative; not absolute. Reference has been made above to the conditions associated with ego impairment; those with demonstrable organic changes associated with senescence, infections, intoxications, etc., and those in which no organic changes can be demonstrated. The latter are called "functional" and are accounted for as ego deficits out of faulty conditioning and child rearing. The manifest expressions of ego impairment from either source are essentially similar. We observed a case of toxic delirium which simply means that a temporary chemical alteration of the ego functions revealed to others latent intentions in the patient expressed in words and actions. If such a person so "affected" should carry out a crime *in delerio*, we would easily accept the fact that mental illness dissipates the ego and not the intent. Thus in this view mental illness does not abolish intent but *releases* it. It is this factor of release of intent that scares us and makes the lunatic real. The suffering of the mentally ill person comes from his own sense of threat and loss of ego to stay the execution of his latent criminal intentions. We will have occasion to refer to the case of the lunatic, Smith, who in the inner perception of his loss of ego control opportuned a policeman with the plea that he feared he would kill someone. We will recall more vividly the frantic appeal of William Heirens, scrawled with lipstick on the wall of the apartment of one of his victims: "For heavens sake catch me before I kill more, I cannot control myself." [77]

The legal denial of intent in the psychotic does not make supportable the realistic fear of either the psychotic or the community for his intentions. The psychotic's ill disguised intent and dispatch illuminate the failure of the counterforce of the ego. From the view of psychiatry in cases of mental illness and crime, the concept of legal intent tied to the notion of "knowledge" erects a barrier to a sharing of experience with lawyers.

Furthermore, the ideal that insane people are not culpable does not hold up because it does not have an universal application. It touches only a select few. What in practice makes the ideal less worthy is the fact that it is not applied in the individual-centered aspect of a case but only in the public-centered aspect of it and then more often in those cases that are "emotionally satisfactory."

Emotionally satisfactory cases are those that involve crimes which are regarded as *mala in se,* murder, rape, treason, etc., in contrast to forgery, embezzlement, burglary and violations of prohibited acts and a host of borderline white collar crimes.[78] Murder, rape and treason are linked to the first footings of our child-rearing, to parricide, incest and tribal loyalty. The emotional satisfaction of crime is also qualified by its source in the position and the power of those who are the principal actors in the drama.

The exculpation of the insane is an ideal which in effect regards insane people as children, but in its operation in criminal matters only those children who *do not know better* are selected. The current method of selection was devised in 1843 in England, following a series of cases involving physical attacks upon English sovereigns and their ministers beginning with the attempt of Hadfield to kill King George III in 1800 and culminating with the attempt on Sir Robert Peel's life by M'Naghten in 1843. Hadfield escaped criminal penalty by pleading insanity. Daniel M'Naghten, a paranoiac, shot Edward Drummond believing him to be Peel. The defense of insanity was raised and nine medical witnesses testified. Lord Chief Justice Tindal intervened at the end of the testimony and argument and gave what could be regarded as very close to a directed verdict.[79] Biggs quotes a letter written by Queen Victoria in March of 1843 addressed to Sir Robert Peel in which she expressed her dissatisfaction with the administration of justice. It is of interest that in this letter she deplored that in the cases of Oxford and M'Naghten, conducted by the ablest lawyers, the Judges did "allow and advise the Jury to pronounce the verdict of Not Guilty on account of Insanity—whilst everybody is morally convinced that both malefactors were *perfectly conscious and aware of what they did!*" (Italics mine.) The Queen complained that the law was put entirely into the judge's hands and pressed for some legislation whereby the "Judges be bound to interpret the law in this and no other sense in their charges to the Juries." [80]

The Queen's observation that "both malefactors were perfectly conscious and aware of what they did," would indicate that possibly she had read the *Treatise* of Isaac Ray or had an uncommon insight which escaped the Judges. The House of Lords took a hand in this and the judges of the common law courts were called upon to formulate the questions of law. The questions were clearly those relating to demanded regulation as a matter of law, binding judges in their charges to juries, less relating to matters of insanity and criminal responsibility, and much to the point as a means of assuaging the anxiety of royal persons. Accordingly, all fifteen judges attended the House of Lords and five questions of law were propounded by the Lords to them. What came out of these deliberations came to be known as "the M'Naghten Rule or the so-called right and wrong test." Overholser remarks that

The test did not actually rise out of a case at all but was the creature of committee work based on a case already decided in which paranoia was an issue erected upon a set of questions which were directly translated out of the current vogue of compartmental psychiatry and phrenology.[81]

Keedy points out that the responses of the Lords were specifically limited to a case "afflicted with an insane delusion" as was M'Naghten, and also that the test announced by the judges was the same as given to the jury by the Presiding Judge in the trial of M'Naghten.[82] In this connection the GAP report commented: "In effect what was at first limited to a specific system of paranoid delusions was extended as a declaration of comprehensive law on insanity, applicable to any case presenting the defense of mental illness." [83]

In sum, the M'Naghten Rule is ". . . *to establish a defense on the ground of insanity, it must be clearly proved that at the time of committing the act the accused was laboring under such a defect of reason, from disease of the mind, as not to know the nature and the quality of the act he was doing, or if he did know it, that he did not know he was doing what was wrong.*" Sir James Stephen expressed the view that the authority of the answers was questionable, that they left untouched the most difficult questions connected with the subject, that they were open to misunderstanding. Judge Biggs supplies us with a background of the M'Naghten Rule in Chapter IV of his *Guilty Mind*. He uncovers the current of political and economic forces of 18th Century England which found expression in a formula that had everything to do expediently with allaying anxieties out of public unrest and little to do with the facts of mental operations of mad men.[84]

In theory the M'Naghten rule is applicable as a defense in any crime. It enters almost exclusively in cases of homicide. There have been a few instances in treason trials. The rule prevails in all State Courts except New Hampshire and the District of Columbia and in Military Law it is the main test supplemented by the "irresistible impulse test." It is the ruling principle in Federal Courts. Two applications of test questions are employed in the state courts. In one the defendant to be excused must be incapable of knowing the *nature and quality of the act* and in the other he must be incapable of *knowing right from wrong* as to the act charged and some courts have held that there is no distinction in meaning between these two phrases.[85, 86]

Commonwealth v. James Ernest Monroe

Let us take a trial run with M'Naghten in the following case. James Ernest Monroe, a middle-aged, married postal employee was observed to undergo a change in personality marked by moodiness and withdrawal. Those about him offered the following observations of his change of personality which became visible in the year preceding his offense. The defendant would take turns between moments of agitation and unresponsive remoteness to others when he wore an expression of inner preoccupation and absorption. At times his responses were either inadequate or far afield. When his mother received insulin injections he would run out of the room. During the mother's illness, and at the passing mention of it, he would spontaneously burst into crying spells which at times were seemingly intractable. Once during a thunderstorm the defendant rushed out of the house and remained secluded for a long time.

One day he proceeded in the direction of the river without announced purpose. Near his intended destination he stepped into a small real estate office occupied by two women to whom he was a complete stranger. Without uttering a word he drew a gun from his pocket and leveled it in the direction of the women. One promptly emptied a cash box within his reach and again without a word he automatically withdrew the contents of the box—some fifty dollars. We do not know what the terror of the women meant to him beyond the fact that no threat was verbally communicated. Again without hint of motivation he fired at random and walked out of the office; upon observing someone coming at him, he broke into a run, but was caught. After a momentary struggle he meekly surrendered, was arrested and placed in prison.

The question is why did he kill one strange woman and wound another? The first answer implying purpose was supplied by the prosecution. He did so in order to carry out an armed robbery in "cold blood" because he needed money and this raised his crime to first degree homicide. Much evidence was introduced to sustain this answer. His actions spoke for his intentions. His crime was dramatically repeated in fantasy step by step in the evidence and the Commonwealth concluded its case. The defense conceded that the prosecution had narrated the evidence correctly. The defendant had not denied it. It was clear that the issue of the defendant's liability to the penalty of execution did not turn on the question of his having carried out the killing. The issue was not the outside events; it was centered on something inside the accused. This called for experts on inside problems; on the inner movements of wills. The shift of interest moved to psychiatry. The prosecution engaged two reputable psychiatrists. The defense did likewise and balanced the opposing teams. The psychiatrists came to the trial with their medical data which among them had more or less a rough correspondence despite the fact that the contending experts had examined the accused separately and at different times. They could not have rendered opinions on the same facts, since the same facts could have been secured only if all the experts sampled them together. This would be scarcely permitted by either side. When the experts appeared for testimony those for the defense could only assume that the prosecution experts had the same data, and vice versa.

In his contact with the defense psychiatrists the accused communicated little of an outward pathological nature beyond the existence of a depression of mood, fantasies of suicide both before and after the offense and only a hint of mystical hallucinatory promptings from his deceased mother who had died in a mental hospital a short time before the visible onset of his personality change.

By necessity the law was concerned for the outside events which purported to explain purposeful causality, but the defense had erected an exculpatory plea of insanity which implied an answer of deterministic necessity. This answer was to the effect that the accused was acting out an old score in the present against a surrogate of his deceased mother, all within the frame of a fantasy of rejoining her in suicide. We don't know what was the momentary transaction between him and the woman victim that completed the connection which released the destructive impulse. The testimony of the defense experts implied that the accused actions were carried out by deterministic necessity on the basis of past experiences and that they were carried out in an individual who was undergoing a process regarded as a mental disease of clinical dimensions.

Each psychiatrist would be expected to make answers inferred from a communication coming from within the accused. Four psychiatrists paired in opposing sides drew their inferences. I think it is proper to say that with their inferences drawn from their examinations each in a private capacity would have been moved to accept the accused as a patient in need of psychiatric help. There was something wrong with him which could be inferred at least from his apparently unmotivated behavior with two strange women. Even the taking of the money proffered by the victim did not fit into a standard technique of armed robbery. He expressed regret for what had taken place but could offer no common sense explanation for it. The psychiatrists took oaths to tell the "truth" which the jury would presently know from the inferences of the opposing witnesses. The defense presented to his experts a lengthy hypothetical question which chronicled the prior personality change as observed by others, the events leading up to the killing and finally posed to the experts a question of the mental condition of the accused at the time of the offense. The experts were already convinced that the accused presented a picture of a person within whom there had been a psychotic process unitary with the killing. Having so convinced themselves, they were ready with their answers. They answered that the accused was mentally ill. The right and wrong rule was then put to them. At the time of the killing, did the accused "know the nature and quality of the act that he was doing, or if he did know it, . . . did he know what he was doing was wrong?" Now the accused knew what he had done and he knew it was wrong insofar as he could convey his "knowing" in words in answer to these same questions put to him. Here the psychiatrists were faced with a problem—how to answer the questions from words of the accused and at the same time come to grips with the facts of his mental illness. In the opinion of the two psychiatrists here was a psychotic person who "knew" what he did and that it was wrong. The only way out of this was for the psychiatrists to convince themselves that inside the accused a psychotic process must in some occult way effect the cognitive faculties to set apart the accused from non-psychotic killers. In words, the accused had knowledge; what about his actions? His actions had equivocal significance. He grabbed money, yet had some. He shot at random at strange women killing one and wounding another, but there was no evidence of a move or threat to tie to the shooting; he ran out as if in a design of escape. His manner of resignation and distance from the examiners spoke for no effort to rationalize in words his deed even delusionally. On the stand the psychiatrists sensed that to testify to the words of the accused would push his psychosis out of reach. The tie between psychosis and his knowledge had to be rearranged to reconcile their data of observation with the requirements of the law. The defense psychiatrists answered the question; the accused did not have the requisite knowledge and on cross-examination they defended their answers with their inferences of the existence of a mental disease in the accused.

The two experts for the prosecution were duly qualified and sworn. They related their examinations of the accused and both came to the identical conclusion that he suffered with no mental illness; one expert volunteered his opinion that the accused was faking mental illness in order to escape justice. This opinion was explicit that the accused, an untutored person, had either come upon a facile compliance with instruction or had found hitherto untapped native sources of intuitive dissembling. [87, 88] Both the experts declared flatly that the accused had requisite knowledge. Their answers made sense to the jury. The accused was found guilty and condemned to die in the electric chair. A short time after conviction he was found in his prison cell hanging dead by his own hand. His passing denied us further knowledge of how much he really knew.

Jerome Hall has admonished that psychiatrists should be on "tap and not on top." In afterthought the psychiatrists who took part in this case might well ponder their contribution to social order. Was it psychiatry and was it scientific? Is being on *tap* really being *used* to move a public moral issue which had no necessary connection with scientific inquiry?

United States of America ex rel. James Colbert Smith v. Baldi

In *The Guilty Mind,* Judge Biggs gives us a comprehensive account of how one James Colbert Smith whose "knowledge" of right and wrong set in motion a prosecution for homicide which came before six Courts of Record, once before a State Board of Pardons, once before Oyer Terminer Quarter Sessions Court of Philadelphia, once before Kings County Court of New York, twice before a United States District Court, twice before a United States Court of Appeals, twice before the Supreme Court of Pennsylvania, three times before the Supreme Court of the United States, and once before a Sanity Commission. At least thirty-five Justices and Judges of Federal and State Courts and fifteen attorneys never extricated themselves from a "footless question"; the cost to New York, Pennsylvania and the United States was at least $250,000. The whole business was eventually settled when the convicted defendant was examined by competent medical men who were unencumbered by the M'Naghten test questions. They found within an hour that all the time criminal law had been dealing with a chronic lunatic.[89]

There are two ways of viewing this chronicle. First, by the appearances of things, James Colbert Smith acted "as if" he were a normal and fully accountable person like ourselves most of the time, and that at other times he was either a mental case or a criminal. This fits into an either/or logic which comes not from adequate knowledge of Smith but merely out of the record of how he was manipulated. At one time he is in a hospital, at another in a penitentiary and in each appropriate labels are attached to him. The second views the chronicle as a continuum in which an essentially unitary psychic process of human adaptation is in operation. In the light of Smith's child-rearing, his heritage and formative experiences, we could think of his adaptive process as one hardly equipped to cope with surrounding reality. It did more or less, but the chronicle would indicate that his margin between magical and realistic adaptation was indeed narrow and sometimes the magic surfaced to express itself in psychotic symptoms with acting out. In the movement of higher though from magical origins, Smith never advanced beyond a stage of perpetual twilight. He did not have far to go in retreat to magic. It is not hard to imagine in him an active predisposition either to adaptation by outright attacks upon his environment or by retreat into psychosis or both. We know little if anything of the stresses that precipitated either adaptation. Whichever way you look at Smith's behavior, it was one and the same of a unitary psychological process. This is well perceived in the dissenting opinion of the United States Court of Appeals:

Whether or not Smith was a schizophrenic at the time he committed the crime for which he is about to be executed, there can be no doubt that he showed at least one major characteristic of the schizophrenic, a complete inability to adjust himself to the requirements of a life without supervision. That he has shown many other similar characteristics can scarcely be doubted. The headless woman who stood by his bed at night, the hallucinatory voices and the numerous signs of personality disintegration are symptomatic." [90]

In Smith's communication with his environment, no one caught on and believed his symbols and he never understood those of others. Smith did not know what or how to do with others, and others were likewise joined in confusion about what to do with him.

Recall that Smith was previously adjudicated as insane and committed to a hospital in Brooklyn, that he was later discharged October 11, 1945 on a medical order which overruled the staff opinion. On this order Smith was formally restored to his "sanity" by the court and set out once more into his environment. Seventy-nine days later Smith sensed his own imminent loss of control and sought it in some outside agency. He went to a policeman and told him that he was afraid he would kill someone. He committed himself to a hospital, the record of which indicated that others shared Smith's own apprehension of homicidal impulses. From this fragment of his history emerge vital questions of both legal and psychiatric interest. Was Smith really "recovered" from his psychosis? How much correspondence existed between Smith's mental condition and the legal manipulations and labels attached to him? How much change, if any, took place in Smith in the interval from his hospitalization as insane in 1945 to the time of his crime of homicide in the first month of 1948? If there was a real inside change, there is no documentation of its observation; he continued to repeat actions which engaged community response. Yet the record of judicial actions in this case indicate a change was conferred upon him from without. Upon discharge from the Brooklyn hospital he was "changed" to a "sane" person. In subsequent events it appears that it was necessary to believe and insist that he really had changed, and here psychiatry played a part. The legal manipulations of a person are one matter; psychiatric realities are another. The problem was how well were psychiatric realities communicated consistently to the law for the furtherance of legal aims. In this communication entered a formula about which the dissenting judges had this to say: "A very large part of the confusion which almost invariably results in the trial of the criminal defendant alleged to be insane, lies in the fact that the law insists that the psychiatrist deal with mental states and conditions which do not exist save as legal conceptions." [91]

Here the dissenting judges are referring to the M'Naghten rule which turns on the question of "knowledge" of right and wrong. In the Smith case the law was dealing with a person who from the age of 16 had been a chronic schizophrenic, whose magical adaptation to his environment made life hazardous and expensive to others and himself. The manipulation of him in criminal law failed to lessen this hazard and greatly augmented the expense.

The M'Naghten rule enters the public-centered phase of the drama of law enforcement. In the murder trial it comes to a culminating gesture upon which life will hang. For its expression it requires the oracle of psychiatry. The oracle of psychiatry entered the case of James Colbert Smith. On the day Smith entered prison following the killing a prison physician examined the prisoner. He testified, "The first day he (Smith) came in I made an examination of him and decided he should not be sent to a mental hospital but put in a cell as an ordinary prisoner." The physician stated that he had examined and talked with Smith altogether about "an hour and a half, *because he was a normal case* . . ." [Emphasis mine.] The physician was asked, "Are the principles that you use in determining a man's sanity the same as those used by psychiatrists?" He replied, "By sane psychiatrists." [92]

I call this testimony to attention not so much for what it reveals in an attitude towards psychiatry or rather towards psychiatrists, but rather that the position of this physician early erected a controlling obstacle to a competent inquiry into Smith's mental condition. It remained for Smith's counsel to pursue the inquiry. At a second hearing records of Smith's history of probable psychosis were introduced according to an agreement at a previous hearing in which a plea of guilty was entered. Following this hearing the Court engaged a psychiatrist to examine the accused. In due course, this psychiatrist reported his findings at a hearing. He expressed the view that the prisoner was fully sane both at the time of the killing and at the time of his examination and was "faking" for the purpose of avoiding penalty. Thereupon the Court entered a judgment of guilty in the first degree and fixed the penalty at execution by electrocution.

The dissenting opinion relates that: "Smith's symptoms were almost classical," [93] yet, the sole court-appointed psychiatrist testified that Smith was sane, recovered "completely" and that Smith was a faker and an exhibitionist. The latter two qualifications of fakery and exhibitionism in themselves confused the issue. We can draw our own inferences. They could mean that the psychiatrist had need for some special emphasis to lend credence to his opinion of Smith's sanity. In paradox such behavior itself would alert his observers to a possible question of his sanity. Moreover, they stood only as a gratuitous opinion which placed Smith beyond the issue of sanity before the court; it placed him in a shadow of another accusation. The psychiatrist's finding of sanity was supported by the conclusion that Smith was able to tell the difference between "right and wrong." The dissenting opinion noted that the examination of the accused had been an exceedingly limited one. "Prior to giving his testimony he had examined

Smith on two occasions for about an hour in Smith's cell . . . about eight and a half months after the commission of the crime. The examination consisted largely of *talking with Smith, observing his demeanor and reading his confession to him to discover whether or not he could distinguish between right and wrong.* He also had the advantage of information concerning Smith's condition given him by a guard in Smith's cell block who told him that (Smith's) behavior was normal." Apparently no other collateral tests or examinations were made and "he had no consultations with any psychiatrist." [94] I quote an excerpt from the Pennsylvania Law Review pertaining to such instances:

If the doctor's civil liability is predicated on failure to use reasonable care according to the standards of the medical community, surely a state permitting the defense of insanity owes an indigent prisoner on trial for his life an examination meeting a comparable standard.[95]

The dissenting opinion was moved to qualify the position of the lone psychiatrist and remarked that he made small use of modern psychiatric tests and seemingly preoccupied himself with a method of anticipatory questions and maneuvers leading to a question surely to come to him as an expert: namely, did Smith know the difference between right and wrong? The law compelled his answer and the lone psychiatrist readied himself for it.

My general thesis is that criminal justice is a continuation of child-rearing indoctrination and ideals and that it is a religious operation which comes into full focus in the public trial.

In considering the magic employed in Western child-rearing, the M'Naghten right and wrong test of responsibility may now appear less as an invention of the Judges of England in 1843 and more of a restatement of a formula probably as old as the Talmud, in direct lineage from the earliest juridic test procedures for determining guilt. Much of the criticism of the M'Naghten rule of right and wrong has claimed support on the ground that it is based on obsolete theories of mental diseases, and that there exists no correspondence of the test elements with known data of medical psychology. The only exception to this criticism is found in one authority's opinion that the M'Naghten test of knowledge is applicable in cases involving actual disturbances of consciousness.

The test questions may be given responsive answers in cases involving actual disturbances of consciousness as in epilepsy, intoxications, deleria, fugue states, true amnesias, and in organic encephalopathies. The grossly feebleminded person is presumed not to have acquired the knowledge of a responsible person.[96]

In these there is not even a faint echo of Daniel M'Naghten, the paranoic, who never relinquished his belief that the Tories were his enemies, who by his acting upon a delusion did surely become his enemies.[97]

Those who framed these tests had no concern for medical or scientific verification; they framed legal concepts which they regarded as workable within the existing moral system. The M'Naghten rule has no medical or scientific application except as noted for the infrequent case of disturbed consciousness which is mere coincidence. The Judges of England resublimated all of the old tests, and with an adornment of their own, articulated the M'Naghten rule, whereby a moral system was reaffirmed. The validity and usefulness of the M'Naghten test as a legal concept and operation is a matter eventually for philosophers of the law to decide. In the voice of Isaac Ray, psychiatry long ago found the rule vexatious.[98]

But a criticism of the M'Naghten rule on the ground of its alienation from modern psychiatry does not meet the issue squarely. If we did not have M'Naghten we would surely have something else as a test. Legal resistance to an attack upon M'Naghten is a resistance against the idea that moral problems can be solved without the use of moral tests. This is understandable since the trial itself is a probative or a testing process. Such tests, in fact, any testing formula, employed in the public-centered phase of criminal justice actuates the trial. The trial is a testing, which is not founded upon disciplined observations and experiment, but upon articles of faith. In the face of disciplined observations such tests may be illusory. In sum, the psychiatrist should recognize that the M'Naghten rule has relevance to mental disease only by accidental association. The rule defines when and in what quality "mental disease" negates responsibility. In the same manner the law sets the age of criminal responsibility in a child. This is arbitrary and has no relation to invariants of human maturity. This is to repeat the often heard argument of those who defend the rule that such are matters of law and not within the province of medicine. This is indeed true. One cannot pass beyond this point without remarking that criticisms centered on the rule itself have served only to divert our attention from a more basic issue, namely, that the rule as a matter of law in action does not remain in the realm of law. It imposes upon medical men answers to a question of insanity, a legal matter, rather than upon a judge or jury who are charged with making legal decisions. This criticism was voiced almost from the time the M'Naghten rule came into existence. It appeared in Justice Doe's opinion in the Pike case.[99, 100] This imposition serves to gloss the fact that criminal justice by jury is popular justice and will continue to be as long as lay persons are put to making moral decisions.

The questions put by the M'Naghten rule are answered by the medical witness and his answers are said to guide the jury. The answers do guide the jury but in matters relating less to mental disease and more in determining legal consequences to the accused. The jury must have some guide in such decision making and a partisan medical man could ". . . in the absence of an independent court of experts," contribute to a ". . . process of constantly and intelligently bringing rules of guidance for juries into harmony with advancing scientific thought." [101] Yet under the M'Naghten formula no such harmony with advancing scientific thought has been achieved. True, the psychiatrist may bring to his testimony the latest scientific data establishing mental disease in the accused, but these are not the guides for the jury. The psychiatrist's testimony may be a clinical lecture on mental disease, but it is delivered to those who do not wish to learn psychiatry but to dispose of another matter. Even if the lecture is understood, the juryman is in the same position as the psychiatrist. He may have the clinical facts but his instructions narrow him to a view that criminality does not exist if the same "mind" lacks knowledge of right and wrong. Mac-Niven tells us that, "The mind upon whose capacity to know wrong a medical man is asked to express an opinion is not a real mind but an artefact, an ingenious invention of the judges who made the rules." [102]

The juryman and the expert have the same clinical data but how to determine the capacity of the accused for knowing right from wrong. Here the juryman and the expert are on the same level and share the same dilemma. One course is to assume that the manifest symptoms said to have existed at the time of the crime must in some manner impair capacity. But this is an intellectual exercise with which the psychiatrist may have greater facility, but the juryman may have trouble with it if the accused in court "looks" sane. If we bear in mind that the criminal trial is a public-centered drama, that under the surface play of words and ceremony it is animated by common emotion, it may come to us that science and reason are mere decoration. I am inclined to share Alexander's view that the average lay or jury recognition is probably governed by Aristotle's criterion of good drama, namely its capacity to arouse awe and pity. Apparently, insanity like the drama, is convincing only if it arouses awe and pity. This, of course, is basically dependent on the capacity of the public to be awed to feel pity.[103]

To bring the jury to awe and pity, the accused should have the appearances that inspire awe and pity and the evidence must be in keeping with such, less in terms of words but more in actions and setting. If the actions of the accused were such as if he seemed to know what he was doing was wrong, no amount of scientific evidence of psychosis can set aside an emotional conviction. This was the case of our postman. Davidson makes this point clear in the case cited of the elderly schizophrenic who sexually assaulted small children, killed them, cooked and ate parts of them. But the case was filled with elements of his design for eluding detection which indicated he "knew his actions were wrong." No amount of medical evidence of the existence of a profound psychosis in this defendant prevailed.[104] Davidson remarks that

"... citing the offender's words seems naive ... However, before a psychotic defendant can be acquitted on this theory it must be shown—by his actions, not by his statements, that he did not consider the act wrong. In the original M'Naghten case for instance this is exactly what happened. M'Naghten perpetrated his murder openly with no effort to escape concealment or disguise and with a good deal of avowed self satisfaction that he had brought about a great public benefit. Here the *offender's actions* were in conformity with *his statement* that his killing was not wrong.[105]

Now it would seem that a lay jury has some means of determining knowledge in the accused; his actions will tell and if his words are consistent with his actions he is surely lacking knowledge of right and wrong, he is insane and not responsible. I suspect that this kind of intuitive thinking is probably the only way the jury can decide the issue. Certainly no syndrome of mental illness by medical criteria can transcend it. This intuitive thinking is probably linked to offender, which in turn is tied to the guilt problem attending what we may call the *unconscious identification* with the those who, as law abiding, have imposed upon them the duty of inflicting punishment upon a fellow being. This is tantamount to repeating the crime in talion equivalence. A juryman cannot easily inflict damage upon the offender without some device of rationalization. This conflict is resolved in common with that of the irate parent who inflicts punishment upon the child with the belief that it is good for the child. As an expression of prevailing beliefs in child rearing, the law structures such child-parent relationships so that those who inflict retaliative damage on others in the name of an ideal may do so without experiencing guilt. [106] The decision of the jury will be a common reflection of how the jurors unconsciously do or do not identify themselves with the offender. The demand that a transgression be expiated in punishment, shields the juryman from an identification with the law breaker who is the exponent of the repressed law breaker within ourselves. The more the actual law breaker resembles the repressed, the more the law abiding is moved with inner stirrings of unconscious guilt. This is alleviated by direct retaliatory repression of the actual law breaker, who serves as an effigy of the inner image. Bertrand Russell comments that, "We never feel so good as when we are punishing someone." A punished law breaker threatens the trier unless the trier be relieved of his guilt by an attenuation in number as by twelve in the case of the jury or by direct displacement of it onto another. If the actions and words of the law breaker are so framed that they do not form an image wherein the trier can place and mirror himself, he can retain his sense of "innocence" without inflicting damage upon the lawbreaker. In this case the law breaker does not serve as a deterrent example for his triers who stand for the commonality. The law breaker and his triers share the same exculpation. I have been describing the probable unconscious relationships between the accused and his triers and the unconscious motivations influencing the decisions of jurymen. These have the meaning of analogic communication, which may be independent of what is going on in the trial on a conscious level of verbal communication which is rigidly structured in the rules of a game. In this game certain persons selected by the rules as "insane" are not to be punished. The psychiatrist is selected to identify them. We have no assurance that the part played by the psychiatrist is controlling of the decision; there is a higher likelihood that the psychiatrist merely carries out a vocative gesture affirming an unconscious exculpatory process within the triers. He acts as a functionary on whom the guilt can be sympathetically displaced. This is brought into clearer relief by Szasz who comments:

> It is suggested that probably the chief unconscious function of the psychiatrist in the court of law consists of taking onto himself a large measure of the guilt which the court (judge, jury, prosecution) would feel in sentencing (i.e. damaging) a man. Once there develops a widespread recognition that persons who are "mentally ill" should not be punished it becomes necessary for the court to be assured—whenever there is doubt on this score—that it is "playing the game" according to the rules. It is for this purpose that the services of the psychiatrist are enlisted. Accordingly, the psychiatrist is asked to render an opinion as to whether the defendant is sane or not—a judgment which in fact has no meaning other than whether he may be punished with a clear conscience. It would seem that when psychiatrists testify—irrespective of the nature of their testimony—they in fact participate in this complex, unconscious "game" of dissipating and projecting feelings of guilt unto others.[107]

We can return to our lone psychiatrist in the Smith case, to our psychiatrists who served on a Sanity Commission in the case of the college student and to the four psychiatrists paired in opposing sides in the case of the postman. How did the doctors determine whether the accused lacked the capacity of knowledge of right and wrong? [108] The method of determining such knowledge is not taught in medical schools. Science provides no method for equating mental illness with innocence. In our courses in forensic medicine students are merely told that the M'Naghten rule will be posed and to be ready for it. The method comes out of our apprenticeship in child-rearing and in our adaptation to a moral order imposed upon us by those who judged our words and actions in terms of an implied capacity to know right from wrong. The M'Naghten rule is already inside of us operating in the unconscious. It dominates our moral decisions without our having awareness why we feel and think as we do. In this, the psychiatrist, the juryman, and accused, have a common genealogy of morals.

In criminal justice a difference is supposed to separate the psychiatrist from the juryman. The juryman has his intuition. The court confers upon the psychiatrist something beyond intuition—he is endowed with an expertness which can be none other than a higher order of clairvoyance. The psychiatrist is asked to examine the accused and he does. He collects medical data which relates to the relationship of the accused to his social environment. He decides that the accused was or was not suffering with a mental illness, having some temporal connection with his unlawful act. Actually this is as far as he can go. So far, his function is clinical. How can he ascertain directly the defendant's knowledge responsive to the M'Naghten questions? Not from his medical data except for the instances of loss of consciousness as before cited, and therein is constituted a small class of persons who seldom commit crime anyway.

In the cases cited the psychiatrist examined the accused by necessity *after* the act, in the Smith case some eight and a half months later. In this case the psychiatrist talked with Smith, observed his demeanor and read his confession to him to "discover whether or not he could distinguish between right and wrong." This is actually all we have by way of a statement of what went on between the psychiatrist and Smith.

A person commits a crime. After the act the doer and those about him attempt through language to grasp the meaning of the event. By the appearances of things it has an obvious meaning of wrong doing and accountability. But within the doer other meanings exist of which he is unaware and it is out of such inner elements that, with the passage of time, the event becomes contaminated with secondary elaborations which have the aim of reconciling the crime with the individual's conflicts and "needs." [109] The crime itself is an expression of both conscious and unconscious needs and has the character of a dream which the doer wishes to forget and he does so by the same psychic mechanisms of distortion, repression, condensation and after elaboration. This process of forgetting and neutralizing guilt is cogent in the face of legal consequences.

It must be apparent that the only direct way one can determine whether the accused has "knowledge" of right and wrong is to place the question to him. The only expert witness in the Durham case ventured to impart this simple directive in his reply to the question whether, in his opinion, on the day of the offense, Durham knew the difference between right and wrong. He replied: "As I have stated before, if the question were propounded to him [Durham], he could give you the right answer." At this juncture the Court interrupted to inform the witness that the question was not whether Durham could give a right answer to the question but whether he knew the difference between right and wrong. The witness replied finally that he was unable to answer for the accused.

It is rare indeed for mentally ill persons not to answer such questions. In fact, many psychotics have a hypertrophied sense of right and wrong which characterizes their illness. Mental hospitals are full of such people. Now if a mentally ill accused answers the questions that he knew the difference between right and wrong and can express judgments on hypothetical examples and even states that his own crime was wrong, he is inviting his own undoing. In some instances this is the case as with the would-be regicide, Hadfield. Freud once remarked that when an accused confesses to a charge the judge believes him; if he denies the charge, the judge disbelieves him. If our accused answers questions which show that he can distinguish right from wrong, we believe he is sane. But this is not clinical reality. If the psychiatrist finds that the replies of the accused convey either denial or an ignorance of right and wrong the position of the accused is untenable, for how could a person as a product of our ethic be ignorant of the very foundations, however imperfect, of his social adaptation? He would be likened to some aborigine brought into our midst who practiced cannibalism and who is totally unaware that taboo systems exist other than his own. We are aware that some persons are deficient in ethical sensibilities, persons who have had either deficient training, who have been arrested in the progress of higher thought, or have regressed. Yet they are not totally lacking in conscience and some code of conduct. The verbal answers of the accused may be so unintelligible that the psychiatrist might conclude from unintelligibility alone that the accused is unable to distinguish right from wrong. Such unintelligibility means that communication is already at a minimum and it would reflect a kind of psychic delirium. Yet such a finding would render the accused untriable and the legal test applied by the psychiatrist would be out of place. Unintelligibility alone would suffice. Unintelligibility is a clinical element which permits the psychiatrist to infer the existence of a psychotic process in the accused; yet it warrants a conclusion that the accused cannot distinguished right from wrong only in words. Here we are dealing with incapacity of communication of the moment from which we can infer no more than mental illness. Again we seek the answer here in the actions of the accused which, if also unintelligible, (i. e. at variance with what we imagine one would do under similar circumstances) strengthens not the inference of the lack of knowledge of capacity but only our inference of the existence of the psychotic process. But the psychiatrist examines the accused after the alleged crime. The accused is now a different person, he has assimilated an experience the inner full meaning of which is beyond his conscious awareness and usually beyond our understanding. Now, he is confronted with a threat of penalty. At the time of the offense he may have been manifestly ill of mind, and is likely to have made some recovery from it; both internal and external stresses associated with the crime have remissed and the reality of the crime exists more in the recorded official memory than in his own. He is questioned in terms leading to answers of his capacity of knowledge. If he admits his act was wrong, he is condemning himself as a sane criminal although he may yet have an active psychotic process within him that was directly connected with the offense. This was the case of our postman. If he denies his act was wrong, he has no means of corroborating his denial which comes face to face with the facts of his moral adaptation in life previous to the crime. Now a curious complicating fact of psychology enters here. The legal guilt of an offender is one thing; his inner guilt is another. The two may not have equivalence or correspondence. Without painstaking and often prolonged analysis the psychiatrist cannot be sure whether his determination of the offender's capacity for knowledge is influenced by the external peril associated with the legal guilt or the inner threat associated with unconscious guilt which William Alanson White referred to as the offender's "secret." The disquieting fact remains that the determination of capacity for knowledge in one accused of crime is neither science nor art. It is a form of communication which is fraught with uncertainty and mischief. In final analysis it is a moral inquiry between the accused and a psychiatrist who, at the time he is examining the subjective element of a criminal act, is also examining himself.

There are two methods of obtaining knowledge. One, by *induction* which is direct cognitive experience. By repeated associations with similar experience we can draw some conclusions leading from particular to general cases. The second, *deduction,* is not related to direct experience but to assertions not about the world but about language. Deductive knowledge is accumulated by use of logic and rules for making assertions about assertions. In the light of these epistemological rudiments we may ponder what kind of "knowledge" either James Colbert Smith or the psychiatrist obtained singly or jointly in the reading of a confession, "in talking to and observing his demeanor, to discover whether or not he could distinguish between right and wrong."

I have asked the reader to examine the nature of the psychiatric examination which goes beyond the determination of mental illness in the accused into a kind of moral inquiry by the psychiatrist to assertain the capacity of knowledge responsive to the M'Naghten rule. In criminal law there is a well established doctrine of self incrimination. When the police catch an offender he is warned that what he says may he held against him and the accused in court cannot be forced to take the stand. Yet, when statements are elicited from the accused, which lead to the psychiatrist's judgment of the capacity for knowledge, a vital legal matter, the accused is not informed of the significance of the M'Naghten rule or of his answers.

The psychiatric examination partakes of a kind of communication between two persons who initially occupy polar positions; one, the accused who stands as the errant child; the other, the examiner, the parental figure who judges. The accused has overtly broken the law; the examiner cannot ignore the immediate evaluation of the appearances of things. This evaluation will tend to color his inquiry into the subjective life of the accused and the evaluation will arise out of the examiner's own social experience. The psychiatrist cannot attain an absolute objectivity; his unconscious bias will show at some place. He cannot detach himself from his own background and orientation. The psychiatrist with liberal political bias will tend to look upon economic factors in his reckoning of ethical problems; the conservative will lean to the idea of congenital perversity, laziness, willfulness, fakery, etc. as the ingredients combined in human illness and antisocial motivation. Prosecutors tend to select psychiatrists who are conservative, more or less rigid and who tend to identify themselves with authoritarian viewpoints and with ruling class ideology, and who have never questioned their premises. The same psychiatrists tend to appear regularly for the prosecution and they find little difficulty with the M'Naghten rule which is so expressive of a rigid, paternalistic formula and which, in the authoritarian personality, lends itself so readily to intellectual rationalization. The intimacy of the examination, the direct recital of the criminal deed, and the sense of contact with it even in its denial, are not likely to bring the conservative psychiatrist to an awareness that within himself there exists a covert counterpart of the deed; that in fantasy he lives in it, now as the doer, again as the victim, again as the spectator, very much as we participate with the principals in the mystery play. Without this empathy in fantasy, communication between the psychiatrist and the accused would be tenuous, and a "psychiatric" examination could easily become a formal gesture. In an examination of the subjective life of a wrong doer emotional, unspeakable, or non-discursive elements loom large; communication is more often on a viseral level of feelings which can be pieced out only in terms of one's own controlled identification with the accused. Reduced to an elementary moral formula it reads: "What would I have done under identical influences and circumstances?" Out of this in an adversary setting on one side of the line the psychiatrist will tend either to become one with the accused or to remove himself from a tabooed object. By his training, the psychiatrist is presumed to possess a greater self-awareness and in such he can reach a more discriminating balance of his unconscious identifications and thus approximate objectivity. I speak of the covert counterpart of the crime within the unconscious life of the examiner. In capital cases this comes nearer to the surface in the psychiatrist who knows that his opinion may set in motion a retaliative penalty, in which a crime will be undone by duplicating it.

Commonwealth v. Edward Lester Gibbs

> The law in the matter of insanity is not incapable of being so interpreted as to do a terrible injustice.
>
> LORD CHIEF JUSTICE COLERIDGE

In the early part of 1950, Edward Lester Gibbs was tried in Lancaster, Pennsylvania for the killing of a young woman, found guilty of first degree homicide and subsequently electrocuted. Gibbs, age 26, World War II veteran, was a married student at Franklin-Marshall College. This case is reported by Richard Gehman in *A Murder in Paradise*,[110] from which I have drawn the following narration.

Edward Gibbs voluntarily confessed to the killing of a young woman employed as a secretary in the College Treasurer's office. On the appearances of things, except for his voluntary confession, his actions spoke of a designed, premeditated homicide. He had taken the girl to a secluded spot, murdered her, had attempted to conceal his victim and had returned once to the scene of the crime ostensibly to efface his traces. The discovery of the victim came by chance. Gibbs made a full statement implicating himself and re-enacted the homicide for the police. There remained an enigmatic element: the subjective part of his criminal act. He supplied no answer to this beyond his statement that he did it on "impulse." The accused plead "not guilty" to the general charge of murder. No formal plea of insanity as a defense was entered into the trial but the defense counsel did engage a psychiatrist of eminence to examine the accused and testify for the purpose of introducing opinion for the mitigation of penalty. Upon request to the court for permission for psychiatric testimony for the defense, the prosecutor likewise made a similar request, and a man of comparable distinction and authority was secured to testify "as to his technically, legally sane mind." [111] The prosecution declared, "We wouldn't have introduced it if he hadn't," having previously expressed on occasion that he had little respect for psychiatrists. The prosecution and defense counsel exchanged copies of the reports of the respective psychiatrists and "each doctor helped his attorney to prepare a list of questions to ask the other attorney's doctor. As it happens, their disagreements were in degree principally; and as it also happens, psychiatric testimony became a kind of legal football in the case . . ." [112] The defense attorney had never before used psychiatric testimony and ". . . he was uneasy about the prospect of presenting the doctor's report simply because of his unfamiliarity with the field." [113] A psychiatrist on each side now set the stage for the introduction of partisan testimony intended to inform the jury of the facts beyond the visible evidence of the crime; the subjective element of the doer of the deed would be assessed. In legal concept the subjective elements declared to exist in the accused at the time of the crime were conveyed in the language of the indictment—"That Edward Lester Gibbs (did) . . . willfully, feloniously, deliberately and premeditatively, with malice aforethought, slay and kill a certain female person . . ." The psychiatrist for the defense would provide the jury with a different concept of the subjective elements intending to show that Gibbs acted upon latent, morbid motivations implied in the killing, and which were beyond those of conscious choice. This was implied in the terse statement of the accused . . . "I did it on impulse." Later in his testimony he said, "We sat there for, I don't know, it was a very long time, and something just happened inside of me, I don't know, I don't know what happened, I can't explain it, but I just reached over and grabbed her and started to choke her." The remainder of his testimony relates a hiatus after the victim's attempt to elude him. "After I came to myself again, I can remember how it was, but I am not absolutely positive about it . . . the next thing I actually remember is looking down and seeing blood on my hands and the lug wrench alongside me." The impulse set in motion actions which carried through to completion the atrocious slaying of a young woman who was believed to be little more than a casual acquaintance.

The psychiatric testimony for the defense attempted to uncover the subjective element of the crime. The intent of the accused was clearly implied in his actions, but there remained a question posing the inner determinism of his act. The defense introduced the testimony of the psychiatrist. The personal history of the accused was narrated in detail. It was a chronicle of an unsuccessful personal development of higher thought and adaptation. The existence of organic brain disease could not be established. Gibbs did not present to his outer world the symbols of mental disease in the sense that his adaptation had or would require any social sanctions; even in the conventions of psychiatry he was not psychotic in the sense that he was committable as an insane person. Yet, as in our case of the postman who killed a strange woman and wounded another, one could not regard the accused as a "normal" person and fully accountable for his offense. The defense psychiatrist could not accept Gibbs as a "normal" personality. He said, in reference to his findings:

> I will say he did not show any marked outspoken symptoms of actual mental disease or insanity. On the other hand, I could not by any matter of means regard Edward Gibbs as normal mentally since there was so much evidence against it... The examination confirmed the evidence of the history and of my conversations with him that he was extremely immature, very insecure and very inadequate in his personality. Furthermore, I felt it revealed that his emotional reactions were not often in keeping, not strong enough for the content of thought. Psychiatrists speak of this as dissociation. They sometimes call it schizophrenia which means some splitting, some disproportion between the emotional reactions as expressed by the patient and the content of his thoughts.

A request had been made for a Rorschach [114] examination of Gibbs and had been done. The findings indicated a schizophrenic process which supported the psychiatrist's inferences from his own material that there was a latent, morbid, chronic mental process at work within the accused, having a probable connection with his offense. The defense psychiatrist continued:

> While I do not believe Eddie Gibbs was totally irresponsible or completely incapable of distinguishing between right and wrong, yet I believe very strongly and very definitely his degree of responsibility both medical and legal must be assessed at very much less than that of a normal person and that in both the psychiatric and legal sense, he has an abnormal personality and at this time has a latent psychosis or mental disease, schizophrenia . . . Therefore, I [say] his responsibility must be assessed at much less than the average person . . . I therefore believe he did not have sufficient or average capacity to understand the nature or quality of his act.[115]

It will be remembered that the issue of insanity was not entered as a defense and that psychiatry was introduced for the purpose of penalty mitigation. Yet, the prosecution shifted the medical testimony to the M'Naghten formula. The psychiatrist's last statement here was to convey to the jury that Gibbs by reason of a defective personality development should not be regarded as fully accountable. No claim was made that his mental condition was such as to fully exculpate him. Yet, I believe, at this point communication became obscured. The defense psychiatrist's statement was in answer to a question of a diagnosis of the subjective element of the accused. The answer was both in psychiatric terms and in the language leading to moral judgments. He referred to the capacity of the accused to distinguish right from wrong and to understand the nature and quality of his acts and to the degree of the responsibility of the accused. His answer in psychiatric language was that Gibbs suffered with a "latent psychosis or mental disease, schizophrenia . . ." [116] The language of psychiatry would convey little to a jury; the judgment of Gibbs' responsibility would convey much. For the moment it was a statement of how the jury ought to dispose of the accused. The defense psychiatrist spoke frankly of his inability to establish that Gibbs was mentally ill in manifest symptoms familiar to the man on the street who views such matters in terms of an either/or behavior; either the accused is insane or he isn't. This view does not identify the not inconsiderable number of ostensibly "normal" persons abroad who are ambulatory schizophrenics, whose mental illness may become apparent only by hindsight after they carry out an "impulse" which calls attention to them. The defense psychiatrist was pressed to identify those attributes of mental illness which would set off Gibbs from normal people. The language of psychiatry was not easily reduced to operational description. Testimony referred to the accused as being "emotionally immature," as having an "inadequate personality," "a personality deviation" and "emotional dependency." These are art terms which have some meaning to psychiatrists but are unlikely to convey the same meaning to lawyers or jurymen. The prosecution made quick translation of them for the jury. The accused was merely lazy and was a "spoiled brat" who had lost his temper.

The ludic element of the trail reached a climax when later without warning the defense psychiatrist was replaced on the stand for futher cross-examination and given a surprise question. Gehman reports this incident. The prosecutor ". . . in a voice that rang through the room said, 'Doctor, I have just one question. Do you feel that this defendant, Edward Gibbs, might kill again?' The psychiatrist hesitated only for a moment then he said, 'I think it is possible that he might, you couldn't be sure.' The effect upon the jury and the audience was plainly visible. There are many who believe that this question decided the case." In recalling it the prosecutor said, " 'It was one of those perfect questions —either way it was answered, it didn't matter. It was the kind of perfect question they tell you about in law school.' The affirmative answer was damaging, but a negative answer would have been equally so . . ." The defense attorney ". . . was totally unprepared for the question. It caught him so by surprise he did not object . . ."[117] This question posed a prediction. The answer was honest but not definitive, nor could it be. In fact, the question was unanswerable. Here is an instance in an adversary proceeding in which a question communicates anything and the answer either way joins it.

The prosecution placed its psychiatrist on the stand for rebuttal. He did not agree that Gibbs was a latent schizophrenic and based his conclusions on the absence of manifest behavior of the well developed adaptive failure found in classical cases. He concluded,

> He seemed to me like so many other boys who have had the experience of emotional immaturity, showed a great deal of frustration in trying to do something he didn't want to do. Therefore, he showed what we refer to as personality deviation in the direction of emotional immaturity, but that was as far as I felt I could go on the basis of calling him a sick person. I think he was a disturbed person.[118]

In direct response the prosecution psychiatrist indicated that he was familiar with the Pennsylvania rule on legal insanity and in reply to a direct question stated that Gibbs was legally sane. He said, "From the standpoint of responsibility he is the same as anyone else in knowing right from wrong. From the standpoint of having personality deviations which we call emotional immaturity, he would be somewhat below normal." He regarded Gibbs as a normal person except for being "an emotionally immature person." He agreed in response to the direct question that Gibbs was able to distinguish between right from wrong and to one final question that . . . "legally this man is fully responsible for his actions." The jury returned a verdict of guilty with the penalty of death. Sometime after the trial, the defense attorney said without bitterness but with noticeable regret,

> I wish I had kept psychiatry out of the case. If I'd had my way completely I'd simply have had Gibbs tell his story. The prosecution would never have introduced psychiatry if I hadn't brought it in first and the verdict might have gone another way. Still, I

don't know, the story Gibbs told doesn't make sense to a rational man. As each year passes, I am more and more convinced he wasn't telling the whole truth.[119]

The defense attorney's reflections were significant. How can we now consider the psychiatry of this case? The introduction of partisan psychiatry in this trial conveyed little to the court or to the community of the psychology of homicide and, in the view of some, its employment to influence mitigation of penalty had the probable opposite effect. It is to be recalled that no formal plea of insanity had been made and for this reason alone M'Naghten had no proper place in the trial. The judge reminded the jury of this fact and that therefore the defendant's sanity was presumed. The instructions were clear that the psychiatric testimony was to be taken into consideration in fixing the degree of punishment if the defendant were found guilty of murder in the first degree. In the trial the issue of Gibbs' insanity was never raised although the judge made passing mention of it in his instructions; that the test for insanity was the ability to distinguish between right and wrong and that insanity had to be a complete defense or not at all.[120] We should ask, if insanity was not an issue in defense, how do we account for the M'Naghten formula getting into the evidence? We have to bear in mind that the psychiatric evidence was introduced to show that Gibbs was not a "normal" personality and that such evidence could not be used by the jury in the judgment of guilt but only in its direction of penalty. The M'Naghten formula got into the testimony in the offerings of the opposing experts. The evidence supplied by them was intended both as a description of the subjective element of the crime and as an interpretation of what was implied in the defendant's "impulse." The testimony of both psychiatrists had a double alignment; each gave an opinion which was an estimate of Gibbs' degree of maturity and adaptation to his society. The defense psychiatrists introduced evidence to establish that Gibbs suffered with a latent psychosis (schizophrenia); the opposing psychiatrist did not deny that Gibbs was "below normal," but minimized it. If the evidence had been confined to this issue of some "defect" in Gibbs, the jury could have considered it accordingly most likely in terms of which psychiatrist succeeded in reaching them. But the evidence was not so restricted. The testimony broke down because in the effort to reach the jury both psychiatrists used the language of the M'Naghten formula. The moment M'Naghten entered the picture psychiatry became a mere vehicle for the processing of a ritual. The repeated use of such two-valued emotionally charged words, "right" and "wrong," with calculated climatic use of them at the terminal summary of expert opinion, could have no other effect than to distract the jury from the individual-centered issue of the doer to the public-centered issue of the deed. The medical facts receded from focus and we find both experts making opinions as to the responsibility of the accused. This state of affairs closed off our view of the subjective element of the crime, obscured the meaning of it, and the fact of Gibbs' illness was lost to the jury. Reduced to jury terms, the experts merely testified to their own beliefs regarding how much penalty should be imposed. In final reduction these were the only guides to the jury on matters of psychiatry. In this case, the trick question probably played a diabolical part.

In this adversary proceeding, which was conducted with commendable decorum and procedural regularity, the psychiatric evidence on both sides was set forth and expert conclusions were made from it. At this point the psychiatric testimony should have been concluded. Towards the end of the expertize, however, and with the fugitive verbal abstractions introduced by cross examination, the original medical facts tended to get lost in a maze of semantic ambiguity. Communication broke down either, as Wiener believes, because of willful sabotage, or out of its inherent tendency to do so. Aside from the vital issue of Gibbs' responsibility and the real consequence to him which were matters for the jury to decide, the communication broke down into a residual of more or less meaningless terms such as "emotional immaturity," "inadequate personality," "personality deviation," "emotional dependency." These are purely verbal and on a jury level can be little else than epithetical. They convey names of *properties* attached to the subjective element of the criminal act but in an adversary proceeding it would be indeed difficult if not impossible to reduce such terms to operational meanings.

It would now appear that any discussion of right and wrong leading to an issue of mental condition had no place in this trial, yet it got into the evidence and had vital influence in the outcome. In this instance it is not a reflection upon the law alone. It reflects the confusion that persists in both the legal and psychiatric professions that the expert witness is expected to employ both the language of science and the language of moral judgments as if the two were equivalent. In charity to both experts, it can be said that they employed both languages in the spirit of conformity with legal usage, but it was a reluctant conformity. Both experts later joined in agreement that the current mode for presenting psychiatric evidence in a trial is unsatisfactory. Dr. Baldwin L. Keyes, the prosecution psychiatrist, said, "I am very anxious that psychiatric testimony become a fair and useful instrument rather than a shuttlecock between attorneys in court." [121] Both agreed that a board of qualified experts should examine the defendant and submit a joint report which could then be introduced in evidence.

The evidence of this case was scrupulously recorded in words, but not the conduct of the participants in a public-centered ritual. The official reaction to the crime is the unwritten part of the evidence. We get a glimpse of its staging in the communication of Dr. Edward A. Strecker, who expressed a view critical of the Commonwealth's prosecution of the case. He writes:

I do believe this trial represented a miscarriage of justice. In the first place there was very definite reason to believe outside my own conclusion, that Eddie Gibbs was a schizophrenic... Unfortunately, the opinion of the leading Rorschach expert in America (Dr. Bruno Klopfer—RG) could not be introduced ... because he could not appear in person... Furthermore, there were other things which contributed to my opinion that the trial represented a miscarriage of justice. With all due respect to the District Attorney, he certainly "waved the bloody rag." He made a great deal of the horrible pictures of the murder and this, of course, does very much impress the jury. He belittled the Rorschach test in an undignified and scoffing manner, with no regard for the fact that this is a well recognized and established test, used constantly in all first-class institutions of psychiatry. Finally, I do not believe a real motivation and premeditation were established. I think it was homicide based on psychopathology in which, in my opinion, while there might have been the capacity to distinguish intellectually between right and wrong, yet there was not the capacity to adhere to the right.[122]

After the passage of over a century the psychiatric profession has yet to become fully aware that the psychiatrist as a witness in the trial of a moral issue cannot be both a scientist and a moralist wrapped in the same qualifications. If he has a claim as an expert in matters of the mind, his competence is within the boundaries of his expertness; beyond them he is a phantom in the jury box and he becomes a party to a moral judgment. When the psychiatrist remains within his competence he is a neutral scientist and his ethical position is clear.

The Gibbs case was instructive. The visible evidence of the crime and its doer came into a public-centered process whereby the law abiding could reaffirm the ideal of local criminal justice. Justice as an ideal implies a balance and distribution to both the offender and those whom he has offended. In Pennsylvania, the law of homicide is clear; one guilty of first degree homicide may repay in kind with his own life. In the Gibbs case there was no question of his having committed the crime; he made no effort to deny it. But the law in Pennsylvania places responsibility for the death penalty squarely on the shoulders of the jury which is a token spokesman for the general community, and in Pennsylvania law the jury may mitigate the extreme penalty if certain circumstances of the crime or conditions of the offender appear without disturbing the balance of ideal justice. The jury can move the fulcrum and yet balance justice. The circumstances of the crime fixed the extreme penalty, but the condition of the doer raised a doubt. Psychiatry was introduced into the trial in order to move the jury with such doubt which was implied in the description of Gibbs as a person who did not fit into the technical concept of normality. But Gibbs did fit into a lay concept framed in the beliefs of a rigidly conservative community. His actions in consummating the killing of a young woman were not surrounded with words that would be in keeping with abnormality in the appearances of things. His fatal defect "lay in his inherent inability to betray his sickness." [123] Nor did Gibbs present to his triers those elements which inspire awe and pity.

Gibbs did not and probably could not relate anything of the psychology of his victim. The prosecution persisted in the belief that the sexual element motivated the crime in the sense that it would alone account for its motivation. This is the formula of expedient over-simplification; it fixed in fantasy the level of judgment to a single event to divert the jury from the longitudinal view of a tension-ridden personality. We do not know what Marian Baker communicated consciously and unconsciously to detonate the attack.

On August 18, 1950 Gibbs was sentenced to be electrocuted. On October 2, counsel applied to the Pennsylvania Supreme Court for a new trial; the plea was denied November 20. A petition for reargument was made December 6; it was refused January 12, 1951. The Governor set the date of execution for the week of April 23. The Pardon Board refused the plea of commutation March 21 and again April 18. The arguments before the Courts, the Boards and the Governor were fairly similar. The petitioner "continually re-emphasized the . . . testimony as to Gibbs' irresponsibility and emotional immaturity." The prosecutor "in opposing them, reiterated his charge that sex was at the bottom of the case." The Courts, the Boards and Government merely acted as a blue ribbon jury which never returned to the original individual-centered aspect of the crime. Gehman comments,

> The law being what it is, justice being what it is, and our attitude toward psychiatry being what it is, the learned gentlemen who reviewed the case saw no connection between the sexual attack, if any, and the underlying reasons for it.[124]

On April 23, 1951 Gibbs went to the electric chair with his "secret." [125]

The psychiatric testimony from both witnesses was based on the same material in the essentials of his personal history, his early infantile, child and adolescent developments and upon what could be inferred from his reactive behavior communicated with others after the crime. His physical condition both past and present was without significance. In the assembly of such material certain outlines of maladaptation came into view. Gibbs never succeeded in communicating well with his social environment and in his signals to others there could be inferred the existence of an inner world of mental life which he succeeded fairly well in keeping out of view not only from others but from himself. As I have mentioned earlier, in the development of thought from magic, to science, there may persist in some an inner, primitive, and active, magical organization of the mind which lies beyond reach of ordinary consciousness. We can readily see in Edward Gibbs that the control of this inner primitive self was marginal. We can now reflect that the psychiatric terms such as "emotionally immature," "emotionally dependent" and "inadequate personality" are little more than epithets having no greater meaning than the epithets applied to Gibbs when his behavior was attributed to laziness or willfulness, or even to those in the realm of legal abstraction, namely, malice, premeditation, etc. The "emotional immaturity" and personal inadequacy attributed to Gibbs were only the verbalized appearances of things. They did not convey to us the underside of his personality. His life was marred by performances which seldom reached levels of achievement and durable gratification and we can sense from his biography and the patterns of his behavior that his inner conflicts absorbed the larger part of his energy, leaving little for real accomplishment in the outside world of people and things. In terms of the power of his inner, primitive life, he could be regarded as an "adequate" person with strength of character insofar as he succeeded in holding in abeyance the primitive man within himself. The terms "emotional inadequacy" and "immaturity" placed in juxtaposition with the description of an atrocious killing may have some meaning academically but they convey little more than semantic confusion to a jury. In this case the sense of conflict was not communicated to the jury; only summary opinions of right and wrong which were irrelevant to the dynamics of the subjective element of homicide. From the testimony there are a few hints of the inner life of Gibbs, but they come to us more in hindsight after the trial. I quote from a non-technical account of a journalist:

Gibbs returned to the campus on January 3, 1950. During the following week he was in a terrible emotional state. The worries, fears, guilts and doubts inside of him could be contained no longer. They had to be released; he had to do something—to release them to prove to himself he was a man, and to prove it to the world. He could not have been consciously aware of his need; he could never have articulated it in detail. If it had been suggested to him, he probably would have scoffed. Intimidations of inner violence are intolerable to one so bent upon being socially acceptable. They exist only in others; in less respectable people, not in fraternity brothers or athletes or campus politicians. Yet the powerfully asserted impulses were there and the conscience of Edward Gibbs shut itself off, for a time, and obeyed its lower, darker brother. On Tuesday, January 10, 1950, he met Marian Louise Baker, took her for a ride, and killed her... So strong in Gibbs were the twin desires for conformity and approval that he was unable to say, later, exactly why he killed the girl. He must have been aware, if only vaguely, of the nature of the resentment stirring inside him. It could not have failed to show itself to him in dreams; but perhaps he was unable to interpret them, or unwilling. In prison, he once said, "I was under great pressure, deep inside me." Yet, he was fanatically anxious to suppress it, perhaps without knowing that he was; or he had to ignore it, to pretend that it did not exist, in order to permit himself the stability he needed to continue to function through the days. He said, stubbornly repeating it, "I did it on impulse." He would not, perhaps could not, say more. The word "impulse" evidently seemed to him to be an explanation and justification enough. In a way, he used it as self-protection; he hid behind it against the evils moiling inside him—the evils which exist in us all, to some degree, but which, in Edward Gibbs' view, could not possibly have existed in Edward Gibbs. The closest he ever came to self understanding, or to admitting that he had become his other nature's tool, was when he said that he might not have killed Marian Baker if he could have done something else, such as hurl a rock through a window. He indicated that this act might have soothed him, at least for the moment. By so saying he *was* again demonstrating his total incapacity, or total reluctance, to understand himself. Breaking a window would not have satisfied him, for in battering Marian Baker's head to an almost unrecognizable mass he was not merely killing her. All his life, women had loomed over him as vicious symbols of authority, tantalizing, shadowy mistresses who controlled him and yet who taunted him by remaining ever out of grasp. While they used him as they wished, they whispered that he could dominate them—but he could not. They were too tricky, too elusive, too ultimately unattainable. Every mundane problem confronting him on the afternoon of January 10 was in some way connected with a woman. He could not bear it. The hostility, festering perhaps from the time that he had been trained to the toilet, screamed for release. He did not simply kill Marian Baker. He killed his mother, teachers in school who had twisted him into learning, nurses in the Army Hospital, whores in Italy, laughing and witless Pitman girls, his wife, his wife's friends, his friends' wives and girls, girls he saw on Lancaster and Pitman Streets, girls that he observed while at work in his various part-time jobs, every girl and every woman he had hated and simultaneously wanted. He murdered them all. He did not know it, and few others did. He said "impulse" and society, while convinced he was lying, had to take him at his word—conceivably for the same self-protective self-deceptive reasons that prompted him to say it.[126]

Gibbs was aware of what he had done and aware of its wrongfulness. After the act and the release of his tension his conscience impelled him to let himself open to suspicion by way of several significant maneuvers and finally his conscience impelled him to confession which in turn gave him release from torment. The event of the killing quickly closed off from consciousness like a nightmare which cannot be graphically remembered the morning after; only the anxiety lingers.

Menninger and Mayman speak of the "already stretched, overtaxed, wearied, exhausted ego . . . that seems to give way; some of the dangerous primitive impulses whose pressure is so largely responsible for the tension, which . . . elude its restraints. They escape; they are enacted; they go toward targets and they wreak their destructive purpose. And in so doing they incur dangers and high penalties for the whole organism. The level of achievement . . . falls, and reactions in the environment are stimulated which force changes of many kinds. The internal tension has been relieved, but the external tension mounts. The organism now becomes burdened with the secondary consequences of its "relief." He continues, "Shall we consider this ego-failure? Certainly it is a failure in the sense that maladjustment has been worsened. But we must remember that the ego strives constantly to make the best of a bad bargain and this it does, even in its apparent gross defeats and failures. The *aim* of the destructive impulses has been somewhat deflected, their original purpose somewhat modified, their primary destructive quality partially neutralized. Even acts of the most frightful consequences and fearful destructiveness must be recognized as being *in the judgment of the actor,* less terrible than that which he was basically impelled to attempt." [127] In commentting on this fact, Menninger and Mayman continue:

In this latter sentence we have introduced a complication representing differences in value judgment of the patient and the outside world. It would confuse the issue to become further involved at this point with ethical and philosophical discussions. *Clinically,* we see the emergence of destructive impulses of varying form and intensity and we can assume that such emergence always seems imperative to that individual at that moment. The vast majority of these aggressions are disapproved of by society. Most of the time, probably, they are disapproved of also by their perpetrator. But sometimes, though he has fought against their insistence, he loses and they emerge. When aggressive impulses in considerable quantities elude ego control, (that is to say, they elude repression, suppression or effective neutralization or redirection), they cause wounds, destruction and excitation in the environment. The environment correspondingly strikes back and the clinical picture is always complicated by the battle that has been joined. Depending upon the temper and tradition of the environment and many other factors, the result may be the prompt extermination of the individual, it may be punishment, it may be avoidance and it may be effort at therapeutic management.[128]

In this paper, Menninger and Mayman reach two general clinical distinctions of *episodic dyscontrol,* which they designate as a third order of stress adaptation. First, those who show organized and consciously rationalized behavior, and second, those who carry out disorganized aggression which they do not attempt to justify or rationalize. In the latter type, the break with reality is obvious in the chaotic nature of the ego rupture ... even to the *loss of consciousness and memory.* From available knowledge of the personality of Edward Gibbs, there is little doubt of his maladaptive suffering which in a given circumstance reached a point of rupture descriptive of ego dyscontrol which in his own terms was an "impulse" *à outrance.* Criminologic literature is abundant in such cases of sudden impulsive attacks which may be sometimes either homicidal with or without rage, or suicidal. These attacks do not come out of nothing; they do not happen in stable people, and they have remote, if any, connection with "knowledge" of right and wrong. Edward Gibbs appeared to fit into that group of impulsive killers who carry out uncontrolled, massive, disorganized aggression from which they are "isolated" and they cannot, nor do they attempt, to rationalize or justify. Such explosive discharge of accumulated aggressive impulses may have a kinship with the phenomena of convulsive disturbances of consciousness which serve a similar purpose in dissipating unsupportable tensions.

Gibbs' "impulse" cannot be viewed as a fabrication of the moment, *de novo,* nor can we view him in isolation from his environment of persons identified with the transactional events of his life, who formed an unbroken line from the moment of his "impulse" back to his beginnings. The "impulse" was fabricated in the cradle and he covered it in the kindergarten. Throughout his formative years the greater part of his psychic energy was absorbed in neutralizing it. He maintained only the appearances of "adjustment" to his society. He did most of the things that others do but seldom with the accent of accomplishment and self esteem. Accumulative failure leads inevitably to some break with reality; either in outright attack upon it or by disintegration of the self. We do not have the symbolic means, a kind of arithmetic, of expressing the multivalued process of the mind which in final pathway emerges as a destructive impulse. We observe that the symptomatic struggle, whether condensed into a single event or diffused in psychic suffering, is a retreat from *our* reality back to the magical orientation of the cradle and the infant's reality. In metaphor one may say that Marian Baker was slain by a baby. The terms "emotionally immature," "inadequate personality" and "emotional dependency" failed to convey to the jury the reality of this metaphor. This is nearer the language of the *how* of some behavior which implies deterministic necessity. At this point we do not ask *why* Gibbs killed the girl, but we inquire into the *how* of it. Once having learned something of the *how* of it we can then ponder the means of modifying our child-rearing practices that bring a certain number of persons to kill on "impulse," and failing this of devising means to reach such persons before they burst.

On reflection, it would seem that an understanding of the life problem of this young man would find little cultivation in the adversary setting of a courtroom. This is likely true if we consider understanding in the sense that we describe transactional processes between the individual and his society, and that we impose on his triers some awareness that Gibbs was the instrumentality of the "emotional immaturity" and "inadequacy" of the environment that shaped him. Such understanding does not diminish our abhorrence of his act nor our commiseration for his victim: perhaps in such understanding we could bring justice closer to its ideal.

The irony of this boy's illness and fate is that his "sanity" was his undoing. The impulsive attack is itself descriptive of an eruption of instinctual forces, which means "crazy" to the man on the street, and psychosis to the psychiatrist. But in such cases, the ego is not obliterated in the path of the impulse; in alliance with it it seems to have rendered a compliant if not purposeful direction to the impulse, and after release the ego reassembles the personality into at least makeshift intactness. In the appearances of things the individual is normal. It is highly probable that such an apparent restitution of the personality can take place only if there is some degree of impaired consciousness during the eruption. In the generality of violent criminal acts, this is a too frequent observation to be ignored and invites searching investigation. Gibbs was conscious of what he had done *after* the killing and was driven to confess it; but he was not able to revive his part during the killing itself. We are left with the conjecture that either his amnesia was genuine or that he consciously withheld the "truth" as his defense counsel complained. If he did so, we are compelled to conclude that in "secret" his conscience welcomed the death penalty. In psychiatric definition Gibbs' "impulse" was an unequivocal manifestation of psychosis. It is difficult to communicate to the law that a psychosis can exist in a person without conspicuous outward actions of it, as it is for the law to regard a person as criminal until he commits an outward unlawful act. Nevertheless, there are a good number of people who are psychotic, not always more than dimly aware of their condition, and there are a good number of people who harbor strong, criminal inclinations, not always aware of them. Sometimes the psychotic process and the criminal inclinations are one and the same thing. It remains for circumstance and forces of the environment to determine the ultimate emergence of the underlying, destructive impulses either against the outer world or against the self. I commented that the "sanity" of Gibbs was his undoing. Gibbs was psychotic as correctly diagnosed by the defense psychiatrist and confirmed by the ancillary tests, but in the outward, eruptive manifestation his psychosis was ephemeral. An impulse can be none other than ephemeral. It does not define the total dimension of the psychosis; it is only an eruptive expression of it. The psychosis designates a kind of reality manipulation structured on magical foundations. Gibbs failed to meet our stereotype of psychosis because his psychosis was not sustained in outward appearances. The destructive force was channeled to the outside target; little of it touched him. If it had, we would have witnessed an accused with patent symptoms of personality disintegration with the underlying magical elements coming to the surface sustained long enough for anyone to see. He would have inspired awe and pity, but the residual of his ego covered him with the appearances of normality. If he had shared his destructive impulse with his victim, he would have presented to the jury the picture of a marked man.

We ponder the devious ways that suffering people solve their inner problems. Gibbs solved his in a most tragic manner; he exploded and an innocent symbol was destroyed. He had taken some flight from surrounding reality, but not enough. The terms "emotional immaturity" and "inadequacy" applied to him in the trial conveyed this. Had he developed more conspicuous symptoms of mental illness and had his destructiveness only turned on himself, the chance of a killing might have been lessened, and if not, the law would have not been put to the undoing of one killing by another.

The case of Edward Gibbs imposes on lawyers and psychiatrists alike a reckoning with psychological realities. We can pose several questions. If Gibbs had not killed the girl but only had made an attempt or threat, would the psychiatric testimony have a different meaning in this setting? In an environment of educators, if Gibbs had come within the range of professional observation, would there have been any doubt that he labored with the burden of a larval schizophrenia and that any psychiatrist would have accepted him for treatment? Would a Rorschach examination be summarily dismissed in a clinical setting as it was in the courtroom?

These questions are left to wistful speculation after the game is finished and its principal player has been silenced. But from the case we can come to some conclusions regarding the communication between law and psychiatry. It is clear that psychological data cannot be communicated in an adversary setting of a moral issue in the language of science. Under present rules no matter reported by the psychiatrist about the subjective element of the crime can be separated from the idea of guilt which is a moral issue, in final reduction a matter of penalty to be imposed upon the doer. All of this comes about because a psychiatrist is required to speak in the language of moral judgments of right and wrong. Psychiatry was introduced into the Gibbs case to save Gibbs, but it was also to save the community. On reflection it had the purpose of bringing to public notice and understanding that a crime of "impulse" has a social meaning and a lesson for those who live in a world full of things made by science but who have yet to learn how to live scientifically; that tragedy could move a community to a humanistic deeper insight into individual suffering and thereby advance in wisdom a step in its higher development from magic, through religion to science. A procedure yet rooted in magical formulations formed an invisible barrier; the community returned to the magical formulation designed to undo one loss of life by taking another, and when it was taken, great care was observed that the spell of magic would not be broken.

"Early Sunday morning, Gibbs' head was shaved and he was given as a part of the State's inscrutable and single-minded devotion a physical examination. No one has yet learned why the latter was considered necessary or if his execution might have been stayed if he had been suffering say a cold in the head or even a heart condition." [129] Thus the payment must not be invalidated by a flaw in the magical ritual sacrifice.[130] "When a life must go out, the man of science has the clear aim to make the transition easy. The man of law, however, feels impelled to conduct an execution in a painful, ceremonial atmosphere with a victim who is sane and sober. He is unwilling or unable to escape the ancient myth that the murderer is making payment of a debt. He may, as a man, be willing to turn away his head while some irresponsible official comforts the victim with prayers and chicken dinners, but the jurist does not know how to enter this transaction in his books." [131]

Commonwealth v. Francis X. Ballem

> Our fight is against some devilry that lies in the very process of things, against something that we might even call demonic forces existing in the air. The forces get men into their grip, so that the men themselves are victims in a sense, even if it is by some fault of their own nature—they are victims of a sort of possession.
>
> H. BUTTERFIELD [132]

The quest for the subjective element of a crime can never be purely objective. When we search for the inner motions of crime we are also searching ourselves. What we discover will depend upon the method and its language. By necessity the language and model of the law mediates the current moral system of the community and by necessity it must be reaffirmed. The moral system stands as an ideal of social regulation achieved in the operation of justice. The operation of justice is vigilant and militant and tends to be mistrustful of any language and method other than its own. The method and language of psychiatry has a scope beyond the immediate moral issue of crime; it reaches beyond the appearances of things into the unconscious private world of the individual, to discover in it the latent amoral elements common to all. I suspect that psychiatry is mistrusted and feared because it holds up man's private, amoral world to us, and threatens the illusion that the criminal is different from ourselves. The militancy of the law is like the reactions of our patients who actively resist recognizing that part within themselves so necessary to deny. It is better to believe and act upon the malice, willfulness, and evil intent discovered in the "knowledge" attributed to others, than to recognize that such matters are already within ourselves hidden behind a curtain of appearances. It is better to adhere to such irrational projections of one's private world than to view one's fellow men objectively and discover that a less violent society might come out of it.

The conflict with and resistance against self awareness has the full demonstration in the communication in the public-centered operation of criminal justice. The communication between law and psychiatry can be likened to a complex game in which language conveys more of the basic conflict and resistance and less of objective reality. In this communication the accused recedes into the distant point of perspective, his crime remains in focus in short range and once again an immemorial problem is relived and joined in battle with the forces of good triumphant over evil.

On April 23, 1954 a 27-year-old man carried out a torso slaying of a 33-year-old dishwasher.[133] Parts of the victim's dismembered body were discovered four days later wrapped in two plastic sheets inside a small trunk in a trolley station. The slayer was arrested, hiding in the attic of his home. He admitted the killing and signed two confessions. He contended at first that he shot the victim in "self defense." The question of robbery later entered into this circumstance. In Pennsylvania law a killing which takes place during the commission of a felony raises the general charge of homicide to first degree. In this case the "robbery" element was introduced into the charge by way of the second of the two confessions but, like that of "self defense," it came to life only in the statements of the accused. The physical evidence of homicide was at hand, none of either "self defense" or "robbery." In the first confession the accused erected an account of self defense which had dimensions other than the obvious one of a critical face-to-face physical threat and reaction of personal survival. The element of self defense had a more cogent latent psychological exertion between the lines of the second confession which contained the admission of robbery presumably attempted by the accused upon the victim. In the interval between the confessions the accused found himself referred to repeatedly as a "queer" and homosexual by his prison keepers. One reference centered between the confessions adhered to his recall: "You know what we do with homos; we lock them up and throw away the key." In the sequence of confessions we note the metamorphosis of "self defense" into "robbery." In the private idiom of the accused "self defense" and "robbery" each meant one thing; in the idiom of the law something else. Why did the accused shift from a laudable defense to an aggravated offense? Here we cannot escape the inference that for the accused "self defense" is revealingly close to his conflict and struggle with homosexuality. The fatal rendezvous points to the revelation. In flight from his nuclear problem he switched his role from one, passive and defensive, to one active and aggressive, from one threatened to one who "robs." In the language of the law one who robs is a felon and one who kills while robbing faces a capital penalty. In the private colloquial language of the accused one who "robs" is not a homosexual.

Psychiatry entered this case at a time both before and during the trial. The accused was convicted of first degree homicide and at the time he came up for a passing of sentence he slashed his wrists in court. Previously he had been on a "semi-hunger" strike at the County Prison. Following sentence of death by electrocution he was transferred to the Eastern State Penitentiary as a "security risk." On June 15, 1956 the Pennsylvania Supreme Court upheld the conviction, but granted a stay of execution in July to permit an appeal to the United States Supreme Court. On December 3, 1956 the United States Supreme Court declined to grant a hearing.

Our problem of communication begins with the discovery of the dismembered body of a man which invoked an immediate anxiety in the community at large. A hideous killing had taken place and the first evidence pointed to a design of concealment. In due course, the slayer was ferreted out of hiding. These circumstances implied an awareness of legal consequences, of the nature of the act and of its wrongfulness, and of a further effort to escape detection. When the slayer was known and detained, the sentiments of the community could find formal expression within the psychological formula of the law and the working through of the community tension could be achieved in the ceremonial of the trial and a condemnation. This case carried more than the fact of a killing; to it was added the repellent features of the disposal of the victim. Such features invited interpretations which were forthcoming from different levels of response and experience. Certainly the man on the street could ponder homicide in its forthright aspect and no doubt identify in fantasy with a killer, but in this case the character of the disposal would dispel such identification. It was awesome and alien even to fantasy. So estranged were such actions from a common sense apprehension that there was indeed something mentally wrong with a person who would do such a thing.

This view of the killer was pervasive and had such exertion as to move the triers in the direction of psychiatry which is regarded as authoritative in such matters.

The slayer's actions after the killing conveyed two meanings; on the one hand, they spoke for a logical design against detection and for the escape from lawful penalty; on the other, they spoke in an archaic language of something beyond mere manslaying, of something mystical and atavistic. Both meanings were emanations of the subjective element of the crime. The subjective element of the crime could be framed in two languages. In one, the legal frame of language spoke of the killer as follows: "With force of arms, etc., feloniously, willfully and of his malice of forethought did make an assault in and upon the body of one John Dopirak in the peace of God and the said Commonwealth then and there being, and did then and there kill and murder the said John Dopirak contrary to the act of General Assembly . . . and against the peace and dignity of the Commonwealth of Pennsylvania."

Thus the killer's mind contained an *intent* described in terms of *willfulness* and *malice,* actuated into a channel of homicide by a conscious choice of one goal and action out of several. This language implies that the accused could have refrained from his unlawful acts, if he had so chosen, or if we take a step to the antecedent position before the unlawful acts, he could have chosen not to entertain such willfulness and malice or, at least, encapsulate them in thought. The choice he made entailed the risk of summary punishment and he knew this. Having chosen to carry out his intent, in face of such knowledge, the accused added contumacy to his offense. In this frame the killing is explained in terms of purposeful causality: the accused chose what he did because his mind was filled with willfulness and malice aforethought. His acts indicated that he was at one moment animated with willfull, malicious and evil intent . . . against the peace of God and the peace and dignity of the Commonwealth. All of this explains why he killed John Dopirak and joins with the logic of St. Thomas Aquinas that, "The disorder of guilt is not brought back to the order of justice except by punishment."

In the other frame, the subjective element of the crime could be in the language of psychiatry which spoke of the killing as an outward behavioral expression of an inner mental process, that the behavior was shaped by both internal and external events in a time span both reaching to the earliest of the killer's formative experiences. The behavior of the accused could be framed in either the language of the clinic or of the law, but in either it had not only a different meaning but also different consequences; the unlawfulness of the behavior shifted it from the clinic to the theater in which a moral issue is once more played. In the clinical language of psychiatry value judgments would be minimized; it did not explain the purposeful *why* of the behavior but would attempt to relate the *how* of it in terms of relative deterministic necessity. Thus in these two languages the defendant was split into two personalities, one, the clinical patient, the other, the moral derelict and each in his own language so appeared before the jury. The burden of the defense was to prove "insanity," to translate the language of the clinic into that of the theater, to bring these worlds together into at least proximate orbits. In this, communication between psychiatry and the law traversed a difficult terrain and led into an unchartered wonderland.

In the language of psychiatry the data elicited in this case fell into a kind of order and assembly which could be called a syndrome. From experience with similar species of behavior an observer could predict that any person from whom similar data could be elicited would have a large potential for destructive behavior. In sum, the language of psychiatry said that it was almost inevitable that the accused would kill someone sooner or later; it only remained for a sufficient and not always predictable stimulus to unbalance a very slim margin of control from within. In the language of psychiatry the subjective element of the crime was not viewed in isolation as something within the actor projected from the observer, but regarded as a functional integer of communication with the external world of persons and events. In this communication the victim played an unrecorded role in his own undoing. We do not know what went on at this time between the killer and his victim on a level of unconscious communication which made this particular interaction the vital key. All we know of this is from his remark, "he (the victim) said, I didn't have the guts to shoot."

The court-appointed defense counsel was the first to move to psychiatry. The accused was examined. From the first of several contacts the examiner was convinced that the accused suffered with a chronic mental illness and that the crime could not be dissociated from it. He recommended that defense counsel petition the Court for a Sanity Commission. The psychiatrist also expressed the hope that the members of such a Commission would avail themselves of his data and perhaps confer with him. He was confident, that if all concerned shared the same data and experience with the accused, a consensus could be developed and a battle of experts could be avoided. This was a suggestion that translators use the original text. A chronology of this translation follows: From June 2, 1954 until the early part of December, the psychiatrist for the defendant made several examinations. His conclusion of the existence of mental illness was reached after his first examination but, before advising counsel, he made subsequent visits to the prison to confirm his original decision. On September 10, 1954 counsel for the defendant presented to the Court a petition for the appointment of a Sanity Commission. A Commission was appointed and it examined the defendant. The report of the Commission was filed on October 22, 1954 and its findings accepted by the Court. The Commission reported the following:

> He is an abnormal, immature, paranoid personality. *He is mentally ill . . . he is not insane.* He can *distinguish right from*

wrong despite his mental illness. He is able to comprehend his position with relation to the crime of which he stands accused. *Despite* his mental illness he is able to confer with his counsel in an intelligent manner to prepare his defense. *Despite* his mental illness he is able to make a rational defense to the crime for which he stands accused. He is of criminal tendency. [Emphasis mine]

The Court ruled against exceptions to its order based upon the findings of the Commission and stated that it was not proper or required that the accused be committed to a hospital for mental illness.

In the meantime, the District Attorney employed another psychiatrist to examine the accused on behalf of his office. The defense counsel waived objection to such an examination. Accordingly, the accused was examined by this psychiatrist in the office of the District Attorney on several occasions; on each, however, there were present besides the psychiatrist and his associate, both counsels for the defendant, two Assistant District Attorneys and either a detective or deputy sheriff who had the accused in custody. I have previously remarked that such a setting militates against an objective psychiatric examination. It is not an examination of the accused, but one of him in a larger communication of the moment not only with the psychiatrist, but also with figures who embody the symbols of a vital game. In this larger dimension there can be little of a face-to-face interpersonal communication between the accused and one who is neither for nor against him. The mere presence of either attorney or both imparts to the event less of a psychiatric examination and more of a trial which carries the same agonal elements of the courtroom. An examination in such a setting is unthinkable in the work of psychiatry which is dependent upon privacy in both diagnosis and treatment. The accused came to trial.

The trial was initiated by the Commonwealth's demand that the defense announce beforehand the expert testimony it intended to present to the jury. The defense knew that whatever was introduced in substance and in opinion would be opposed by the prosecution. Up to this moment all preparations clearly set the separate languages of the clinic and of the theater in antiphonal positions. It remained a problem of what would come of the original text translated by sectarians.

In chambers the defense made novel proposals which merit our attention. Counsel said:

We expect to show by his testimony (the expert) that in the legal definition of the law in Pennsylvania the defendant was at the time he committed this act, and for some time prior thereto, and at the present, insane.... We do not expect to ask the doctor necessarily a legal question; we expect to have him give those medical factors which either the Court or the jury could then determine the legal question of whether the man is sane or insane; in other words ... all of the factors which from the medical standpoint may be put into medical conclusions which a jury may conclude the question of sanity or insanity.[134]

At this juncture the District Attorney raised the question whether the proof of insanity would involve the question of whether the defendant was able to distinguish between right and wrong. The defense replied:

In answer to that I think that is a question for the Court to determine at a later time in charging the jury as to what constitutes insanity; whether he knew right from wrong, and so forth and so on is a legal question which *I cannot ask the doctor.* I can only ask the doctor to give the evidence which the Court can then later instruct the jury... this is our position in this case... when this matter came up with this particular doctor, I asked him, if in his opinion the accused was insane? He said, "... I cannot answer that question because the whole proceeding is a legal proceeding to determine a legal conclusion; I can only give you medical factors..." The doctor will not state whether he is sane or insane because that is stealing the prerogative of the jury in the case or the court in certain other types of cases ... He will limit himself in testimony to the answers to specific questions.[135]

The District Attorney declared that the psychiatrist was not taking the stand as a witness to testify regarding facts but to testify as to an opinion: "When we say insanity we speak of legal insanity . . . the knowledge of the distinction between right and wrong. . . . If he does not intend to testify to that, there are many things we contend are not admissible." [136]

The proposals of the defense were significant. First there was a clear recognition that the determination of insanity is a matter only for the Court and for the jury to ponder. The M'Naghten rule imposed a first step determination of it upon the psychiatrist. In this instance the psychiatrist made a proper stand in declaring that he had neither concern for nor competence to meet M'Naghten. He was limited to the presentation of the clinical data and limited to an interpretation of them in the language of the clinic. Second, the defense passed M'Naghten by an outright statement of fact that from the appearances of things the accused knew what he was doing and the wrongfulness of it. The remaining probative device centered on that part of the subjective element having to do with "control." This took the triers at side bar through the badlands of "irresistible impulse" with eventual appeal to the Court for a dictum on the matter, to wit:

> In order for insanity to be a legal defense to the commission of a crime there must be (a) such a perverted and deranged condition of the mental and moral faculties as to render a person incapable of distinguishing between right and wrong, or (b) he must be unconscious and unaware at the time of the nature of the act he was committing, or (c) where though conscious of it and able to distinguish between right and wrong and to know that the act is wrong, yet his will or governing power of his mind has been otherwise involuntarily so completely destroyed that his actions are not subject to it but are beyond his control.[137]

In this case the Court conveyed the latter point and did so charge the jury. In this reference to "control" the psychiatrist could speak grammatically in his own language, but unfortunately in the legal channels his communication to the jury suffered a heavy entropic loss. The abandonment of M'Naghten by the defense appeared to clear the way to an objective appraisal of a mental illness of which a crime was a part. Uncertitude filled the void left by M'Naghten. In its place some device of explanation was found in the concept of "control" which is closer to the dynamic model of psychiatry, based upon deterministic necessity and probability. Even so, in the language of the theater the concept of "control" was not free of its demonological implications, that is, that some kind of agency of the mind turns free will on and off.

The psychiatric testimony in this case had some features which merit extended comment. In brief, the initial defense psychiatric assessment was as follows:

> The patient was demonstrably a schizoid personality throughout his developmental years, that he had struggled for adequate defenses against the stresses of latent homosexuality, that these defenses collapsed shortly after his marriage and ushered in a phase of decompensation; the separation from his wife was followed by some degree of restitution, though not complete. He then entered into a phase of overt homosexuality but was never compensated at this level. The conscious abandonment of homosexuality was accompanied by more profound paranoid symptoms of the highly organized and systematized type. The patient remained at this level of organized paranoia shortly before the homicidal act came to pass ... the homicide occurred during the course of an acute, precipitous homosexual panic, of the type that is observed daily in any psychiatric institution of any size. I refer to the so-called relapsing reactions that occur in paranoid patients whose repressions are inadequate to maintain sound integration but who had, up to the point of precipitous disorganization, been presumably "progressing satisfactorily." The dismemberment of the body was obviously a further acting out of his psychopathology rather than an attempt to conceal the crime.[138]

This is a compressed statement descriptive of a long-standing process of personality growth and disintegration of a tenuous balancing of contending adaptive expressions, culminating in an atavistic slaying. In the direct testimony the expert concluded from his examination that the accused was mentally ill, and to this statement added a definition of mental illness which he took verbatim from the Mental Health Act of Pennsylvania: "Mental illness shall mean an illness which so lessens the capacity of a person to use his customary self control, judgment and discretion in the conduct of his affairs and social relations as to make it necessary or advisable for him to be under care. The term shall include "insanity," "unsoundness of mind," "lunacy," "mental disease," "mental disorder," . . . etc." [139]

The witness expanded his conclusions by stating that the accused was suffering with a psychotic process, specifically marked by a paranoid interpretation of the environment and of the inner self. The defendant's view of the world was delusional in the sense that like his primitive ancestors he had endowed it with the same magical animation exteriorized from his unconscious. The witness indicated that the psychotic process had been manifest for at least four years before the killing, that it had its roots in the early formative life of the accused and had a slow and insidious progress in the major part of life and that an open psychotic break with reality was inevitable, "almost natural, logical outcome. . . ." This expert's testimony conveyed a well ordered clinical development of a singular instance of social maladaption, which, in a less surcharged setting, would scarcely have left a doubt that some intervention with treatment would have been indicated. And, with all the facts known, commitment to a hospital would have been indicated not only for the safety of the community but for the patient himself: His case came within the reach of mental illness as defined in the Mental Health Act. As it happened, this defendant's psychotic process had remained beyond critical evaluation until unlawful behavior occurred.

The psychiatrist for the prosecution related that the term "schizoid" is one commonly used, "especially in patients that you don't want to diagnose as schizophrenia, and that they are really psychopaths." He defined a psychopath as ". . . a group of individuals, it is a serious defect in the social and moral spheres; the British call them moral imbeciles." He went on to relate that in moral imbeciles the intelligence is usually good, in fact, often above normal. "As long as they are under good authority at home or elsewhere they may fit into the scheme of things, the scheme of life, but practically always they get into difficulty, especially if they are thwarted or frustrated. They cannot complete jobs, they are trouble makers, so-called needlers, . . . they are floaters, they often show all degrees of—now remember all of them do not have all of these symptoms but this is a sort of a description of the group; they have sexual irregularity, they often take to the use of drugs, especially alcohol and they often take to the use of alcohol if they do not get their own way. They often have a paranoid personality and they are often of a schizoid type. Now some may even finish college but cannot as a rule hold jobs commensurate with their education although some of them do. They become radicals and nonconformists; they have a code of their own. And as I said, if the atmosphere is good they may go through life without great difficulty; but that is not the rule. They show great emotional imbalance and lack of self control. And they are also likely to exhibit persistent misbehavior. They are socially maladjusted and as I said they often show sex irregularities, they are eccentrics, cranks and hoboes, and they are liars, and forgers and swindlers. They demand much and give little and because of this they are extremely selfish, when they are blocked in their desire they drink to excess, they sulk and often go into fits of temper, they often have a tendency to project their own sense of inferiority and insecurity into blaming others. Now as far as actual mental illness in this group is concerned they do not become mentally ill any more than let's say the general run of the population; but they do have the great things as I say are in the social and emotional sphere." The witness then declared that very few of such persons that he had described could be considered insane. He then placed the accused in the category of "constitutional psychopathic inferior." He described the constitutional psychopathic inferior as "a well known group that makes up all of these people and probably a large part of those in prisons, the repeaters especially . . . one of the great things about the psychopath is that he never learns from experience and under present laws and modes of treatment, it is impossible to achieve any sort of a cure." The witness replied affirmatively to the question whether an intelligent psychopath would be a very dangerous person and supported his view with the statement that such persons are leaders in prison riots. In summation this witness's testimony indicated his opinion that the accused could distinguish right from wrong. He added that he disagreed with the previous testimony to the effect that the accused did not possess adequate control.

In the redramatization of the crime, the prosecutor frequently cautioned the jury not to be moved in outrage, not only in the recall of what probably happened in fact, but also what, in words of the prosecutor, served as a prefatory support for, and exculpation of the jurors for what they would materialize as an actual killing of the defendant. The prosecutor remembered in small detail the evidence of his own expert; he had less recall of the evidence of the defense experts and implied that most of it was "over my head." That part he did remember and understand was that which was the easier to manipulate semantically. Thus, a schizoid person did not after all have a disability nor did such a term have real implications in the premorbid personality. Paranoid was only a "horrible" sounding name and many people are successful who are tainted with schizoid and paranoid features. Delusional thinking was reduced to mere suspiciousness. The defendant's replies to psychological test questions did not really represent what he actually felt and thought but were only accommodating replies to test questions reported by the experts and mere hearsay. The central conflict of the defendant's life was his failure to establish a firm sexual world, his perception of himself as a male or female; yet the clinical findings of this conflict were dismissed as mere figments. The data elicited by an expert by means of testing procedures, the Rorschach and Thematic Apperception Test, etc., became merely something "predicated upon a book written by somebody," and the statistical norms which have established the fairly high reliability of such tests were derived from a large sampling of "people . . . where they came from or who they were I do not know . . ." The Rorschach findings were dismissed as so much picture playing to which the prosecutor commented ". . . I will use that horrible word in this case—*projection.*" Each element of the testing procedures came in for separate treatment and was dismissed as having no meaning and contribution to the total assessment of the defendant.

The tests employed by trained experts are not infallible and no claim is made that they are, but they do represent methods which have a fair degree of accuracy and validity. They met with rebuttal which in a clinical setting vital to the personal welfare, would be likened to a clinical staff submitting the test findings of a disturbed child to ultimate judgment of its untutored parent who had only one solution to the child's problem, a summary conviction and punishment.

In this case, all of the clinical data was offered as a description of a unique instance of social failure which in its own development and eventual behavioral configuration came to climatic public notice. A killing had taken place and with it were the demonic features of necrophilia, a feature alone which spoke for a deeply centered primitive magical process immediately identifying the defendant as suffering with a profound mental disturbance. In the assembly of such a process there could be little doubt that it could be named, paranoid schizophrenia. If the naming could not convince the community of the disability of the defendant, it could at least regard him as an object in need of treatment, even if his acts were repellent.

The prosecution carried the defendant out of his disability and made him into a creature which came within reach of identification with the sane man in the jury box. At the same time, his psychosis was kept out of reach. Within the span of this summation the defendant emerged as a person possessing only a mind made up entirely of an entity called will which in some demoniacal fashion chose to do something the nature of which and the wrongfulness of which he fully knew. Probably most of the psychiatric information lost its meaning and articulation. The prosecutor said, "Regardless of what you may have said to you, the law is straight down the line, that if you understand the nature and quality of the act, if you are able to distinguish between right and wrong that you know the consequences, that is, you are legally sane." [140]

The prosecutor then gave quick dispatch to the notion that the defendant's mental processes could be structured in terms of control, although as a lawyer, he must have known that the Mental Health Act of Pennsylvania clearly erects the definition of mental illness on this concept. In this model, the mentally ill person has lessened control, but in the model of common law a mentally ill person who breaks the law can have only lessened knowledge. As long ago as 1838, Dr. Isaac Ray cautioned all mentally ill persons to be reasonable and have a care how thew manifest their illness: "If you are caught tripping in your logic; if in the disturbance of your moral and intellectual perception you take a step for which a sane man would be punished, insanity would be no bar to your punishment." [141]

In the courtroom, psychiatry appears in two forms, one that is in agreement with the prosecution, the other that is in agreement with the defense. On reflection, it may be that in Court neither form is psychiatry but mere advocacy. Our prosecutor could not remember much of what the defense expert had offered and what was remembered was not well understood, but he was confident that if psychiatry as offered by the defense were accepted it would be tantamount to inviting psychiatry and psychology to take over the criminal courts. However, no such threat came from the expert for the prosecution. The prosecutor remembered and understood all of his offering and was moved to remind the jury as follows:

> I did mention his testimony to you and I want you to bear in mind how explicitly, how clearly, how methodically, he stated to you that from his examination of the defendant, he did know the difference and had the capacity to know the difference between right and wrong and that he knew the quality of his act and his consequences and also that there was nothing in his make-up ... that would have prevented him from exercising his self control if he wanted to do so. And ... he said in effect according to this legal definition of insanity, which I have given you, that the defendant was sane.[142]

In final appeal to the jury the prosecutor declared that there were valid reasons for restraining and deterring others from manslaying. No mention was made of restraining or deterring others from becoming mentally ill. In his final utterance he made a disavowal of the spirit of vengeance placed in juxtaposition with the demand that the jurors find the defendant guilty and that they impose the death penalty.

After a forceful refutation of the defense contention that the accused could not control his alleged criminal actions, in summary rebuttal the prosecutor with equal vigor declared:

> There is this matter of deterring some one else and restraining a defendant and they are important ... This defendant ... cannot be deterred from commission of another crime of this sort even if you accept their theory of homicidal tendencies and so forth, he cannot be restrained except in one way, namely, the imposition of the extreme penalty.[143]

In the charge to the jury the Court pointed out that opinion evidence is considered of a lower grade than the positive testimony of actual facts. The Court then went on to relate that the observation on the part of several lay people of the defendant's behavior after the killing and the statements made by such witnesses that the defendant did not appear unusual to them were entitled to more credence than evidence of an expert who based his opinion upon an extended examination also after the killing. It did not occur to the Court that such lay witnesses at the time of their observation were not looking for oddities or for the existence of mental disturbance in the defendant. The Court continued:

> This type of evidence is factual in character and therefore entitled to greater credence than opinion evidence even from the most expert of experts who come to Court prepared to testify as to the defendant's mental condition and probable conduct before the killing, at the time of the killing and after the killing.[144]

Further on in the charge to the jury the Court went to considerable length in cautioning the jury that the statements made by the psychiatrist elicited from the defendant in a private examination could not be considered as statements of fact but hearsay of the worst kind. The Court continued,

> So that we have this situation, we have a person who is come into court by the undisputed evidence says that he killed a man; he says that because I killed a man I want you to delve into my life, I want you to read my mind and I want you to learn my complexes, my emotions, my desires, my frustrations, my inferiority complexes, I want you to delve into my personality so that you will be able to say that I killed because I am an habitual criminal inclined irresistibly to murder not one person but a class or the whole human race.

The jury was not informed that none of the statements elicited by the psychiatrist from the defendant was at any time regarded as facts having a separate existence in themselves. They were statements and no attempt would be made to give them the evidential habiliment of objective fact. But in assembly they had a profound symbolic meaning which was lost to the jury. The Court's statement could have no other effect than to imply that the data offered by the defense psychiatrist were nonsense and that the employment of psychiatry for the defense had no other purpose than to find an excuse for a crime.[145]

The Court further instructed the jury on the doctrine of moral insanity and indicated that if the jury should find the defendant not guilty on the ground of insanity, the defendant would have to be placed in the class of morally insane persons who are irresistibly inclined to kill and that it would have to be proven by a fair preponderance of evidence that the inclination existed, that it was habitual, that it was continuous over a long time, and that it was evidenced by more than one offense or one killing. As an illustration of such a condition of moral insanity the Court related to the jury the case of "Jack the Ripper" who terrorized London in 1888, who was said to be responsible for the killing of some ten women and who subsequently disappeared and was never apprehended. This item of the Court's charge conveyed the novel implication that the defense of insanity could be available only to those rare instances of "habitual" multiple killings over a considerable time. Only habitual killers could enjoy immunity; the commonplace case of a single killing would be barred from mental illness.

The Supreme Court of Pennsylvania has divided insanity three ways. Regarding the first, general insanity, the Court declared:

> If a prisoner at the bar, at the time he committed the act had not sufficient capacity to know whether his act was right or wrong and whether it was contrary to law, he is not responsible, that is, in fact, general insanity so far as the act in question is concerned and it must be so great in extent and degree as to blind him to the natural consequences of his moral duty, that it must have utterly destroyed his perceptions of right and wrong. The test in this instance . . . is the power or capacity of the prisoner to distinguish between right and wrong in reference to the particular act in question: for although a man may be sane upon every other subject, yet if he is mad, to use the expressive phrase, upon this subject and so far as the act under immediate investigation is concerned, he thereby loses that control of his mental powers

which renders him a responsible being. In reference to the second aspect of insanity the Supreme Court spoke of "partial insanity, hallucination and delusion." But suppose that the prisoner was able to distinguish between right and wrong and yet was laboring under partial insanity, hallucination or delusion which drove him to the commission of the act as a duty of overwhelming necessity, is he in such cases responsible for his act? If the delusion were of such a nature as to induce the prisoner to believe in the real existence of facts which were entirely imaginary but which if true would have been a good defense, he would not be responsible. We, however, desire at this stage of our remarks to refer rather to other delusions than the class thus spoken of reserving for future consideration our remarks on this branch of the subject. That partial insanity, hallucination or delusion coupled with the power of discriminating between right and wrong is an excuse for crime was held in the charge of Chief Justice Gibson (that was where he placed the defendant or the prisoner in the category of moral insanity). It, the insanity, must amount to delusion or hallucination controlling his will and making the commission of the act a duty of overruling necessity. The law is that whether insanity be general or partial it must be so great as to have controlled the will of its subject and to have taken from him the freedom of moral action. We cannot, however, leave this branch of the subject to doubt or uncertainty and our conclusion is after a somewhat extended investigation of the law, that the proper rule to be adopted upon the point in the question is the following... If the prisoner, although he labors under partial insanity, hallucination or delusion did understand the nature and the character of his acts, had a knowledge that it was wrong and criminal, and mental power sufficient to apply that knowledge to his own case and knew if he did the act he would do wrong and would receive punishment; if further, he had sufficient power of memory to recollect the relation in which he stood to others and others stood to him, that the act in question was contrary to the plain dictates of justice and right, injurious to others, and a violation of the dictates of duty, he would be responsible.[146]

In this charge to the jury the Court pointed out that the law therefore looked upon the defense of partial insanity with reservation and even if the defendant suffered with "delusion or hallucination" he would nevertheless be responsible if he understood the nature and the character of his acts and had knowledge of its wrongfulness. The Court continued in exposition of the doctrine of partial insanity:

You may be partially insane, you may be so partially insane that you do have hallucinations, you do have delusions, you do have the earmarks of insanity in certain categories, you can be said to be queer in your actions and so forth, you may make wild statements, you may be subject to fits of frenzy and all that sort of stuff—I am trying to point out in lay language what partial insanity might be considered—but if the offense that you are being tried for is unrelated to the hallucinations, to the delusions that you may be subject to, you are responsible. So that is the reason that partial insanity is frowned upon by the law.

Supposing that a fellow who believed that his wife was about to poison him had that hallucination which of course was not true and he is crazy over that hallucination; he goes to work one morning and he discovers that one of the fellow employees was searching his locker. Now the fact that he found that that employee on one occasion appeared to be stealing from him bothered him an awful lot so he kept watching everything that was being done around the place and over a period of weeks or months or maybe years he built up within himself all those various feelings which eventually became so strong and so powerful that he came to a feeling that the man that he had originally seen trying to steal from him was out to destroy him, actually out to cause his complete physical disintegration and because over that period of time he began to have the hallucination and delusion that those conditions existed in his place of employment he went out and got a gun one day and killed the man. Now, supposing you could prove that. That is what is meant again in law language, partial insanity. True it is he had the hallucination against his wife of poisoning him, she never did, and he never died of poisoning, but another facet of his mind, he went to work and he got these circumstances around him over a period of time so that eventually he not only believed his wife was going to poison him, but he believed that the fellow workman was going to destroy him and he was impelled, . . . his reason, conscience and judgment were so entirely perverted as to render the commission of that act in question an overwhelming necessity. This is what is meant by partial insanity. Now you can see it is a dangerous thing for a jury to accept in many instances the defense of partial insanity and again I say that it is the reason that the courts disapprove it. Total insanity, yes, a defense. Partial insanity, yes, a defense under certain circumstances though under the circumstances where the insanity points to the act itself that is the question.[147, 148]

A comment on this rule of law is in order. This is the 1879 legal model of psychology and the mental operations it portrays exist only in the language of the legal model. The terms hallucination and delusion do not have precise meaning here and are spoken of as if having some corporate foreign body existence in the person who is otherwise normal and intact. This is a demonic concept of possession which may indeed confound lunatics who seek exculpation for their acts, as it will confound psychiatrists who attempt to shape their own concepts into conformity with it and as it will indeed confound juries.

The third wing of the law of insanity in the Court's charge to the jury referred to "homicidal mania," which the Supreme Court of Pennsylvania declared as a "moral or homicidal insanity"; this seemed to be an irresistible inclination to kill or to commit some other particular offense. "We are obliged by force of authority to say to you that there is such a disease known to the law as homicidal insanity; what it is, or what it consists, no lawyer or judge has ever yet been able to explain with precision. Physicians, especially those having charge of the insane, gradually it would seem, have come to the conclusion that all wicked men are mad, and many of the judges have so far fallen into the same error as to render it possible for any man to escape the penalty which the law affixes to crime." This opinion was entered in 1879. The Trial Court charged the jury that the same language could be applied "to what we know today and that was the testimony of the experts in this case on both sides; they don't know what it is." [149]

The jury returned the verdict of guilty with the death penalty. In discharging the jury the Court was moved to commend it for the verdict with which the Court expressed hearty agreement.

Thus was the law of insanity brought to the jury. "General insanity" implied the raving lunatic in the locked ward or strait jacket as he might have been believed to exist in an asylum in 1879. This did not fit our accused although, at the time of his sentencing, he did make a stir in court by an attempt to cut his wrists and restraint was applied to him. "Partial insanity" in which "hallucinations and delusions" are the partitioned elements set off from an otherwise sane person, had to have a fixed reference in the outside world. The hypothetical case cited by the Court to the jury implied that the man who killed the fellow employee after a long paranoid brooding made a fatal error. He should have killed his wife about whom he had the "hallucination and delusion" that she had slipped poison into his food. If he had killed her, his isolated "hallucination and delusion, his reason, conscience, and judgment would have been so perverted as to render the commission of the act a question of overwhelming necessity."

The jury was cautioned against considering the plea of partial insanity. Moreover the accused did not fit into the 1879 phenomenon of a sane person going about with an appendage of "partial insanity." The third category of "homicidal mania" was a disease discovered by legal authorities and legally registered in 1879, the same legal authorities then and since never having been able to explain it with precision. The Court advised the jury that the "experts in this case on both sides—don't know what it is." This was more than a dictum; it was an observation of a verity. No one knows what homicidal mania is.

We can make the observation that when the testimony was brought down to the residuals for decision the meaning of the accused's behavior had evaporated and all that was left were conundrums presented to the jury posed by the law of in-

THE CRIMINAL TRIAL 157

sanity and the law of homicide. The "general insanity" of the raving lunatic certainly obliterated knowledge of right and wrong, etc.; "partial insanity" was labeled as a doctrine frowned upon by the courts, and as for "homicidal mania" not even psychiatrists know what it is, and even some judges have fallen into the error of believing with some doctors that "all wicked men are mad."

In the forepart of these lectures I borrowed Robinson's thought that the world is not made up of scientific and unscientific people but of scientific and unscientific approaches to social problems provided by our culture. The persons who conducted this trial and those who gave testimony did so honestly within the formula and range provided by our methods and language. I have pointed out that the distance in language between law and psychiatry is variable depending upon which operational phase the two find themselves. The distance is greatest in the public-centered phase of criminal justice, the least in the pre- and post-trial phases. Inherent in the public-centered phase are the deeper human motivations which impel the "official mistrust" that Llewellyn speaks of and the agonal and game elements that Huizinga traces to their earliest historical sources. In this element are revenants of the magical religious foundations of our child rearing and our penal codes. In our time "official mistrust," the agonal and ludic elements have their highest intensity when a psychological discipline enters into the trial of the issue of mental illness and criminal responsibility. Indeed in the setting of such tensions, psychiatry as a science and criminal law as a moral system are incompatible. This invites a question whether such incompatibility and its attendant confusion confirms the belief of some that justice in this area is achieved, a justice consistent with 20th Century social needs.

In this case the jury returned a verdict of guilty of first degree homicide and imposed the death sentence. There remained an open question. In our climate of doubt and certainty what is the meaning of the testimony offered by the psychiatrist purporting to establish the accused as a mentally ill person and his crime as an expression of it. The accused was neither afflicted with a "general insanity," 1879 vintage, nor with a "partial insanity," nor with "homicidal mania" recognized by the law, but about which little is known by anyone. The accused was said to exhibit a pattern of behavior which is named paranoid schizophrenia, which outside of courtrooms is regarded realistically to identify a profound disability, fairly predictable in its social consequences. Yet, in the naming of paranoid schizophrenia the meaning did not reach the jury. On its way it met head on with the phrase "constitutional psychopathic inferior," given by the expert for the prosecution. This phrase conveyed nothing of an insight into the mental life of the accused; it conveyed only condemnatory value judgments of him, his illness and his unlawful acts. In fact, the statements of the prosecutor's expert had nothing to do with the accused; they were a catalogue of a class of disagreeable hypothetical persons who were not on trial.

What was the nature of the communication in this case? The same words carried different meanings; at one time they seem to report objective phenomena, at other times only the subjective evaluation of them; yet at other times they were antithetical depending upon the nonverbal components which accompanied them. A general configuration of the defendant's probable mental processes was erected by one set of statements by the defense; by another set offered by the prosecution. The prosecution verbally repeated the crime and its after elaboration in minute detail, in word, in picture and exhibit. In this set the accused became known to those assembled only as a demonological personality born at the moment of the crime. To this personality, the actor of the crime, the psychiatric set added the life of the personality before he became the actor in fact. This antecedent life was a long gestation of crime in fantasy which eventually came to crime in fact.

The Supreme Court of the United States refused to review the decision of the Supreme Court of Pennsylvania upholding the verdict and judgment of the Trial Court. Counsel applied to and appeared before the Pennsylvania Board of Pardons in an appeal to commute the death sentence. The basis of the application was that had the jury been aware of the findings of the Sanity Commission in addition to the psychiatric testimony presented at the trial, it might well not have imposed the death penalty. After argument, the Board took the matter under advisement.

On the basis of a more recent examination a psychiatrist advised that Ballem's mental illness was advanced and required hospital commitment. Accordingly, counsel determined to proceed immediately pending action by the Board of Pardons, with an application for the appointment of a second Sanity Commission as provided under the 1956 amendment to the Mental Health Act of 1951. The petition was presented to the convicting Court, two Judges of which voiced strenuous disapproval of a move "which provided a loophole for his escape." Finally, the Court consented to the appointment of a second Sanity Commission. As before, this Commission consisted of two psychiatrists and an attorney. The first Commission had found Ballem "not insane . . . *despite his mental illness.*" This finding actuated his trial. The second Commission would determine how long the Commonwealth could postpone the execution. If Ballem were found "insane" he would be committed to a hospital for "mental illness" until such a time when he had recovered his "sanity" which would then qualify him as an "example to others." In this case the problem was to bring "insanity" as defined by law into consonance with "mental illness" as defined by psychiatry, whereby both could see the real Bailem as both insane and mentally ill and in need of *care.* This was not achieved.

In 1956 the Pennsylvania Mental Health Act of 1951 was amended [150] to instruct a Sanity Commission in the examination of a prisoner under judgment of death imposed by a court upon conviction on indictment charging him with murder in the first degree. The instructions order the Sanity Commission to consider "insanity" as having an existence only after the fixing of penalty, and to determine its existence exclusively on the basis of the following questions:

1. Whether the prisoner is insane and does not have capacity to understand the nature and object of the proceedings against him.
2. Whether the prisoner is insane and does not comprehend his own condition with reference to such proceedings.
3. Whether the prisoner is insane and does not understand the nature of the punishment to be inflicted upon him.
4. Whether the prisoner is insane and is unable to confer with his counsel with reference thereto.

In this amendment the definition of insanity applied to a condemned prisoner specifically eliminates any consideration of mental illness as defined by the Act originally passed by the Legislature. This definition is as follows:

"Mental illness shall mean an illness which so lessens the capacity of a person to use his customary self-control, judgment and discretion in the conduct of his affairs and social relations as to make it necessary or advisable for him to be under care. The term shall include insanity, unsoundness of mind, lunacy, mental disease, mental disorder and all other types of mental cases."

The second Commission examined Ballem. One psychiatrist and the attorney member of the Commission submitted a majority report in keeping with these requirements which barred considering the prisoner in the light of either legal or medical criteria of mental illness used by physicians in ordinary commitments.

The report adhered to the four common law tests set forth in the 1956 amendment, cited two cases in other jurisdictions and quoted Blackstone as follows: "If after judgment he become of nonsane memory, execution shall be stayed;

for peradventure, says the humanity of the English law, had the prisoner been of sound memory, he might have alleged something in stay of judgment or execution . . . For, as is observed by Sir Edward Coke 'the execution of an offender is for example, *ut poena ad paucos, metus ad omnes perveniat*: but so it is not when a madman is executed; but should be a miserable spectacle, both against law, and of extreme inhumanity and cruelty, and can be no example to others.' " (4 Blackstone 25)

The guiding principle of their examination and findings was cited from the Pennsylvania Supreme Court: *"Expert medical opinions are especially entitled to little or no weight when based upon insufficient or (partly) erroneous facts or a feigned state of mind or an inaccurate past history, or upon unreasonable deductions."* [151]

The report also cited the language of the Pennsylvania Supreme Court in its interpretation of the Mental Health Act of 1951 as follows: "At first glance the wordage of the Act would make it appear that every conceivable type of mental illness with the exception of those specifically excluded would fall within its scope and require commitment. Upon closer scrutiny it becomes evident that the *controlling factor is the degree to which the mind is affected by the mental disorder and not the bare existence of symptoms which would induce the psychiatrist to diagnose a mental illness.*" [152] [Emphasis mine.]

The report concluded that the prisoner was "sane" by common law which posits the separate existence of a "mind," which can be affected in degree by another separate entity called a "mental disorder," which, however, is not to be confused with a "mental illness," which is merely the bare existence of symptoms which induce a psychiatrist to make a diagnosis.

Great value was attached to the letters written by Ballem to his counsel during incarceration. More than any other evidence (the letters) showed the "true state of the prisoner's mind and the extent of his comprehension." Ballem's letters were interpreted to satisfy the four tests insofar as they demonstrated his awareness of his predicament, his knowledge that he faces execution, his understanding of the nature and the object of the proceedings against him, his comprehension of his own condition with reference to the proceedings and his capacity to confer with counsel.

The prison psychiatrist offered an *expert medical opinion that Ballem was mentally ill,* but his opinion did not satisfy the four criteria, because Ballem *"realized* he had been found guilty and sentenced to death and *knows* what death means." One witness, a prison guard, stated that the prisoner "expresses himself intelligently with regard to his needs," and established the time when the prisoner started to put on an "act."

The report related that on direct examination, the prisoner was hostile, refused to be sworn, refused to answer questions relating to the crime; but the prisoner *"knew* his name, his lawyer's name, the judge before whom he was tried, . . . had written letters, *knew* that his parents were dead, that he had no brothers or sisters, and that he had married, etc. . . ." [Emphasis mine.] The prisoner's resistance was penetrated to the extent of eliciting a few laconic admissions of the shooting and the attending circumstances. But he refused to answer questions relating

as to why he was in prison, of what he had been accused, what sentence was imposed upon him, whether he cared what happens, when he was supposed to be executed, whether he would like to go on living, what he would do if freed, whether there was ever anything wrong with him psychiatrically, whether he remembered certain persons bringing in papers for his signature, what the victim wanted to do before the murder, whether the Court had decided he had not killed in self defense; whether he felt they were going to execute him, whether he had talked to his counsel's assistants; his impression of life after death; whether his parents were nice to him. This report concluded: . . . he was hostile and refused to answer many questions regarding the crime, his trial and subsequent events. However, he answered many other questions *intelligently,* as set forth in the summary of the evidence, and *when caught off guard,* answered some questions regarding the crime. It is evident he *knows* he killed a man, feeling however, it was self defense. He *knows* he was tried and sentenced, and *knows* what fate awaits him unless some action intervenes . . . [Emphasis mine.] *As stated above, the prisoner is mentally ill from a medical viewpoint, suffering with paranoid schizophrenia, and under ordinary circumstances the majority members of the Commission would recommend commitment.* However, under the circumstances of this case, the Commission is governed by Section 344, Clause 3, of the Mental Health Act, and the majority members realize that their findings must be governed by the definition of insanity set forth therein.

In lawyer's language the two members of this Sanity Commission arrived at a moral judgment of Ballem's "sanity" strictly within the prescription of the law.

The dissenting medical member of the Commission submitted a separate minority report that the prisoner was a chronic schizophrenic, that his behavior before the Commission was consistent with his psychosis, and that the circumstances of the examination were not "conducive to bringing out the quality and quantity of material that could be elicited in a psychiatric interview." This member accommodated his findings of psychosis with the four criteria, and so testified that Ballem was insane.

Ballem's *physical* contact with our world is reduced by a self-immurement which is beyond the isolation imposed as a "maximum security." As a "show off" he remains continuously alone in a cell with door closed. He lies naked on his cot, sometimes sits in Hindu fashion; occasionally he walks about in bare feet. He is indifferent to the untidiness of his cell. His daily nourishment consists mainly of fruit and vegetable juices and six raw eggs. Save for daily brief contact with the prison psychiatrist, who brings his nourishment, occasional visits with outside persons and a few visits with the prison dentist, he exists in a dimly lighted enclosure with access to the outside world limited to either a cell corridor or to a narrow ventilation slit in heavy masonry, and these he insists be closed. He has no communication with fellow prisoners and minimal contact with his keepers, who are content to let a sleeping dog lie. For many months since his conviction he has left untouched a full beard and head of hair which impart to him an image of some gaunt anchoritic figure from the age of asceticism.

Ballem's *psychological* contact with our world is tenuous and fleeting. No consecutive communication with it is sustained. His attention wavers and is interrupted by intraneous promptings; at times he is far away in thought which in surface fragments conveys his clinging to past events with an inner theme of mystical experience.

As with many certified insane, Ballem has variable surface accessibility insofar as he is compliantly "responsive" to insistently pressed leading questions touching upon immediate circumstances, on fragments of his personal history, on his crime and trial—to questions designed to elicit his "knowing" such matters as would satisfy the legal criteria of his sanity. In these matters Ballem is undoubtedly "sane" as are many psychotics in mental hospitals who write letters which show "the extent of their comprehension," adhere to hospital regulations, have nominal awareness of their circumstance, express themselves "intelligently with respect to their needs," and unless otherwise adjudicated as incompetent by a separate action, can make valid wills and transact business.

In the Court accepted majority report there is no mention of a psychiatric inquiry into how the inner side of Ballem relates to his outer world, into his emotional deficit, into the meaning of his retreat from life, his absorption in a communication in "one's connections with God, flowing through a spiritual umbilical cord into one's being from God," short of "beatific visions." In this uterine isolation Ballem lives out passive, mystical communication with his inner self in paranoid interpretation of our world, in withdrawal from the evil that "comes from without, materialized in doing wrong things," from his deep instinct that "others dislike and want to hurt me," from an unspeakable feeling since childhood that he has been pursued by "ill luck of an unbelievable nature"; that he has been a victim of his uniqueness and superiority. "I was born in the wrong age which doesn't appreciate me and instinctively tries to destroy me." He is aware of the totality of his adaptive failure since his earliest beginnings. We get a glimpse of his flight from human contact wherein he speaks of himself as guided by a kind of blind fate, a driving impulse over which he fears his lack of control, a kind of separate destructive personality which has a mind of its own and which was his undoing. He identifies this personality as "sensuality" which in him is aroused to activity when he attempts to establish a human relationship. He succeeds in the suppression of this demonic entity as long as he isolates himself from others. In this rigorous avoidance of human contact he takes refuge in an intense fantasy world of words. Words are people and he lives with them linked to persons long dead. In these personified words he finds double meanings; homologues of double motivations in living people. When he tried to reach a living person in the present, "something had gone wrong," as in his marriage and in his crime. He is now tied to the past and to the dead. In surface exchange with others, his words have another function; they form an intellectual screen which filters out and makes less visible his inner emotional dilapidation. In this regressive necrobiosis only the shell of a social creature remains, a verbal shell out of which a "sane" Ballem exists in the island universe of Section 344, Clause 3 of the Mental Health Act.

Efforts to rally Ballem's attention to his present predicament are unrewarding. He is detached from his physical person. As one putting on an "act" his contemplation of his own death or of others arouses no appropriate emotional response. In his acting he has succeeded in feigning sanity. His manifest mental change began early in adolescence with unquestioned schizophrenic features showing in his later twenties, punctuated by a slaying and continued today, marked further by a bizarre retreat from human contact, by symptomatic return to an atavistic mode of life in ascetic darkness and nudity and to an inner mystical fantasy, his "liberation through introversion," to an increasing occupancy in the world of dreams which are in color and "harmless and nice," and by a flight from "sensuality," in the alignments of which he cannot determine whether he is male or female. He maintains a superficial verbal contact with others which enables some to discover the "true state of the prisoner's mind and his comprehension."

The procedures of this inquiry and the conclusions of the two members of the Sanity Commission invite further comment on the problem of communication between criminal law and psychiatry. The examination was accusatory in procedure, vocabulary and spirit. Testimony was centered exclusively on the imposed legal criteria of "insanity," governing a special instance. Medical evidence of "insanity" by psychiatric standards was cast in the shadow of a dictum in which there is no room for expert medical opinions based upon sufficient and correct facts, accuracy of past history, and reasonable deductions, and which ". . . calls in experts to solve a problem and then discards their conclusions for the opinions of a passerby." [153] The offering of an experienced prison psychiatrist was "especially entitled to little or no weight," and given none. Witnesses were placed under oath (the prisoner refused to be sworn) and the prisoner reported that during the examination he was flanked by two "giants" (guards). There was no concealment of a readiness to dismiss the prisoner as a "show off" and his symptomatic behavior as an "act," and in the examination technique, emphasis was recorded of the weight of his replies when he was "caught off guard," all in keeping with an attitude which defined Ballem's position as a defendant. It does not appear that the inquiry went beyond the acceptance of a diagnosis of malingering suggested by a prison guard.

If we view this event in terms of its concepts, language and aim, it could be regarded as having the effect of both a reiteration of Ballem's trial and an appellate finding vindicating the original adjudication of his guilt and his penalty. A Sanity Commission which must consider an "insanity" with time boundaries only after the penalty is fixed and only on the basis of four elements of "knowledge," is within the same restrictions as the medical expert who, in the trial, must determine a kind of "insanity" based upon M'Naghten.

In Pennsylvania a prisoner not under penalty of death has recourse to a kind of "insanity" provided by law, which allows the psychiatrist comprehensive inquiry within his model of science. The condemned prisoner is strictly limited to another kind of "insanity" which limits psychiatric inquiry to a residual of surface communication. Ballem has been cast into two roles; one the paranoid schizophrenic, "insane" by the legal criterion of *care;* another, the condemned murderer, "sane" by Section 344, Clause 3 of the Mental Health Act. Meanwhile, Ballem as a person remains retrenched, self-contained in his world of words and "harmless, nice dreams," of his umbilical "connection with God," with scant interest in either role, in how the game is played, or in which side wins.

Ballem has been the meeting point of two systems of viewing the phenomenon of behavior which is called both criminal and psychotic. The legal system enabled the majority to find a *knowingness* inside of Ballem; the psychiatric system had less concern with what was or was not inside him, and more of the aim to describe the profoundly changed relationship taking place between him and ourselves. Both views were properly adduced and correct insofar as each employed its own model and language. Within each is validity insofar as each system is self-contained, but there was no sharing of experience.

The social and economic implications of Ballem's "sanity" may attain the measure of those of the "sanity" of James Colbert Smith, discussed in the forepart of this chapter. The difference between them lies in the fact that since 1956 the Commonwealth of Pennsylvania has taken the determination of sanity of a condemned prisoner out of reach of scientific inquiry.

> The first of these is the recognition that scientific concepts and generalizations are not literal transcripts of reality but highly selective constructs of the mind; not discoveries in the strict sense, but inventions, products of the creative imagination of men of genius.
>
> MAX OTTO [154]

Criminal Law Is Moved by the Hand of Man Alone

Mid-20th Century criminal law is moved by the hand of man alone, but it is a wavering hand. It is a wavering that comes with the beginnings of self-awareness, a wavering that man experiences as he stands alone between the child's world yet within him, which is alive and permeated with intentions and finality, and the outer uncertain reality of the scientist. The world of the child in us with its "subjective adherences," those fragments of internal reference which cling to the external world, and from which come our allusion of certitude, will be found also in our social institutions.

Such "adherences" are the Idols long ago described by Francis Bacon; pictures taken for reality, thoughts mistaken for things: "For it is a false assertion that the sense of man is the measure of things. On the contrary all perceptions as well of the sense as of the mind are according to the measure of the individual and not according to the measure of the universe. And the human understanding is like a false mirror, which . . . distorts and discolors the nature of things by mingling its own nature with it." [155] "For everyone has a cave or den of his own, which refracts and discolors the light of nature . . . men look for sciences in their own lesser worlds and not in the greater or common world." [156] Bacon spoke of the Idols formed by the "intercourse and association of men with each other . . . for men converse by means of language . . . and words are imposed according to the apprehension of the vulgar. And therefore the ill and unfit choice of words wonderfully obstructs the understanding. Nor do the definitions or explanations wherewith in some things learned men are wont to guard and defend themselves, by any means set the matter right. But words plainly force and overrule the understanding, and throw all into confusion, and lead men away into numberless empty controversies and idle fancies.[157]

"Lastly there are Idols which immigrated into men's minds from the various dogmas of philosophies and also from wrong laws of demonstration . . . stage plays representing worlds of their own creation after an unreal and scenic fashion." [158] Bacon spoke of the Idols of the Tribe, the Cave, the Market Place and the Theater, and thus in modern idiom we might identify these Idols as the "subjective adherences" congenial to our child rearing, to our symbolic environment, and which play a part in the maintenance of a moral order.

From the beginnings of moral order men have been applying their Idols to the problem of explaining the appearances of things in persons who deviate either by way of mental disorder or criminality. We can trace these Idols in their direct lineage under their different names. They began with *mana,* then to *demons* possessing or obsessing, then with *witches* in "criminal conversation" with the *devil*; later the devil became *original sin,* oftimes identified as "constitutional" *orneryness,* and in more recent origin reduced to a pallid abstraction of the devil invented by the moralists called *responsibility.* Responsibility is one of the Idols of the

Theater, which has "immigrated into men's minds from the various dogmas of the philosophies." Menninger speaks of the evolution of such Idols in these words:

> They linked up all behavior, good and bad, with a mystical metaphysical essence called *responsibility*. According to this solemn theory, it isn't God or lack of God, or sin or the devil or witches or anything celestial or mundane that makes men saints or sinners. It is a single, solemn imponderable called *responsibility;* millions of dollars are spent annually to determine who has it or who hasn't it. If one is found to have it, he is locked up; if he is found not to have it, he is also locked up. Thus is demonstrated the pragmatic beauty of a doctrine, which is neither fish nor fowl, but which is still the shibboleth and the fallacy of the lawyers just as the doctrine of original sin was a fallacy of the clergy.[159, 160]

Responsibility is an Idol of the Theater with which the psychiatrist in court is faced, but for which he has neither comprehension nor concern. Responsibility in the sense that the criminal law employs it as a mystical property possessed by some and not by others, as something that can be reckoned to a scale of *none* to *total,* divisible and variable in time and place, is derived from the primitive organization of the mind which magically equates injury in the talion principle. It is one of the "subjective adherences" having no existence other than in the minds of those who talk about it.[161] Mercier expressed this tersely when he said that "responsibility is therefore not a quality of the person who has inflicted pain, but a demand on the part of the others that he shall suffer."[162] In sum, when we speak of responsibility we are speaking of a practice of looking not *at* but *past* the behavior, and past the behavior we are contemplating our own behavior toward the offender, what we intend to do to him. Beyond this, responsibility becomes what MacDonald calls " 'the ghost in the machine' that is held responsible for the individual's conduct or misconduct." [163]

Much of what has been written of responsibility and the moral order continues as an Idol of the Theater; little has been written about it as a realistic device of balancing tensions between the law breaker and the law abiding. Scarcely a line has been written of responsibility as a functional process in which both wrong doer and his triers are mutual participants. This is to say, that when we speak of the responsibility of the criminal we are speaking of an inseparable element called guilt and in the same breath we are also speaking of the responsibility and guilt of those who make judgments upon the criminal and who inflict injury upon him in imitation of his crime. In the trial, only the responsibility and guilt of the accused are in focus; those of the triers are obscured in the formal procedures, in the paragraphs of the law books, in the attenuation in number, and in displacement to the experts. The guilt and peril of the accused are borne by him alone; the guilt of his triers is divided by number and dissipated in abstractions. Thus, in the name of responsibility a jury can actuate a legal injury. In a practical, operational sense, responsibility merely denotes an action to be taken by some against one, some tension relieving exaction of payment or compensation imposed on one who, in breaking a rule of the game, has set up tensions in those who have succeeded so far in adhering to the same rule.

Law and psychiatry are making an effort to improve the Idols of criminal justice. Within the past decade there has been an acceleration in the output of literature from both legal and psychiatric sources. The preceding recipients of the Isaac Ray Award have made distinguished contributions to the communication between law and psychiatry and have set the pace and direction for a re-evaluation of our Idols. We are in times when science has reached a point where it has outdistanced man's self awareness and when more than ever before we are concerned for the survival of individual human values and freedom. The symbols of criminal justice are beginning to undergo a shift from a public-centered to an individual-centered jurisprudence and in this shift criminal justice will shed its magical anachronisms. Psychiatry has had a hand in this shift and with it criminal justice will be in time slowly liberalized from the grip of social and political demonologies. But self awareness and re-evaluation of our Idols do not come easily; they require a rugged objectivity and invoke the anxiety that comes when certitude is threatened, even a certitude that has no substance beyond indispensable and fatal words. The anxiety of uncertitude impels us to cling to old formulations even when we acknowledge them as impediments to justice, and the same anxiety will show when we enter upon change and novelty.

I have spoken of the concept of responsibility as an Idol of the Theater and in the same token we can speak of the means we employ in determining it. A formula or testing device is indispensable as long as it is determined in a public-centered procedure, as long as we impose upon unsophisticated persons the task of making juridic decisions, and as long as we place a high value on a test as a check against the abuse of power. The Royal Commission on Capital Punishment spoke of this need:

> The advantage of a formula is that it serves to limit the arbitrary element and to promote uniformity as well as to help the jury to decide between conflicting views. It is as much a safeguard for the offender in some cases as in others; it is a safeguard against unjustifiable acquittals on the ground of insanity. To have no rule at all would be to leave the decision on which often a man's life depends to the uncertain variations of ethical standard and emotional reaction which may influence the minds of members of the jury.[164]

There is a belief in some that psychiatrists carry in their opposition to the M'Naghten formula a wish to abandon any rule of responsibility in cases where insanity is a defense. There is substance to this belief. As matters now stand in such cases the test is first directed to the psychiatrist and then secondly delivered to the jury to accept or reject. Psychiatrists should be opposed to any test of responsibility that is imposed first on them under the guise of a medical desideratum. Psychiatrists would not presume to abandon any testing device as long as it remains a legal communication restricted to those who make moral judgments. The psychiatrist employs tests of his own in the area of medical inquiry. Psychiatrists would not complain of the M'Naghten formula if it were put exclusively to the jury, which, with the medical facts in evidence, in all probability would do no better or no worse with it than the expert. In sum, the psychiatrist is not opposed to any legal test as long as it is put to the right people. He is not opposed to any test which is a medical desideratum and within his competence. The M'Naghten test is not a medical desideratum and it is outside his competence.

Some may think that it is not desirable to isolate the psychiatric expert from the moral issue because the expert's evidence must be communicated to laymen and must lead to a moral decision. It may be that expertness itself implies a civic obligation to relieve the layman of full, personal, moral responsibility for the decision. The trouble with this is that psychiatrists are not learned in moral matters. Again it may be argued that any medical evidence given by the psychiatrist will be inescapably tied to the ultimate question of penalty; that medical evidence of mental disorder of any description communicated to the jury will have less meaning as objective data and more meaning as a moral instruction to the jury in making a verdict. This issue of responsibility is clearly at the center of our problem of communication between psychiatry and criminal law.

Anything said in an adversary setting will drift to partisan alignment, pro or con, and will have the meaning of an instruction to the jury. But there is a difference between something said which is a scientific instruction leading to a moral decision, and something said which is a moral instruction leading to a moral decision. Objective medical data in transit to a jury are a scientific instruction leading to a moral decision but they carry no moral instruction—the moral instruction comes properly from the law. It is our desire that the jury receive correct and meaningful instruction which is uniform, consistent and leading to an ideal of "equal justice for all." However, as matters now stand there is only exceptionally a recognition that objective medical data expressed in the language of science can be as meaningful an instruction, if not more so, than one limited to the moral language of knowledge of right and wrong which comes improperly from psychiatry. M'Naghten stands in the way of our discovery that scientific instruction may meet the criteria of a good formula as set forth by the Royal Commission on Capital Punishment. M'Naghten now casts a spell on objective medical data and transforms them into a moral instruction with a label of psychiatry.

The shift of criminal justice from a public-centered to an individual-centered operation meets a resistance common in all of us and we tend to take refuge with those who find ". . . it is necessary to sacrifice both scientific validity and legal logic in the interest of certainty." [165]

In his *The Urge to Punish,* Weihofen devotes a chapter to the search for certainty and relates the quest for a formula for the determination of criminal responsibility. He says, "There is no doubt that a clear and simple rule would be a Good Thing. Clarity and simplicity are always desirable and in law they are rare and precious jewels among the heaps of scoriaceous dross produced by the legal mind at work." [166, 167] Weihofen then turns his attention to the M'Naghten rule, to find that its simplicity and clarity are illusory. The words "nature" and "quality" have yet to be reduced to operational meaning; as verbal symbols they continue to revolve in juridic orbits of their own high above the realm of objective data of experience. Likewise, with the words "wrong" and "know," key words in the M'Naghten test. These words have spawned other words into an imposing creation of reversible errors, dicta, opinions and dissertations. Weihofen states: "After one hundred and twelve years we still don't know" what such words mean. Thirty years ago, in his authoritative book,

Mental Disorder and the Criminal Law, Professor Sheldon Glueck said: "Perhaps in no other field of American law is there so much disagreement as to fundamentals and so many contradictory decisions in the same jurisdictions. Not a modern text or compilation begins the discussion of the subject of insanity and its relation to the criminal law without a doleful reference to the chaos in this field." [168]

Despite this chaos the drift to individual-centered jurisprudence continues and those who shape our legal rules are accommodating themselves to it. Two trends are noted. In English and Scottish procedure three steps have tended to soften the M'Naghten rule; (1) more persons are found "unfit to plead," (2) a liberalization of the interpretation of the words of the rule, even to the point of making irresistible impulse a defense, and (3) the Prerogative of Mercy used particularly to reprieve condemned murderers. Weihofen believes these three developments in English and Scottish law have had the effect of reducing M'Naghten to a minimum. He notes such tendencies in American law with the exception that no American State has a pardoning power comparable with the English Prerogative of Mercy.

The second trend comes through the influence of a philosophical re-examination of our conceptual tools. In this rereading we come upon the discovery that the search for a rule in the field of responsibility and mental disorder is futile. It is futile because such rules are by necessity circular verbal definitions born of words which in Bacon's reflection are the definitions or explanations wherewith in some things learned men are wont to guard and defend themselves but "do not set the matter right." We come to the view that general concepts do not have a reality of their own, such as *mind, intent, will, insanity,* etc. but that they must be regarded simply as names. Any exercise of reasoning establishes merely an hypothesis which must be verified by concrete experience. We are reminded of the dictum of Gasset, "Hence, if we penetrate to the true inwardness of a concept, we find that it tells us nothing of the thing itself, but only sums up what one can do with it or what it can do to one." [169]

I can find no better statement of the discovery that the evidence of science does not support the "pictures taken for reality," "thoughts mistaken for things," than in Weihofen's summation:

> The search for a clear and certain rule in this field is a misguided one, a manifestation of the all-too-human yearning for certainty and order in an uncertain and chaotic world ... Perhaps this is part of a more pervasive craving for unquestioned standards and psychological security which Max Lerner has called "the most corroding development in the American character." It is a manifestation of that anthropomorphic view of the world that reads purpose and design into the working of natural forces, and that leads ultimately to a picture of a rational universe governed by law. The great spread of scientific knowledge during recent times has produced no evidence that supports this picture. The evidence it has produced tells us the picture is false. We shall make progress faster when we abandon this delusion and proceed on the basis of what is ascertainable. But if the yearning for certainty is not peculiar to law, it seems to be particularly strong with respect to law. There is a widespread feeling on the part of the public that the law ought to be clear and definite. Even lawyers share this feeling. Although they must know that all law is a good deal less definite than laymen suppose, lawyers make heroic efforts to maintain the illusion of certainty. When bar association leaders make speeches about the law, we rarely find them talking about the dynamic and adaptive character of law. Rather, they emphasize its antiquity and its unchanging permanence. This is what Jerome Frank called the basic myth of the law.[170]

We have reached a place where there is a consensus that the M'Naghten test of responsibility in the defense of insanity is no longer useful. The Royal Commission on Capital Punishment conceded that "The test of responsibility laid down by the M'Naghten rule is so defective that the law on the subject ought to be changed." [171] In this country the Criminal Law Advisory Committee of the American Law Institute has likewise viewed the M'Naghten rule.[172] To these views now expressed from the side of law may be added an almost unanimous expression of dissatisfaction on the part of the profession of psychiatry.[173] But a few psychiatrists remain who accept the M'Naghten rule in its present application. In this connection Wertham submits that,

> Criminal guilt is, first of all, defined by law. By definition, therefore, it is a social phenomenon. In view of a widespread tendency to the contrary, it is important to realize that no social phenomenon and no social problem can be directly and simply translated into a psychological one. A great deal of the difficulty in the relationship between psychiatry and the law has come from the fact that the psychiatrist makes a pronouncement on a social category as if it were a psychological one... The law chooses what it designates as criminal guilt. From the whole undistinguished mass of guilt it selects its own criteria of criminal responsibility and segregates legal guilt from guilt in general. The question, therefore, arises whether and to what extent this is defensible in terms of the data of modern psychiatry and psychoanalysis. In this sphere the law operates with such terms as *insanity, irresistible impulse, irresponsibility, incompetence, lucid interval, transitory insanity,* and in some degree also *clemency* and *mitigating circumstances.* This gives the psychiatrist the task of evaluating the psychology used in the law.[174]

I think Wertham would find others in complete agreement with him if the "psychology of the law" he states exists were kept within the bounds of the legal communication with those who make moral decisions and if the psychiatrist were excused from working with a psychology not his own.

Two developments are taking us beyond M'Naghten. One is the area shaped by new proposals for change notable among which is that submitted in the tentative draft of the Model Penal Code of the American Law Institute. The other is the Durham case [175] which marked the passing of M'Naghten and the irresistible impulse test in the District of Columbia, and the adopting of the essentials of the New Hampshire rule which in sum determines that one cannot be held responsible if the evidence considered by the jury shows beyond a reasonable doubt that the unlawful act was the product of mental illness or defect.

I shall leave the legal analysis of both the academic and decisional departures from M'Naghten to qualified hands. I shall venture some comments upon them within the compass of my previously stated viewpoints which must be regarded as my own and not necessarily the consensus of psychiatry. Both Professor Weihofen and Judge Biggs have scrutinized the tentative proposal for a modern penal code by the American Law Institute, submitted at its 32nd Annual Meeting. It follows:

Mental Disease or Defect Excluding Responsibility.
(1) A person is not responsible for criminal conduct if at the time of such conduct as a result of mental disease or defect he lacks substantial capacity either to appreciate the criminality of his conduct or to conform his conduct to the requirements of law.
(2) The terms "mental disease or defect" do not include an abnormality manifested only by repeated criminal or otherwise anti-social conduct.[176]

Judge Biggs regards the first paragraph of this proposal as a restatement of M'Naghten, aided by the phrase "or to conform his conduct to the requirements of the law," in which phrase he detects "substantially the same rule of responsibility as that laid down by the Durham case or *State v. Pike,* the New Hampshire rule, though the reporters . . . in their comments, expressly repudiate the doctrine of the Durham decision." [177] The second paragraph is designed to exclude the so-called psychopathic personality as a category of mental illness or defect. Judge Biggs believes that this matter should be left open and that no hard and fast exclusionary rule should be attempted at this time.

Weihofen likewise notes that the proposal adheres essentially to M'Naghten, that it makes changes in wording and that it adds a second element which recognizes impairment of volitional capacity as a defense but which is not expressed in terms of *irresistible impulse*. Weihofen welcomes the abandonment of the controversial words "know," "nature," "quality," and "wrong," and the adoption of the word "substantial" which removes from the formula the requirement of an *all* or *none* alternative of cognition imposed by M'Naghten. "Nothing makes the inquiry into responsibility more unreal for the psychiatrist than the limitation of the issue to some ultimate extreme of total incapacity, when clinical experience reveals only a graded scale with marks along the way." [178]

The code draftsmen provide in the word "substantial" relief to the expert witness. But what the word "substantial" adds in relief to the psychiatrist it subtracts in definiteness to the jury. This would impose upon the judge an onus of jury instruction, of something pointing to a mark along a graded scale. The judge would in turn need instruction from the expert witness upon whom the task of determining what is clinically "substantial" would be equally onerous. My comment here is that the word "substantial" as a measure of clinical demonstration would likely throw the psychiatrist in refuge to the "ultimate extreme of total incapacity," as does M'Naghten and limit the range of cases to a relative few, as does M'Naghten. The criterion of commitability might better serve, but if the accused were so affected as to require commitment he would be "unfit for trial." This begs a question how far do the framers of the code wish to go in order to reach that group of persons in whom psychiatrists recognize the existence of mental disorder which does not always appear in the bold relief of classical example. The proposed Code, as with M'Naghten, may exempt the idiot, or a person with impaired consciousness. It may reach a few but not all psychotics including paranoiacs and schizophrenics. Will the code fulfill its purpose and ideal if it leaves untouched a larger segment of persons afflicted with conditions medically recognized as incapacitating, namely, those suffering with anxiety states, hysteria, depressions, compulsive disorders, ranging to psychotic degree, and the so-called psychopathic group? The framers of the code have made themselves clear on the exclusion of the "psychopath." I would venture the comment that the framers of the code are closer to a class theoretical orientation to mental disorder, which tends to dominate the thinking of many psychiatrists as well. Legal literature abounds in such an orientation which erects static identities of mental disorder by classes which by being named seemingly acquire definite boundaries and separate existence. Legal literature is weighed down with older static concepts of mental disorder of which a good number have acquired a quaintness with age.

It should be borne in mind that since time of M'Naghten the manifestations of mental disorder have changed. Today they are more diffuse and less articulated in outspoken symptoms, and we suspect that such departure from the classical pictures of mental disorder has some relationship to the sociological and ideological changes of our era, to the general unrest of our times, and to the change of values in human affairs.[179]

It is difficult for me to see how the proposed Code would reach our case of Edward Gibbs or others like him to come.

Class theoretical identities give the illusion of certainty; they do not reveal the hidden properties of nature, but are at best only properties of language. To some it may seem that in abandoning some words and replacing them with others the Code points to the promised land. But a real change can scarcely be effected by the use of words which bear a dictionary synonymity with those erased. The same verbal circularity remains and in time, through the process of judicial interpretation and scholarship, such circularity will ascend heavenward in ever increasing spirals as did the words of M'Naghten. The framers of the proposed Code do not live and work in the same climate of doubt and certainty as the Judges of England in Victoria's reign. Their task is harrassed with much doubt. Weihofen is ready to believe that "The Model Code formula is a recognition that definiteness in this field is a mere *ignis fatuus*. The most significant and most hopeful thing about the Institute's formula is that a group of eminent lawyers have at long last recognized this fact, and are ready to stop chasing will-o'-the-wisps." [180]

I pass on to the suggestion of the Code framers that ambiguity will be minimized with the substitution of the word "criminality" for the word "wrong." The accused must lack "substantial capacity either to appreciate the criminality of his conduct or to conform his conduct to the requirements of law." Weihofen is emphatic in his view that the criterion of "appreciation of criminality" would alone condemn the "most wildly disordered persons ever seen . . . who kill believing that the deed is commanded by God . . . may even commit it precisely *because* he knows it is criminal . . ." [181] I would join Weihofen in this view and venture further to state that it is highly improbable that any mentally disordered person who commits a criminal act is ever "substantially" unappreciative of its "criminality," as revealed in the case of Ballem.

Exceptionally the contrary would obtain in cases of criminal acts committed during delirium or within an epileptic fit or its equivalent. The framers of the Code believe that the second part of the proposed test would exempt the persons cited by Weihofen. It reads: ". . . or (substantial capacity) to conform his conduct to the requirements of the law." He does not think that the "capacity to conform" covers such situations and anticipates that such a criterion will come to the same battle of experts as does M'Naghten.[182] I would agree with his objection. M'Naghten's Cheshire Cat has vanished but the grin lingers. The "capacity to conform" part of the Model Code appears to lengthen the reach of the insanity defense to that of the "irresistible impulse" which is already accepted in at least thirteen States. Again Weihofen regards this proposed terminology as an improvement. He says, " 'Irresistible impulse' is an unscientific term . . . another example of the 19th Century penchant for using absolute terms as 'rhetorical flourishes.' " [183]

I would comment that many persons act out as if by some imperative that transcends all common sense and rationality and that the term "irresistible impulse" is descriptive of the imperative.[184] To reckon such actions with a lack of substantial capacity to "conform one's conduct with the requirements of the law" is a dubious improvement, if for no better reason that the criterion has more equivocal words to ponder. Clinical literature is replete with observations of irrational behavior which in the appearances of things is impulsive. Professor Edwin R. Keedy has written a comprehensive monograph on the legal aspects of this subject.[185] If we are guided by the data of objective observation, people certainly appear to act impulsively. The element of "irresistibility" attached to the impulse is more defining of our attitude towards such impulsive acts than it is of the doer's subjective element that we wish to identify and measure. Irresistibility conveys the *all* or *none* concept tied to the notion of unlawful intent which in the lunatic legally doesn't exist. Implied in the acceptance of the idea of "irresistible impulse," is a latent recognition in ourselves that under given circumstances we are not "free agents," and in this recognition we can find a thread of identification with those who act out impulsively and "irresistibly." In this identification we also achieve a kind of humanistic understanding and a sense of empathetic justice. In fact, it is not difficult to relate all irrational behavior to the concept of impulsiveness and irresistibility. Engage yourself in communication with a person who is actively psychotic and discover for yourself that his productions both verbally and in actions are impulsive in the sense of their apparent disjunctive irrelevance to the content of the communication, and that they often issue against any resistance which either the patient or another can erect. Suppose that we observe a schizophrenic with catatonic features of apparent withdrawal and indifference to his surroundings. One day without apparent provocation and notice he suddenly jumps to his feet and touches a passerby and as suddenly returns to his prior state.

It would not be difficult to accept this action as impulsive or as irresistible since we know we are dealing with a schizophrenic within whom there is an active psychotic process at work out of view. We know that we cannot assess the impulse in terms of our own values but must look for its connection with a different set of values within the patient. The emergence of the impulse alien to our value system can have a meaning only in symbol which provides a clue to the inner life. Such symbolic impulses do not come by caprice, but represent in symptom the patient's way of attempted resolution of his inner conflict, a loosening of it and an effort to restore contact with the outside world. It is a form of communication.

Now all people to some extent are given to symptomatic impulsiveness, which is not resisted, witnessed every day in the common slips and mistakes of forgetting and accidents, etc.[186] Words come out of us and we may not know what we have said until after we hear them. Yet another class of individuals have variable awareness of conflict within themselves which is so structured that relief of inner tension is obtained only by repeatedly carrying out certain ritualistic acts, some of which may be unlawful. In point are the cases of impulsive stealing, fire setting and some sexual perversions, notably exhibitionism. Yet the awareness of inner conflict does not itself enhance the "capacity to conform," which can be restored only by working out the meaning of the conflict in therapy.

There is a courtroom gambit known as the "policeman at the elbow test" employed to rebut the defense of irresistible impulse. When this test is put to the expert witness, it is put with the demand for a yes or no answer. If the witness answers that the irresistible impulse would not occur with a policeman at the elbow, the defense collapses. If the witness answers that it would occur, the witness collapses. Yet the "elbow test" can and must be qualified. It is improbable that a person driven to irresistible impulse, for example in the case of the exhibitionist, with the materialized ego and monitor at his elbow would then and there consummate the act. He would be "crazy" if he did. But now he has an alliance with another who augments his control and repression of the impulse. His defenses, combined with an ally, render the impulse resistible, and for the moment his anxiety is bound. This is a commonplace experience for many who, when alone, sense in themselves an uneasiness which is relieved when they are "with somebody." There is no virtue in such an alliance save as a momentary expedient. The true answer to the "elbow" question would be *yes,* if the policeman were *always* at the elbow. In real life a curious paradox is often observed. When the policeman goes off duty, the impetus is renewed and the actor finds a way and a time for the release of the impulse. But his action is not solely within a design to elude detection; within the action itself beyond the relief of tension, there is as often a companion gesture beckoning the policeman to return. We observe in cases of repeated "irresistible impulse" which remain undetected, that in time the individual continues to invite detection sometimes to the point of recklessness. His offense appears at once to be both a law breaking and an appeal; the "irresistible impulse" appears to drive the offender into irresistible acting out, and irresistibly into the arms of the policeman. The "elbow test" could be applied to certified lunatics as well. Ofttimes the most profoundly disturbed persons do not carry out certain symptomatic behavior if an attendant or physician is at hand, and can hold the psychotic impulses in abeyance. Under these circumstances it would not occur to anyone to consider the patient sane simply because he withholds certain symptoms when attended. Irresistible impulse is framed as something that comes out of an individual. This is a limited view. It neglects the transactional aspect of behavior which, in its outward appearance, is a token of an invisible process of many dimensions. Thus a fuller understanding of the act can be achieved in the interactional frame of doer-object or doer-victim.[187]

The liberalization of the M'Naghten test of knowledge suggests several interpretations. The extension beyond knowledge of right and wrong to "irresistible impulse" provides an exception to the criterion of knowledge. Thus, one knows what one is doing and knows that it is unlawful, yet does it anyway as if impelled in spite of one's "knowing." In this is implied some other undefined element of the mind and some alteration of it to effect the control of volition. Even in cases in which M'Naghten is formally applied, juries appear to react as if this undefined element determines the verdict. It is something which touches the deeper identification of the juryman with the accused; the juryman unencumbered with the abstractions of M'Naghten, instinctively senses that everyone acts out impulsively and that such impulsive behavior itself in its more bizarre form has a secular meaning of "insanity." This view is reflected in the statement of a legal writer in the Cambridge Law Review:

> This dislike [of the existing law] now appears to have spread to juries, judging by the verdicts of guilty but insane, returned at the Central Criminal Court in 1936 and 1943, in the face of the M'Naghten rule. If juries persist in recognizing the defense of irresistible impulse, the legislature or the Courts may be forced through pressure of public opinion to recognize it as well.[188]

A second interpretation is that the idea of irresistible impulse, is actually descriptively closer to what we observe as something real. This is to say that it has an objective concrete extension in the act, whereas M'Naghten and the notion of knowledge remain in the realm of the subjective. One is tempted to believe that the impulse notion is nearer to a real test of responsibility insofar as visible behavior is a guide to the evaluation one can make of the subjective element of crime. The "irresistible impulse" is a demonstration. The extension of the M'Naghten test of knowledge (cognition) to that of the irresistible impulse (conation and volition) as a defense has been in keeping with the intuition of juries who somehow sense the argument that a symptomatic manifestation in one aspect of mental life must be a token of a process that affects all of the mental life, and this intuition is in the direction away from the compartmentalized faculty psychology and the vogue of phrenology in M'Naghten's time. It is contended by some that if one function of the personality is impaired his capacity for knowledge would be in some degree also affected. Wertham is an exponent of this view that the subjective element of crime finds its endpoint in "knowledge." In discussing the "product" concept in the Durham decision he states:

> If a crime is really the product, the result, the symptom of a psychosis, it is inevitable that a person who committed it cannot sufficiently distinguish between right and wrong and/or sufficiently know the nature and quality of his act.[189]

This view is also held by the legal writer, Jerome Hall, who quite correctly adheres to the concept that man functions as a unitary being, that the faculties of will, reason, feeling are interdependent, in normal persons integrated, and that there cannot be a distortion in one without a corresponding asymmetry in the others. He says,

> The personality is seen as a fusion of functions and not a mere inter-relation of separate faculties, whether these be designated cognition, will and emotion, or ego, super ego and id; hence there can be no serious impairment of one of these functions without serious impairment of the others . . . It will be seen that, given the premise of an integrated personality, the concept of "irresistible impulse"—of will totally separated from reason and emotion—is untenable.[190]

According to Hall the test of irresistible impulse is superfluous since cases of impulsive behavior come within the comprehension of M'Naghten. He states, "Indeed all action, especially that relevant to the penal law, involves a unified operation of the personality. . . . The M'Naghten rule provides an analytical device for dissecting this action." [191, 192]

The thesis of functional unity of mental operations does indeed serve the argument for the validity of M'Naghten. It says that "knowledge" of the wrongfulness of an act and of its nature and quality is an indicator of a larger dimension of mental disturbance. It is a method of sampling the mind to determine the subjective element necessary to a crime. The theory of functional unity of mental operations is consonant with modern psychiatric thought. The assertion that the test of "knowledge" is truly comprehensive of such unity may be logically valid but I believe it is empirically false. I have previously offered some analysis of M'Naghten in terms of the means available for its verification. When we looked beyond the assertion itself we found ourselves only making more assertions and circular definitions, and when we abandoned our assertions about assertions and looked at the objective data of behavior, we could find little if any correspondence of them with the assumptions contained in our assertions. From this endeavor we could draw two reflections. The first is that, as a critical moral formula, the legal test of responsibility merely tells us that the wrong doer *ought* to have knowledge of the wrongfulness of his act, its nature and its quality. This is in keeping with the moral ideal which need not have relevance to the objective data of experience. The second is that a moral order can exist if a sufficient number of the community subscribe to an assertion of what ought to be and act accordingly. If such be the case it may be that when we make assertions about right and wrong and about the subjective element which accompanies the action of others, about intent, will, malice, knowledge, irresistible impulses, etc., we are actually making assertions about abstractions which are inside of our own heads, assertions having to do with law as a science of arbitrary human relations but not always having to do with a science of objective reality.

When we go beyond these moral prescriptions of our child rearing and attempt to bring them into consonance with our experience with human behavior we find that some persons not only knowingly do things they ought not to do but also that they morally deplore and condemn what they do. Such persons appear to themselves as well as to others to be impelled by an inner imperative to carry out the forbidden behavior. The subjective element attending their crimes remains out of reach of conscious search. These persons experience relief from an inner threat often momentarily and occasionally permanently. The acting out has the meaning of a primary gain which is covered by the surface rationalizations. Such acting out has been characterized as impulsive and its consummation as irresistible. The term "impulse" implies behavior which is spontaneous and in some degree as deviant from common sense standards. Such behavior is not always regarded as pathologic as in the case of the person who by impulse runs into a burning house and rescues someone, or in the case of some soldiers in battle who act impulsively to find themselves heroes. The term "irresistible" can have no meaning other than that which tells us that an action has taken place, something of an event in the past. The term carries an implication that the same impulse is resistible by some but not by others. It also has a latent demonological implication that the doer is a mere agent of some incorporated malignant personality. One often hears the complaint of another who has acted impulsively; "I don't know what got *into* me, that I should do such a thing."

At best, the terms "impulse" and "irresistible" in conjunction imply the existence of a pathological state in the wrong doer who acts out irrationally and yet need not be mad. Maudsley regarded the mad ones under the common term of *impulsive insanity,* and spoke of them as follows:

> It would be a hard matter for those who have not lived among the insane and so become familiar with their ways and feelings to be persuaded, if, without such experience, they ever can, that a man may be mad and yet be free from delusion and exhibit no marked derangement of intelligence. Nevertheless, it is a fact that in a certain state of mental disease a morbid impulse may take such despotic possession of the patient as to drive him, in spite of reason and against his will, to a desperate act of suicide or homicide; like the demoniac of old into whom the unclean spirit

entered, he is possessed by a power that forces him to a deed of which he has the utmost dread and horror; and his appeal sometimes to the physician whom he consults in his sore agony, when overwhelmed with a despair of continuing to wrestle successfully with his horrible temptation, is beyond measure sad and pathetic.[193]

This statement of Maudsley conveys the ultimate of terror that fills the person divided between that part of himself representing the value system of his society and that part of himself which arises from the depths of his one time magical, amoral orientation to the external world. We note this to be the case of James Colbert Smith who pled that the policeman stay *always* at the elbow. In these cases the archaic demoniacal part of the personality is an imminent threat to the mental integrity of the individual. In some the conflict has an insistence and dominance in the conscious life of the individual; in others it is less pervasive; yet in others the instinctual element is attenuated in symbol which may manifest itself in a circumscribed token ritual. Such is the case with many exhibitionists, with the sexual practices of the homosexuals, and with certain persons who compulsively steal and set fires. The observation of uninhibited "irresistible" impulsiveness is unequivocal in some psychotics. In wider scope are included the impulses of the compulsive neurotics, but beyond this the law fears a further broadening to include the impulses of apparently normal persons who may react impulsively with rage or frustration. In this range we can see that impulsive behavior is common to all; only in the degree that it dominates the personality do we have some measure of the morbid process. That the actions of some persons are impulsive and irresistible is a matter in law which will probably remain in the realm of dialectic for some time to come. The fact remains that irrational behavior is manifest in the whole range of mental disturbance, imperceptibly in the "normal" person in gradations to the stark craziness of the psychotic. There remains one impediment to our view of impulsive behavior. The opponents of irresistible impulse as a defense to a crime state flatly that no symptom in psychiatry corresponds to an ungovernable or uncontrollable impulse except for that observed in the clinical syndrome known as the *obsessive compulsive neurosis*. This view is expressed by Wertham which he sets forth in his *Show of Violence*.[194] Referring to the so-called compulsion, Wertham describes it as an act repugnant to the doer who is impelled to carry it out otherwise he experiences psychic pain, i.e., anxiety. Compulsions are deeply rooted patterns having a repetitive and ritualistic character. The outward act is symbolic and has the psychic meaning and purpose of warding off danger from within. An example: A person is compelled to repeat a hand washing ritual. He has displaced an inner conflict between intense, hostile (dirty, forbidden) impulses and the counterforce of moral sentiments. The conflict finds compromise in a symptom which contains token elements both of getting dirty and of cleaning up (atonement, washing away sins, etc.). Wertham says that this kind of syndrome never plays a role in a criminal act—and that "compulsions are always unimportant and harmless acts." No one will dispute this statement but one must go on in order fully to understand the function of the compulsion. One feature of the compulsion is that with time it tends to loss its efficacy, the balance is threatened; it requires re-enforcement by repetitive intensification, or failing this, must give place to other compulsive patterns of psychic defense. Thus we observe in the course of a patient's illness a change in the symptoms; furthermore, when the compulsive symptom fails as a defense the forbidden impulse may break through into an action in undisguised form. This may be the release mechanism of a criminal act, against which the psychic defenses, effective for a time, eventually, and sometimes by fortuitous circumstances, fail and the primitive impulse gains ascendancy. Thus, to a point, we can see that the symptom is not a static entity but dynamically impermanent. In cases illustrative of this we are likely to witness a profound disintegration of the whole personality reaching a psychotic degree, and the change may be only momentary.

A compulsion may be all that a person has between law-abiding sanity and madness. Wertham's argument is correct that the compulsive symptom is itself harmless—indeed it is the very purpose of the symptom to neutralize the criminal (or unmoral) impulse, utilizing the same, if not more, psychic energy that would be required to carry out the impulse. Here we may note a possible contradiction of terms. If the compulsion is a defense against criminal impulses, it follows that it must succeed in its mission and in itself must be a harmless surrogate for the harmful impulse. Yet, how does one account for cases of compulsive stealing, fire setting, exhibitionism and sexual perversions all of which are carried out regardless of consequences, and all of which are susceptible to analyses which demonstrate the mechanisms alluded to above. I think what we often overlook is the fact that the external threat, i.e., legal consequences, has less mandate to the individual than the threat that arises from within him. This is to say that the theft of the kleptomaniac forestalls a greater inner suffering than that which accrues from the outer penalty for theft. The individual yields to the imperative of the inner solution. In Wertham's own case (*Dark Legend*) a matricide was moved by an inner impetus and agitation to kill, after which he experienced an ineffable relief and an apparent sense of psychic well-being and reintegration. In this case there was no pattern of manifest, repeated acts, but the psychic counterpart existed as expressed in Wertham's own words:

> The central manifestation consists in the development of the idea that a violent act—against another person or against one's self—is the only solution to a profound and emotional conflict whose real nature remains below the threshold of consciousness of the patient.[195]

What Wertham describes holds for a number of persons who commit homicide and probably also suicide. In Wertham's case there was something very compelling and irresistible. If Gino had been able to develop a substitute compulsive neurosis and sublimated his mother-hate in some acceptable form, he would have been a very neurotic boy but a law-abiding one. Many criminal acts are carried out in a repetitive way, often heedless of external consequences, and are at bottom symptomatic efforts to solve inner psychic conflict. Like any neurotic symptom, the acting out has a compelling character and has as well a symbolic meaning over and above its obvious social meaning. The offender has no awareness of the real meaning of his offense beyond the fact that he often experiences a curious relief of tension after committing it, which in time builds up again to a breaking point again relieved only by repetition of the "remedy." Fortunately most of the so-called remedies are socially harmless.

The homologue of the compulsion is the obsession which is an irresistible thought (fantasy) which may plague the person. This is what Wertham describes in the case of Gino, in whom the defense collapsed and he carried out the mother-murder in a most compelling, "irresistible" way. The question may be when does the obsessive train resolve into explosive impulsive action, like the chemical solution which reaches the critical endpoint and produces a new entity, albeit the original ingredients remain within the vessel combined in new form. This was the question put to us in the case of Edward Gibbs.

The Idol of Justice

To those who have followed the literature of responsibility, and who have had the patience to follow the foregoing discussion, it may become apparent that our pursuit of truth has been founded more upon the nature of language than upon the phenomena we examine. Pavlov once said that ". . . men are more influenced by words than by the facts of the surrounding reality." It is hard to deny that there has been a good deal more talk about criminals and crime than a disciplined examination of them. Little of what has been said and written about criminals ever gets out of the realm of abstractions which have come down to us as a part of our religious and philosophical heritage. These abstractions are tied to a system of thought and causality set by moral premises inherent in our child rearing and in maintenance of an ideal moral order. These abstractions have no necessary correspondence with our observations of human behavior in a moral system. In this sense, our surrounding reality is cast into two images; one, subjective and in terms of an ideal; the other, in terms of maximum objectification. The former speaks of things as they *ought* to be; the latter speaks of things as they *appear* to be in terms of their relationships to one another. The former provides the comfort of certainty; it is venerable and massive; the latter is yet tentative in the face of the complexity of human personality. Yet when we speak of our surrounding reality whether in moral or scientific terms, we are hedged by the structure of our language and confined to our symbolic system by means of which we attempt to establish objective factuality, and to make reliable predictions affecting our welfare.

In attaining reliable predictions, our hope lies in the method and language of science. We can no longer be content with the method and language filled with the "subjective adherences" anchored to the magical prescientific orientation of the child. In the face of these recognized obstacles in the path of our quest of objective truth, we may be receptive to the suggestion that both lawyer and psychiatrist join in re-examination of our Idols. When we enter the subjective realm wherein dwells our moral indoctrination and the sense of certainty we also enter the world of the *ought to be* where the concepts of "responsibilty," "free will," "intent," "cognition," "conation," "volition," "motivation," "knowledge of right and wrong," "guilt," etc., occupy fixed hierarchical positions in the heaven of criminal jurisprudence. Once we enter into this subjective world of certainty, we tend to cling to it, but it is a self reflexive world that has no more substantiality than the words and symbols out of which it is made, and within its shadowy interstices lurk those archaic magical figures that nourish illusion. The world of objectivity is less hospitable and in it we must endure doubt.

In our present inquiry into the world of how human beings actually behave, we come upon no certainty and we discover that our subjective concepts of the *ought to be* live apart from the objective data of experience. Cohen spoke of these concepts as "supernatural entities which do not have a verifiable existence except in the eyes of faith, and that such rules of law which refer to these concepts are not descriptions of empirical social facts (such as the customs of men or the customs of judges) not yet statements of moral ideals, but are rather theorems of an independent system." From this it becomes clear that a legal argument can never be refuted by an empirical fact. Cohen continued: "Jurisprudence then as an autonomous system of legal concepts, rules and arguments must be independent both of ethics and of such positive sciences as economics or psychology. In effect, it is a special branch of the science of transcendental nonsense." [196] Such concepts then are really statements of the ego ideal which is never realized in mundane matters. Ego ideals have a religious and metaphysical character. It would be one-sided not to concede that psychiatry also dwells in metapsychology, but I believe that we can agree that if its head is in the clouds it has at least one foot on the ground. Cohen further observed: "For it is well to note that the problem of eliminating supernatural terms and meaningless questions and redefining concepts and problems in terms of verifiable realities is not a problem peculiar to law. It is a problem that has been faced in the last two or three centuries, and more especially in the last four or five decades, by philosophy, mathematics, physics, as well as by psychology." [197]

In recent times psychiatry has moved away from classical

theological concepts and come closer to those principles which are at home in modern physics, mathematics and philosophy. To the extent that law moves in the same direction will communication between it and psychiatry become more meaningful and effective? The aim in this movement for both law and psychiatry is a working collaboration based on this maxim: "All concepts that cannot be defined in terms of the elements of actual experience are meaningless." [198]

Despite the recent advances of psychiatry and the trend of criminal justice to an individual-centered operation the problem of selecting those wrong doers who shall not be punished has not become easier and probably will not until the psychological model employed by the law is changed and the role of the psychiatrist more clearly defined. Indeed, with the increasing awareness of general antisocial behavior and of mental disorder disseminated in mass communication, there may be even a greater tendency to cling to the certainty of traditional formulas and to resist change. Yet there is a beginning movement and change. Both trends are noted from the side of law itself. In the field of legal scholarship there is a wavering between the traditional and the novel. In this country witness the American Law Institute's acknowledgment of the inadequacies of the M'Naghten rule and its rewriting of a substitute which is M'Naghten dead but not buried. In the field of decisional law, the break with M'Naghten has been final, and a prosthetic extension of M'Naghten, namely, the Irresistible Impulse, has gone with it. I am referring to the Durham decision.[199] The Durham decision affected a change but not novelty. It merely abandoned M'Naghten with its appendage, the Irresistible Impulse test, and returned to a rule and practice firmly established in 1870 in the New Hampshire courts.[200]

V THE CRIMINAL LAW AND PSYCHIATRY IN ACTION: THE POST-TRIAL PHASE

Commonwealth v. William Conquest

In the preceding sections I have presented some analysis of the function of psychiatry and its communication with law in the pre-trial and trial phases. In the following case I offer a small sampling of the post-trial phase, the penological aftermath. In this, the criminal, as symbol has passed over the stage of public-centered Criminal Justice to re-emerge as a person. He has had "his day in Court" and now he has his days in prison. We will observe what happened to our prisoner when law and psychiatry attempted a post-trial individual-centered manipulation of him.

In Philadelphia, shortly after midnight of April 16, 1927 a shooting took place on a street. The killer became a fugitive. Seven years later in September of 1934 he was indicted and tried in Philadelphia on a charge of murder. On arraignment William Conquest pled not guilty on July 16, 1934. When the trial took place on September 24, 1934, the plea of not guilty was changed to guilty after the Commonwealth's evidence was in.

After hearing evidence defendant adjudged guilty of murder in the first degree with penalty fixed at life imprisonment and defendant sentenced to the Eastern State Penitentiary for the remainder of his life.

At the opening, the Assistant District Attorney stated that the case did not rise higher than second degree murder and that one judge could decide. One witness testified that he saw the shooting which took place a little after midnight on April 16, 1927 on the intersection of 28th and Oxford Streets. The same witness testified before the Coroner that three nights before the killing a fight took place between the victim and the defendant, and that they were separated by an officer, who took the defendant home. He further testified that the victim had said, "Well, I won't get him today but I'll get him tomorrow." The witness testified that he and two others and the victim had been together earlier that night. The defendant got mad in a Chinese restaurant where they had gone to eat and left. He did not know whether or not the defendant had been drinking. Another eye-witness testified there was a short argument between the victim and the defendant before the shooting. He could not remember who made the first motions. The police officer testified that he captured the two witnesses after a chase. A gun was found between some tires in a tire shop. A detective stated that on January 26, 1934, the defendant was arrested in Ohio for vagrancy. Upon being questioned there by the sheriff of that County, he told conflicting stories about his means of support and where he was from. He was turned over to the sheriff of another County. He then made a statement to the latter sheriff that he was wanted in Philadelphia for a shooting in 1927. The defendant was returned to Philadelphia.

The following is excerpted from the defendant's confession: "He kept on tormenting me about not being able to fight and how easy it would be for him to beat me, calling me names and accusations of my character. I was too drunk to do anything." The defendant had gone on to say that he had carried a gun for defense and that "being in a drunken rage, I remember firing at him . . ." Conquest took the stand but was withdrawn. A plea of guilty was withdrawn and he was permitted to plead not guilty. After a recess, the plea was changed to guilty. The Assistant District Attorney concluded with a brief statement that, while the evidence showed guilt rising to first degree murder, yet there were circumstances that suggested that life imprisonment might be a sufficient penalty.

Despite impressions that pointed strongly to a disordered mental condition, no effort was made at the time of his trial to ascertain it and he was committed as if wholly responsible for his offense. On September 23, 1934 he was received in the Eastern State Penitentiary to begin a sentence of life imprisonment.

Some five months later he was called to the attention of the prison psychiatrist.

The prisoner complains that since the time immediately before his arrest, he had gradually developed the hearing of voices which he recognized as being unreal; which were condemnatory, obscene, abusive and which had superficially no relation to his crime and which had reached the point of intensity as to compel thoughts of homicide and suicide. His keeper reported an attempted suicide with glass and open safety pins. He tended to be solitary and kept his thoughts to himself. He volunteered that he required some help because of his ideas. The prisoner is above average in mental achievement and cultivation. He is mild and gracious in manner, but depressed and actively hallucinated.

On the basis of this observation, the psychiatrist regarded the inmate as mentally disturbed and requested a petition for a Sanity Commission. This was done. The inmate was examined by a Commission on March 7, 1935 and two days later transferred to Farview State Hospital, an institution for the criminal insane, where he remained until February 11, 1939, at which time by order of the Court he was returned to the Eastern State Penitentiary as restored from his mental illness.

The prisoner remained in confinement in the Eastern State Penitentiary until March 8, 1943 at which time he was reexamined by a second Sanity Commission by a request of the Penitentiary psychiatrist. This interval of segregation had been more or less uniform; but, from the standpoint of an adjustment in the institution, unsatisfactory. Following his return he was almost immediately placed in quarters with older physically enfeebled men. In due course, he was transferred to one of the segregation galleries, having been unable at any time to find a satisfactory personal adjustment. He remained on this gallery until it became necessary to move him to the mental observation block in the early part of September of 1942. During his confinement on the gallery he remained largely to himself, seldom ventured from his cell, except perhaps on summons to the psychiatric office. He insisted on having his door locked at all times, and from time to time, complained to the officers in charge that he had premonitions within himself and fears that he would harm someone. In his complaints, there was a suggested return to his hallucinatory intrusions which were accompanied by a ringing in his ears, occasioned in part by a chronic catarrhal otitis. From time to time, without apparent provocation, he would explode with a kind of unmotivated, frenzied anger, would shout and curse, only to relapse and then withdraw into isolation.

It was during the early part of his residence, following transfer from the Farview State Hospital, that the psychiatrist had discussions with the prisoner concerning the legal aspects of his commitment. On reference of the psychiatrist, the inmate engaged an attorney in Philadelphia who made an investigation into his legal status and offered the opinion that the inmate was most probably insane from a legal standpoint at the time of the commission of the crime. The attorney then made suggestions for bringing the matter to a legal remedy and it seemed that there was a fair prospect that he would see some promise of his sentence commuted.

At the threshold of this move, the prisoner suddenly became disturbed and withdrew all interest in his own welfare. On similar occasions when efforts were made to give him a reasonable adjustment with the conditions as they were, he made nominal attempts at employment only to become irrationally anxious when in contact with other inmates and in due course he was again compelled to withdraw into the security of his own cell.

So far we have the appearances of a usual case of homicide, except for the fact that this man remained unidentified and unapprehended for some seven years. We could conjecture that he may have so remained longer had he not maneuvered his own surrender. Our attention is drawn to the fact that, within five months following his trial, he came to the attention of the prison psychiatrist. At this place it should be noted that in this prison there had been no organized psychiatric service until some two months after the prisoner's commitment. Within the first several months of this service, and with firmer establishment, confidence, and acceptance of the psychiatric functions in the prison, calls on this service became manifold and there emerged out of the dark interstices of this ancient prison a seemingly unending procession of mentally ill persons, some of whom had been confined for years. There took place a general house sweeping and for some months Sanity Commissions did a land office business. The prison guards suddenly became amateur psychiatrists and so discovered that psychiatry was good for something even if not more than a means of getting rid of many of their difficult wards hitherto unnoticed as lunatics. It was remarkable how so many prisoners, before regarded as a cross to bear in the keeper's life and not uncommonly kept in line with a "discipline," now, by the magic of a new label conjured by the psychiatrist, became special objects of wonder and exempt from repressive discipline.

In the midst of this novel discovery our prisoner was brought to the psychiatrist's attention. Had the psychiatrist not been within easy reach, it is not improbable that our prisoner would have remained without attention beyond the usual call of keeper's duty, his oddity tolerated and his moods met with routine.

So much for the circumstance of our prisoner's career and his introduction to psychiatry. He was duly transferred to a State Hospital for the criminal insane. Our first inquiry takes us back to the time of the apprehension and trial. Why did not the question of mental condition enter into the indictment or trial? Several possibilities arise. Either the prisoner kept his symptoms within himself or no one took the trouble to put the question to an inquiry. The prisoner evidently made no issue of it. In the trial, the change of plea removed the possibility of a revelation by his own testimony and manner in defense. So it passed.

From the appearance of things, our prisoner with malice aforethought killed another in cold blood, took flight from the scene of his deed, and eluded justice for seven years, finally to be caught and brought to it. In the language of the official record:

The prisoner had been doing lettering on cars as well as other sign work for a garage in Philadelphia and had developed a close friendship with the owners who were brothers. There was a man who hung about the garage. He was a bully and would "nose in on the prisoner's affairs with the garage owners" and for some three days had become abusive in his remarks regarding the prisoner. During the early morning hours of April 16, 1927, while walking along the street, the prisoner and the brothers came upon this bully who started to "horn in" on the party, became very abusive towards the prisoner who went straight to his room in the neighborhood, obtained his revolver, returned and shot the bully twice at close range. The latter died enroute to the hospital. The companions took the gun away from the prisoner and he vanished. He made plans to leave the city and went to Washington on an early train. Several days later he was said to have gone to West Virginia and to St. Louis and he returned to Philadelphia in November of the same year to marry his second wife. The two then went westward moving from place to place and finally settled in Detroit where they both obtained work until he lost employment with an automobile plant. He did odd jobs and his wife continued working. While wandering about the city of Detroit, he began drinking to an excess and, while under the influence of liquor, would talk regarding his activities in Philadelphia which led the police to become suspicious and keep a sharp eye upon him. Up to the time of his locating in Detroit, he kept on the go most of the time being fearful at all times of being picked up. He chanced to go to Ohio in June of 1934, where, under the influence of liquor, he became talkative. It was while he was getting over one of these sprees that he was arrested on a vagrancy charge and at the time admitted to the police that he was wanted in Philadelphia for murder. He was then removed to a County Jail in Indiana where he remained some two weeks prior to his transfer to Philadelphia.

In this statement there is an irresistible implication of a willful crime and a design to thwart the ends of justice. From the standpoint of the criminal law, this is sufficient, but criminal justice has extended itself beyond this simple formula and has reached into the field of psychology. When criminal law enters psychology, it must for the moment abandon its moral preconceptions of human behavior and look at the individual offender to learn how humans really relate themselves to their surrounding environment.

But the law turns to the inner events of crime only to the extent that the psychiatrist is permitted to ventriloquize them in his communication of words. His communication is only the husk of the inner events which remain in the realm of feeling, of formless desires and satisfactions, incognito and incommunicado. We are left to the device of inventing an anatomy of inner events much after the manner of the ancients who invented an anatomy of the body and endowed it with four humors. Likewise, law accounts for all moral ills out of the humoral workings of intent, malice, premeditation and unfettered will. Our prisoner killed another in cold blood, premeditated with intent, knowing what he was doing and certainly knowing that it would bring a penalty and knowing it was wrong. Yet, even the prosecution sensed that the event was not unilateral. The victim appeared to act as an accessory to his own undoing. We have no direct evidence from him; only the statements of witnesses who likewise sensed that the meeting of these two men was a critical moment which triggered a complementary solution for each, in whom there must have been a long standing preparatory stage. We do not know anything of the inner events of the victim. To reasonable men the killing could have been

THE POST-TRIAL PHASE

avoided by the simple expedient of avoidance, but some deterministic necessity met and fell into place. Each saw in the other an affinity that he must destroy. We shall soon learn that what our prisoner saw of himself in the bully was perceived on a more primitive magical level. In the language of the prosecutor, the crime did not rise to first degree homicide which could have brought the death penalty at one time contemplated by our prisoner.

Now we can turn to the language of the prisoner:

I, William Conquest, was born of poor parents who were engaged in farm development in the new West. They gave me a good home life free from any sordid thing. Like most others of that place and period they had very little education so could not help me much in that respect. Neither ever used intoxicants. Always I was used to the influence of a good Christian home. Often my only playmate was my sister, two years younger than myself, as homes were far apart on the plains. I continued in school until the age of nine years. I was very large for my age, and as education did not play the important part in the lives of those people that it does today, I quit school and went to work. Before I was seventeen I began to study at home and at eighteen started a career in the postal service, resigning only to enlist in the Navy in 1918. Was reinstated in the San Francisco Post Office after the war. Most of my education was gained during the last eight years in the postal service. It was my desire to combine such subjects as would give me a good general education as well as the technical matter required by the commercial artist. Those subjects included history in general, history of the world, art and ornament, anatomy, theory and practice of color, the photoengraving process, geometrical drawing, perspective and projection drawing, casts, human figure, psychology, mathematics and a wide range of reading. I preferred such periodicals as the *Inland Printer, Arts and Decorations, Atlantic Monthly, International Studio,* and *System.* Commercial law was a favorite subject. Particularly contracts. My mental life at that time was colored by a three-year service in Co. K., 1st Kansas National Guard. My work, studies, social and religious activities and my marriage to a splendid woman of fine family, character and personality who made for me a good home. My philosophy of life is the Christian religion and my political convictions are those of the Constitution of the United States. Following the War and a brief time in the San Francisco Post Office, I worked for many sign and advertising concerns until the tragic event which changed the course of my life. The only notable exception was my second enlistment in the Navy, during which time I was in charge of painting on the U.S.S. Relief.

Concerning the events which preceded the crime: I did not know of any condition or circumstance in my life which would lead to crime, nor do I now. Unpleasant things there were that I did not then know how to avoid. In 1924 my first wife, after four years waiting, and I am sure, hoping, for my return, had at last secured a divorce as I desired her to. An excellent woman of whom I could bring myself to say no evil. There was a difference in our ages, she being older than I, and a son by a former marriage, a splendid boy and a good stepson. I was entirely to blame. I had insisted on marrying a woman older than myself, with a child too old to be my own son. I soon realized that as soon as the boy was able to support his mother it would be best to separate. I discharged my obligation by doing my duty to my family to the satisfaction of my wife and her people. The last I heard of the woman was that she was married and the boy was radio operator on the U.S.S. ———. We were married in 1911, the year I received my civil service appointment and the year of my father's death. All the time I was waiting for my wife to secure a divorce I was drifting without knowing it. I called it waiting. Without the divorce I could not live as I desired. She was the only one I ever loved and I was not strong enough to break away as I was sure I should for our future advantage. That was why I re-enlisted in the Navy in 1920. It would keep one away and give her time to get a divorce if she would. Until I was past thirty, I never drank. For six months in San Francisco after the War I was frequently drunk. Not again until I was thirty-five did I drink. From that time on I was often intoxicated except for one eighteen month interval. Then usually so. I had lived three years at the address on 28th Street, near which the trouble occurred. For the reasons recounted I had become morose, despondent. I had recently been convinced that very bad characters occupied the same apartments and tried to persuade the woman I lived with as my common-law wife that it was best to move to a healthier location. She would not hear of it as she said we were within our rights. I could not dispute that. However, the sense of some possible danger caused me to get a gun. Three weeks later a stranger appeared at the nearby place where I supplied myself with whiskey. A place I had frequented for over a year. His first sight of me brought forth a tirade of abuse. He was not noticeably drunk. He boasted that I did not know him, which was true, but that he knew me, which was not. He was known to the others as a bully who would, they said, "fight at the drop of a hat." It was evident that he was doing his best to force me to attack him in an encounter which would give him every advantage. Had I lived at a distance I would have left for good, but as going home, the only place I had to go, only meant stepping inside the apartment, I felt there was no escape short of a cowardly running from my wife and the only home I then knew. Feeling and being helpless, my drinking increased as did his vile abuse. I dared not play his game by retaliation. I became so drunk I could no longer hear his obscene abuse. The next night after a timid venture to see if I could avoid him and procure more whiskey, I found myself safe and then he came in again. Repetition of the mental torment of the night before. Unable to extract a word from me, he tried and did force a club into my hands. Although near unconscious, I did as he forced me to do and hit him with the club he had forced upon me, at which he made his long-sought attack. A police officer who witnessed my humiliation, seemingly with amusement at the abuse, stopped him and compelled me to leave, much to my relief. He said he should run me in as a drunk. Why the fault is all mine I don't know. Knowing, however, that I could expect no help from the Police until the brute had worked his will, whatever that was, the next evening I armed myself and after as much more mental abuse as I could stand, feeling there would be no satisfactory ending, *I determined to kill him and pay for the crime in the electric chair,* rather than run from the community. Had the officer arrested either of us it could have prevented the ruin of two lives. I can supply no motive for his actions, other than a bully's sadist desire to harm whom he can. I had always thought of myself as worthy, my naval and military service, a man of courage. I could not run as a prelude to a cowardly life of running. *There was no thought of escaping punishment.* I approached him as he advanced toward me and shot him in sight of his friends. I fell exhausted and as his friends called to each other to kick my brains out they tried to get hold of the gun. I surrendered the gun and was allowed to get up, at which the gun in the hands of one was pointed at me and I was commanded to "get going, you——!" Terrorized and utterly hopeless, I ran ... instinctively ... aimlessly.

Quieting myself as best I could as realization of my fugitive state came to me, I became alert to everything which would draw attention to me. From a free man to a hunted one in an hour of aimless terror. The night was one of horror and the day of fear. *I had no sense of guilt.* I considered surrender at once, but having *the feeling that I was not the murderer I was believed to be, that if people could know the whole truth they would not want me to suffer more.* I felt that it would be making them do a thing they would not, if they *could but read my soul.* I believed, too, that having run from the scene of the crime, even at the point of a gun, had lost for me any sympathy people at the trial may have had. I travelled west working from place to place a wanderer. I returned to Philadelphia after nine months and sought out the woman I had lived with as my common-law wife. She was the only one who could possibly care for me and who knew me before I got into trouble. We were married in Elkton, Maryland, on December 12, 1927. I thought I was a bigamist, but found out at Farview that my first wife had a divorce and was married long before. Had I known that I could easily have handled the trouble that later drove me insane and cost another his life. I was joined by my wife, who believed in me and we lived in Detroit six years prior to my surrender. She is still faithful. *Any statement concerning the causes leading up to a crime or insanity must be largely speculative.*

I believe that worry combined with the cumulative effect of alcohol led me to my mental collapse. The first unusual thing I can remember was the unaccountable whispering voices. I listened to the drip of a faucet and could detect the whispering, usually unintelligible, with the unmistakable drip. An idling motor or any soft sound had the same effect. Loud sounds I could not mistake. I could not control my thoughts without conscious effort. Sometimes not then. My efforts to identify or explain the new things which were happening to me possessed my mind. I was then bothered by what I called people talking about me. The whispers had become voices. I moved from place to place continually. My fugitive condition made me desperately try to avoid trouble. When I really heard talking in a nearby place I put other meaning, other words in their mouths than the original ones they said. I could not understand why for at least a year a life that was friendly had become hounded by hate. The depression and loss of work and fear of following my only trade terribly aggravated the condition. I made trips through many states but always the fiends were there as soon as I was. They never allowed themselves to be seen. At last, fearing my presence would in some way work harm to my wife, I left Detroit for Toledo. The fiends followed all the way. I was sure they were in cars on highways alongside the train I was on. Then they were no longer fiends, but good people deceived by the fiends. I became hopelessly insane. I took across country, afraid to ask for food or water, avoiding human habitation. Continuing in the night across strange country in blind terror, across rivers and all. Seeing the folly of such a hopeless chase in which the radio was playing a part, I fell exhausted in the road and dirty, unshaven, starving and insane I lay there all day asking travellers to tell the Sheriff. By that time I was suffering delusions of every kind one mind could have: sex fiends, murderers' voices from those who could read my mind as well as terrorize it. The officers came for me at last and I was taken to Bryan, Ohio where I told them my right name, age, place of birth and all about the crime, its date and place. I asked officers for a gun to kill myself with and screamed from barred windows for help, was beaten by prisoners for accusing them of things they never did or said. I was not allowed to have my safety razor and was after approximately ten days taken for a ride in a car by a uniformed officer and put on the road to Auburn. I could not account for a confessed murderer being so freed. I thought it the old Mexican custom of giving one a chance to run so they could shoot the escaping prisoner. After a day of hasty and grueling hardship I entered the Courthouse in Auburn, Indiana, and asked the Sheriff to protect me from my enemies. He was a kindly, understanding man, and while it was necessary to isolate me I was well treated. All this time my delusions were at their worst. After about ten days I was called for by an officer who brought me to Philadelphia. I felt better after I was on the train, but asked my officer to keep me from being taken from him. The delusions slowly left me, and after the first week in the County Prison only the low notes of the radio and the voices were left. My condition remained about the same until after I had been in Farview for some months, *although I was always changing my explanations of the things which I believed to be going on.* My reason for wanting to be returned to the Eastern was that

I did not want to be considered insane as a patient must be to some degree. The most wonderful thing is the recovery.

I feel that I have had a terrible, and at the same time a wonderful, adventure in the realm of my mind which had at all times much to commend it. My condition lasted so long that I had to fight thought habits of long standing, in the face of hopeless despair and a great anger at the unknown cause of my troubles. With those fiendish thoughts I relied solely on the truth. God's truth. On that higher justice which lives forever. "Know the truth and the truth will make you free." I did not spare myself, but exposed my every vice and weakness to my mind, fiends and all, and I am free in mind. I have had a wonderful experience. I am proud of the fact that I have been honest with the officials and with myself.

Our prisoner physically imparted to us a gaunt, prematurely aged figure, blanched from long days in the darkened cell into which some light entered only in brief cycles through a narrow slit of masonry. He had the mark of immolation self-imposed beyond the requirements of a well ordered penitentiary. In his narration he has made a picture of the facts and he has conveyed them in words of everyday life which can have different meanings. On the surface of language, our prisoner conveys a life which has met with needs, disappointments and frustrations that are common to all. We know only fragments of his earlier years, his phases of higher thought from magic, to science. One such fragment comes from his late childhood; a series of truancies for two years culminating in his removal to a Reform School at thirteen for petty larceny. This occupies a place between previous events in child growth of which little is known save for several moves of the household and the subsequent few years when William changed to a serious and somewhat withdrawn boy much occupied with books. Around seventeen his mother began her mental decline. We have some hints and afterthought that some distortions existed in his developing communication with paternal figures. His mother did not develop a psychosis suddenly at forty-four when he was eighteen; the pattern of the psychosis must have existed long before. We have only glimpses of his early life related by him. Singularly, in earliest recall one memory stands out: his clinging to his mother's skirts and telling her that he was afraid of his shadow. To him his father appeared in two meanings; one, that he was a large man with great strength; the other, that he was incompetent in business and a failure, a weak and ineffectual man. He admitted that complaints could be lodged against his mother but could not bring them to verbal expression; rather, in contrast, he presented her as a person who came from a high-placed family socially, Mayflower descendants, in contrast to the father's inferior origins. Her family had despaired that she had married below her station. We sense his greater identification with his mother, not only in the striking similarity in looks but also in their shared talent in artistic interests. On the first occasion of his Navy service, he had used his mother's name in the enlistment. In his early twenties, during his mother's hospitalization, he had wished her to come to keep house for him. He had picked out a little cottage where they could live. After a prolonged delay he received a postcard, "one of those Madonna pictures." On the head of the Infant was written "1888," the date of his birth and some other undecipherable scribbling. In relating this William broke down and wept. He spoke feelingly of heredity and here one sensed his earliest cleavage of loyalties to the parental figures. What father lacked in strength and effectiveness, mother possessed in family background, in artistic feeling and the appreciation for education and learning. We sense his identification with the mother and that it orients the boy to a woman's view of the world. He never achieved a masculine accent, and he will be occupied with this lack in all of his later relationships with men. Just out of focus, in the background, there is a primal incestuous tie with mother. He clings to her in refuge from a shadow and we will note this in his later flight into the arms of the first wife who was older. But the image of mother and himself, her excellence and ideals, is like the apples of Istakhar, all sweetness on one side and all bitterness on the other. He is also tied to her mental illness.

He continued contact with the mental hospital where the mother was confined throughout the entire period when he was a fugitive. After the trial, he preferred to think of her as dead and also that she think of him as dead. A secondary view of William's identification with mother's values is reflected in his feelings about his sister. She looked like father. When she grew up, she did not have the same moral ideals as he and had no desire to improve herself.

Mother's commitment to a mental hospital took her out of his reach permanently, and he turned to another woman. In speaking of her (his first wife) he had need to refer to his foolishness in marrying one older than he; he described himself as romantic and commented that he reacted more like a schoolgirl in this romantic interest. He had read sentimental stories and pictured a dream girl, youthful, tall, slim, blue-eyed and blonde; actually the girl he found was heavy, had brown eyes, dark hair and was older. It is not without significance that at this place in his recall he should revive in the present an ecstatic picture of his actual dream girl, the one he married, but set in direct opposition to this revived ecstacy, he spoke as if he had made a bargain with God to allow him to have such a love but with the proviso that he should also accept whatever came with it. In a similar heroic style and metaphor of his initial statement of his life and crime, he spoke of his unbounded happiness with the women for which "one gets nothing without *paying* for it." Here is the glimpse of the hard, inner bargain driven by a relentless conscience. He could not accept the happiness with a woman without payment. But here we pause to ask payment for what—"a secret crime"? We sense that this is the answer from his reflection that he had gotten into trouble because he couldn't control his emotions and his emotions seemed to stand in the way of his wish for perfection to which he goaded himself. Yet, in his story, he found that he must in time abandon this woman and we have difficulty in reconciling this flight except that we must think of her in some way as connected with the payment that he must make for happiness.

We have noted previously his return to the measure of others and himself in physical terms; others are bigger or stronger, taller or shorter, etc. This has found its earliest reference to his father—like the child's view of the adult world; its last reference to the victim, the bully. It is a metaphor peculiar to himself: relationships are expressed in those ambiguous terms much concerned for his tallness, strength and at times one senses that he is using his comparisons to express something beyond physical attributes. He remarked that he could find no legitimate fault with the woman that he had abandoned. If he had "been bigger and maybe everything would have been all right." And in this wish for bigness he conceded that he had always felt small and inadequate in the attributes of masculinity beyond mere physical appearances. His view of himself in physical terms varies with his vacillating inner either/or estimate of himself. At one time, he describes himself as small for his age, at other times as large. In either case, he is too small or too large, something of himself doesn't ever quite fit in with others. A separation from his first wife took place in 1917 within six years of the marriage. She had brought into this union a stepson near ten who in time became "bigger and stronger." William took flight into military service and during this service, which lasted some six months, there occurred a first phase of alcoholism. In 1920, his orbit brought him back to reconciliation with his wife, but within two years he again took flight from her and re-enlisted in the military service. This was the end of the marriage. He was discharged in 1922 from Norfolk, Virginia and returned to Philadelphia. In the interval, from this discharge to the time of the homicide in

1927, William had entered into a second phase of alcoholism and we note, from him, that even the year prior to the homicide, he had come upon new psychological experiences that he could not explain, namely, transient hallucinosis. In this period he met the woman who became his second wife. She was tall, slim, blue-eyed and "it was no compliment to her, she looked like me." They were often taken for brother or sister and he found in her a motherly person who babied him. He wept when he recalled her sacrifices for him and how little he had done to care for her. In his developing mental illness and eventual crime, William was likewise to take flight from the second wife, but even after imprisonment there recurred an incident which was to be the final token of his unresolved relationship with the mother figure. He had lived with her in a common-law relationship and not until after his crime, did he legitimatize the marriage.

She writes of her observation of him before the offense. He did not seem moody or detached although there were times of irritability but apparently without resentfulness toward her. His associations with other people were few. Much of his time was spent in reading and in radio construction. However, about two months prior to the offense he had made friends with some men in a nearby apartment. His wife described these individuals as being the "bootlegger type." She noted that he tended to be in their company and ceased to be interested in anything he had been before. This association with these new found friends came with increased drinking. His wife noted that he appeared "to have a persecution complex."

On various occasions, he thought people who were total strangers were making bad remarks about both him and me. If we were in a restaurant, he would think that people at the next table had said things. If we passed two or three men on the street, who were standing and conversing, he would tell me that he had heard them make remarks and would want to go back and argue with

THE POST-TRIAL PHASE 213

them. He did so on one or two occasions. I was worried and perplexed about this attitude but did not know how to cope with it.

On many occasions, William went out with these new friends and left his wife alone. She thought of this as a sudden and almost completely opposite trend in his usual behavior. She remarked that there were only two things that marred her happiness with him. One, the suspicion on his part that others were unfriendly and were talking about him and the other, his possessiveness, expressed in jealous inquiries as to the possibility of her having men friends. His wife expressed the view that she had never sensed any threat of harm to herself in his actions. The wife recalls that on these two occasions prior to the crime William had apparently reacted to what he fancied were remarks made by others about him. On one occasion, a colored janitor was working in a furnace room directly below the quarters of William and his wife. The janitor was humming a song and in it William insisted that there were remarks directed at him. William seized a long saber, went down to where the man was and only the sincere actions of the man and his insistence that he was merely singing at work forestalled the possibility of an attack. On another occasion two women talked outside of the apartment window, William again insisted they were discussing his affairs. He went out and threatened to kick one of the women off the steps. The wife verified later that this woman had made no such statements.

Following William's return from the Farview State Hospital on February 11, 1939, the psychiatrist had greater opportunity to review with him some of his experiences. He related that for almost three years before his conviction and commitment to the penitentiary, from time to time, voices came to him. Our interest here is in the fact that the "voices" that came to William did not actually have the character of what we usually understand as false perceptions or hallucinations. He was aware of the fact that he attached meaning to things which were seemingly conveyed to him as words and in it we appreciate that if we define situations as real, they can be real in their consequences. This was his account of them. He said:

Practically every sound, particularly sounds of very low volume, of any rhythm which could be possibly interpreted as a conversation, and that covers a wide latitude of sounds, because a person can talk rapidly or slowly, or they can speak in any rhythm or in a broken rhythm—my impression of it is difficult to separate from my explanation of it. Of course, there were no words in those sounds but rather they suggested the thought. The thought was in my own words. I got the cart before the horse and thought the words were themselves coming to me from the outside. An example of such an experience was as follows: Low pitched footsteps, although now having no special significance, at that time four footsteps would seem to me to say *God damn your soul*.

In January of 1940, some thirteen years following his crime, William came to the psychiatrist and stated that he had on that day come to a conclusion about his total experience. This was entirely new to him, and it was that he must have been insane at the time of the commission of the crime. And the incident of his experience with the colored man had come back to him. He reflected: "Had he shown resistance, there would have been a killing and I might have been the victim. I now see that this was a display of insanity. Now I'm glad I see myself as others have been seeing me. I realize that I had been a fool but I'm much better off than before because I can see myself in this light." On a later occasion he complained to the psychiatrist that he was unable to concentrate. "I can't do the things it is necessary for me to do to conduct myself in work, in reading, in anything relating to my self advancement. I find that everlasting mental handicap which . . . well, I know that I am crippled in the head and anyone knows that there is something wrong with him . . . You can stand other kinds of physical disabilities, but when you know yourself that you've got something wrong in your head, then you are disabled. I am not especially depressed because I can stand it. I have been standing it for years and I am fully convinced I will have to go on standing it." William again referred to his experience with sounds. He again complained of the "noise." As far as my thinking is concerned I can reason as straight as anyone else. My mentality operations are slowed up and there is some emotional depression and I feel that my case is pretty hopeless. Yet, I'm not abnormally depressed. I know that if anyone else were suddenly attacked with the condition that I have it would drive him insane because it drove me insane. He would probably get used to it the same as I have."

Parenthetically, William supplies us with an example of the state of mind of many criminals who can "think as straight as anyone else," and have a "knowledge of right and wrong," and at the same time know there is "something wrong in the head." He said: "Your knowledge of psychiatry and such things would probably save you but in any ordinary person who was suddenly obsessed with those things, they wouldn't know what was in their mind . . . When a person is taken with something of that kind, they don't know it is in their own head. If you don't know that it is a mental condition arising in your own head you blame other things for it. You imagine things, you know there is something wrong and you can't properly locate the blame. If it isn't you, it must be something else . . . I am adjusted to the struggle with it. I know that the condition is something that arises in my own head and I know that I have got to suffer." William made further attempts at communicating his thoughts and feelings. In referring to the inner physical experiences he said, "It's just the sensation that doesn't seem to be as strong with me as it formerly was. Occasionally there is a feeling of excitement, that is, a sort of tenseness and I feel that there is a rapid beating of my heart like I was very much excited and yet I am not excited at all . . . When my heart beats fast like that I am terribly afraid or terribly angry or some other emotion that would cause a person's heart to beat loudly. Everything I hear is a maze of sound."

It seemed at this point that both William and the psychiatrist were having difficulty in making out the real nature of his complaint. The psychiatrist asked him if he regarded himself as still mentally disordered. He replied:

That's why I wanted to see you. If you can accept my statements concerning the sound and that everlasting present sound when I am sleeping or all of the time—I have to sleep with that sound; I have to live with it every moment of my life, I have for years and years and there seems to be no possibility of its ever stopping. Since it interferes with my powers of concentration I can't read. If I try to read in order to do so and get rid of that sound and concentrate, I pretty near have to talk to myself or move my lips and if I do that, I can't get the thought because all of the attention is devoted to keeping my lips quiet and not looking crazy. If I devote myself entirely to the thought I find myself talking to myself. Now things like that are mental handicaps. They hurt me with other people. I can stay here in the cell the rest of my life which is a terrible handicap in itself, but if I'm going to be around other people I don't want to suffer the handicap and constant constraint of having to watch myself.

The psychiatrist inquired whether William in talking to himself merely repeated what he read or whether he had found himself talking to himself unrelated to what he was reading. He replied that it was a matter of trying to think through sound all the time. Other sounds were different; sounds that wouldn't bother him ordinarily beyond what he described as an everlasting hissing sound. Here he evidently was referring to a sound within his ear that could be related to the chronic ear disease. Even so, this experience was not clearly differentiated. The psychiatrist asked, "I'm still having difficulty in understanding what part of this noise that you hear is articulated in any way. Is it like a voice, or some other personality within you that disturbs you?" He replied, that the hissing part was not but whether it is unrelated to that condition, I don't know. It's like this. There is some loud sound that speaks to you, my ears hear that normally and my mind interprets it correctly, but it is a sound which is just to the level of consciousness, very often that will appear to be as words. [Here William speaks of the frontier between conscious and unconscious.] I knew formerly I was deluded into believing that that came from some external force. I know now that it is a noise which originates in my own head. The sound comes from the outside, my mind puts thoughts to those sounds. I can't help it. I know that it is my fault, that the fault originates in me and that it is an association of words with sound. I can't think of it from force of habit. I can't imagine anything else because I know it is crazy. You see, Doctor, as long as I believe that they came from some external force these words were anything that was suggested. The first words might be "you will." My mind would then follow the suggestion—"you will"—with anything my mind rambled with that.

It was with great difficulty that the psychiatrist could bring William to an attempt to recall what such words convey to him in articulated sentences. He replied, "It's useless to try to describe the thing that has no sense to it." He said, "Just open the dictionary; anything that happens to come into my mind." He was asked if it had a pattern and he replied, "I think I know what you mean." Does it have a pattern of persecution? "It would be, but it isn't. It formerly was a thing of persecution. It contained anything that was abominable because the condition was abominable. I felt that somebody else was doing it. Anybody that was capable of doing it was a terrible person and terrible people say terrible things." The psychiatrist's desire to have an articulated pattern was not met with success. William indicated, "All the pattern that you are speaking of disappeared until there was no pattern, merely the impression and very often if I concentrated on those sounds, I could distinguish one and see very clearly. I can even control myself. I can distinguish sound and I can identify every sound but if I am not concentrating that old memory, that old habit of thought will come up but it no longer has that pattern that you are speaking of. It is just words, senseless, disconnected." William complied with a sample of such disconnected thought. "Some faint sound would just come to consciousness—'What will you think about that?' It's just an echo a lone thought."

William reconsidered and corrected himself to say this was really not like an echo of one's thought that he was merely using a simile. The psychiatrist pointed out to William that perhaps such animation to his thought would come during the time of day particularly in the evening when there was a natural reduction in the number of ambient sounds of life about him. He pointed out that he is more aware of such inner experience after the lights are turned out. Perhaps when the stimulation of the external world is lessened, there is a greater awareness of the summonings of the inner world. William spoke of himself as having control of his emotions and then added, "For instance, I shout around and feel very much mistreated and I always feel that there is very little sense to my existence anyway because no matter how crazy I act I can't make my sentence *one hour longer*. It is a hopeless situation. I know I am never going to get out of some state institution because of this mental condition, because simply I can't do the things that are necessary to conduct myself as I should in order to get out. I'm hopeless in that way and I'm reconciled to my hopelessness. I am not suicidal and I don't want to shorten my life, yet, I have no interest in my physical health. I am contented in the cell." Here William's "mental illness" was his inability to change.

Despite William's power of articulation and his use of language, his communication with the psychiatrist was nevertheless an ordered and controlled gloss in token of what must be a chaotic turmoil within him. One has the impression that his position is as one astride the fence between the unconscious and the conscious, a kind of dream stuff near the surface. Sounds are utilized in the dream economy. In one's sleep, the natural sounds reaching the dreamer are used in the dream, pressed into its service. The sleeper awakes from a dream in which he heard a great explosion only to discover that in actually he perceived in his sleep the closing of a door. Observation by others brought us nearer to a communication more expressive of the inner life of William. It was noted that he remained within his cell and insisted upon having his door locked at all times, giving the explanation that he was afraid that he would hurt somebody. It appeared that William was unable to talk to anyone other than the psychiatrist without becoming angered, as if anger were the only remaining nondiscursive means that he had to convey his thoughts. He did not use vulgar words, but the tone of his conversation was that of distinct anger.

From the reconstruction of the events in William's life, we come first to an apical turning point—the homicide in 1927. During the seven years as fugitive, the psychotic process gradually increased in directing his existence. He was driven to surrender not by what we might fancy to be the guilt of his manslaying in 1927, but by the inner nemesis that had pursued him all of his life. He tells us that he never felt a sense of guilt and, even in later years, he never once expressed remorse for the victim. There seemed to be an inner vindication of his deed. His victim must have been some other representation than that we perceive from the appearances of things. And William will join us in our condemnation of what he did but, for him, it is done and passed. In the deed, something of a great relief came to William but this is deep within him and cannot be surfaced. We vaguely sense that an inner compulsion brought him to it. We had a hint of it in the encounter with the janitor and with the recurrent provocations to others in his reactions to fancied persecution. It remained for the chance circumstance of an appointed victim, the bully, who was no "stranger" to William. He did not immediately give himself up as others do because what he had done was a private vindication of himself that no one would understand. He said:

I had no sense of guilt. I considered surrender at once but having the feeling *I was not a murderer I was believed to be,* that if people could know the whole truth they would not want me to suffer more. I felt that it would be making them do a thing they would not if they could but read my soul. . . I believe too that having run from the scene of the crime even at the point of a gun, had lost for me any sympathy people at the trial may have had.

Such statements taken on their face value would have no other meaning beyond the confession of a deed and of guilt in a legal sense. Guilt in a legal sense connects the doer with the deed and demands of the doer an admission of guilt. William readily admitted his legal guilt but did not recognize his inner psychological guilt probably because it did not flow from the deed of manslaying, but from conflicts long antecedent. He asks if people knew the whole truth would they want him to suffer more? Can this mean that for William the killing was a culmination of a long struggle within the personality, his obsessive symptoms beginning with strong defenses against the instinct only to end with the victory of the latter. He tells us of his inner battle and suffering. The legal penalty for his crime could not compare with that imposed by the inner tribunal of conscience, but he is unaware of its existence in meaning and so are others who cannot "read his soul and know the whole truth." In review of his life before and after the crime, we are impressed with the fact that he was more a fugitive from the nemesis within him than he was from the police. The official account would lead us to believe that he was pursued by a relentless Javert, but so far as one could determine there was no such manhunt. William moved in flight from an inner Javert and his surrender to the police was to seek sanctuary from the enemies which he later recognized as creatures of his own imagination. Arrest and penalty for the legal crime was a Hobson's choice, a purgatory compared with the hell of the unconscious stirrings of the conscience.

As we look back we can at least see the outlines of a long

standing mental illness which he could describe himself as "some emotional depression," and when given the setting and opportunity to examine it we find that it has dogged him for the better part of his life. The depressive pattern is set in the early infantile years of life but we have no direct documentation in William's instance. We do know that the relationship between child and parents and one's sister must have effected tensions of such exertion that William should find himself in a reform school at eleven and that he should escape from his home sometime around fifteen. Here we note in miniature the fugitive pattern. Did the people around him "read his soul and know the whole truth?" At eighteen he did effect an escape from home to Civil Service in a distant town and he recalled vividly that in this period of several years he sensed the "emotional depression." This was incident to his mother's decline which culminated in her commitment to permanent hospital care when he was around twenty-two. At this time he turned to another woman older than himself and, in the following six years of marriage, his depression had lifted only to return to its earlier phase in his late twenties and we note here that he again takes flight into military service. He fully concedes that, as his marriage progressed, his sense of uneasiness increased finally to break through. Flights from the "old woman" occurred twice with his enlistments, and during his "fugitive" years he found in drinking a means of some tranquilizing relief. The turning point in William's life is centered around the age of thirty-four marked by the resumption of drinking following his discharge from the second enlistment. At this point a detail of his conflict about his first marriage has a suggestive interest. He remarked that at the time of his courtship he was a member of a certain gang of young men whose association he thoroughly enjoyed. All of these companions looked somewhat askance upon his intended marriage to an older woman. He remarked that he "belonged to them." We can surmise that his enlistments recovered for him this sense of belonging. It is notable that shortly before the killing William unaccountably found himself associating more intimately with men as if he "belonged to them" despite the fact that they represented the coarser side of life from which he had previously recoiled. In the interval between his discharge in 1922 and the killing in April of 1927, William suffered but he concealed his suffering with the defenses that passed uncritical view. Alcohol served one defensive purpose but, like any addiction, it is often attended by an erosion of inner control which in time surrenders to the magical level of reality testing. He recalls such moments in the period of hallucinosis in which he saw "big faces." Again his allusion to the outer world in terms of size. Who are these "big faces"? William doesn't know, but we can surmise that in his own "littleness," there is offered some clue to the big faces of parental figures who loom large to small people. From his account it now seems fairly certain that what he calls the condition of depression became increasingly a more insistent distraction in his everyday life and he struggled with it. We know, now, that the unconscious magical elements began to interfere with his reality testing for some three to four years before the crime. This was marked by a clear episode of hallucinosis within a year prior to it. He became increasingly sensitive to the world of sound and developed a compensatory, persecutory response. With the direction his behavior was taking, his wife sensed an impending tragedy; but she could not persuade him to a policy of avoidance. The unconscious had already taken over; everything was simply rationalized within what we would call his paranoid system. All of this can be comprehended under the term of his choice, a depression, a patterned something which was founded early, which started in the course of his life to become a dominating force in his reality testing in middle age and which has so remained with him since. Seemingly only two intervals of his life were free from it; a few years following the final marriage and the interval of his escape from the older woman into military service. Yet, such period of relative freedom could not last "... you get nothing without paying for it."

In speaking of depression we are using it as William does in describing his mental illness in a word. If we use the term in a technical psychiatric sense, we speak of depression as descriptive of a pattern of symptoms of sadness and hopelessness, embitterment, retardation of mental processes, associated in variable measure with a sense of weariness and loss of animation. In this pattern, self-condemnation and suicidal impulses are marked. Basic to the outer symptomatic structure of depression is a repressed anger and hate. The manifest symptoms of depression are indicators that the subject is moved from within by imminent hostility held in abeyance by the self-absorption of it. In this sense, hostility is turned against the self. This has its counterpart in the larger social pattern of law enforcement which imposes restraints, regulations, and some measure of suffering upon the individual, so that the stability of the group can be maintained. Each individual must endure some depression for the good of all. If law enforcement is arbitrary and overly repressive we note a kind of sickness overtaking the group and it becomes morbidly depressed, its stability is threatened and we become mindful of the latent revolt and break-through of accumulated hostility. In depression, a sense of guilt pervades. It is aroused by hostile impulses. Guilt is allayed only by the successful repression of hostility which is neutralized by self-destructiveness. Depression has its genesis in the earliest dependent love relationships acquired in the child's development of higher thought from magic, through religion to science. The dependent love relationship is parlous in the fact that inevitably frustration comes out of it. Frustration begets hostility which begets guilt which must be handled lest the love relationship be destroyed. Hostility turned against the self dissolves the guilt and also achieves a secondary gain of sympathy in one's suffering.

How does this evaluation of unconscious love-hate reactions

apply to our problem? There are some suggested elements here. Persons whom we may describe as depressive characters, tend to maintain a reality orientation structured in an obsessive compulsive defense. Such persons erect elaborate devices of living in their struggles against their own ambivalence of love, hate and guilt which make up the inner rhythm of their lives. Fully developed obsessive ideas are asocial and appear as alien to the personality. An individual may find indisguised intrusions of thought like attacking others, doing forbidden sexual things, etc. Compulsions are the final pathways of ritualistic defenses that ward off unconscious, forbidden wishes and unconscious "crimes." Compulsive rituals tend to be exaggerations of social conventions. But here the emphasis is not on the obsessive symptom which occurs in those extreme cases of neurosis but rather as such defense mechanisms impart a dominant trend of character. We are reminded of the overly moralistic, punctilious, industrious, and conventional person given to overcourtesy who imparts to the outside world a behavior that is close to a caricature of rectitude. In such reference, we turn to our prisoner who was inconspicuous in the prison crowd, set apart from them as a matured, settled, middle-aged man who took special means to comply with all rules and regulations. He was solitary and aloof. He was mild, gentle, perhaps womanish; and intellectually philosophical. He possessed a considerable general fund of information (I.Q. 137). He was voluble and precise in his speech, unhesitant and rarely found wanting for words. In tempo, his movements were in keeping with his gentle, almost effeminate manner. Emotionally, he reflected a variable degree of anxiety and the intensity of his fairly well-concealed self-absorption left little for the interplay of humor. In manner, there was a half-conscious apologetic diffidence. The lines of his face reflected more of an inner absorption and perplexity than a soberness; the eyes imparted a nuance of furtiveness and perhaps fear. In physical appearance, the lower part of the face was under-proportioned, imparting a weakness to his profile. His features had a smoothness of outline which imparted no contrast to a suggestive eunuchoid body configuration. Such in brief was the physical and verbal communication of our subject who in characterology would fit into our picture of one whose character armoring has been an obsessive compulsive. The surface is one personality who adapted fairly well with the demands of conventional life; beneath was a personality that carried an old problem for which an attempted solution was made, through mental illness and a symptomatic killing. We must be satisfied with very little information about William, particularly that of his early infancy and childhood development. We must draw large inferences from small material that comes only in secondary elaboration like that which comes in the recall of a dream. In the system of his early love-hate relationships, we can see how some of the lines of force meet to impart distortions in his adaptation. From the very beginning, his reckoning with others invariably brought him to unfavorable comparison; he could not compete with girls mentally and he felt sensitive and inadequate with boys physically. We note an early identification with mother in his physical resemblance to her and their shared interest in intellectual and artistic things. He could never fight. He feared aggressive boys and he feared father who was big and powerful. We note symptomatic behavior at nine; he became truant; at eleven he broke into a store and was sent to a reform school. In adolescence we note a consolidation of his orientation towards the symbols of mother; the preoccupation with social standing, ideals, self-study for betterment, romanticizing of love and the fantasy of his dream girl. In this period we have glimpses of an interest in physical development as exalted by Bernard McFadden but this never came to his service. His companions were few and he found working associates too rough. His identification with mother is now more decisive in his emphasis on her talents and good family. Father is less in focus and we can see a model of masculinity fading from his view.

In late adolescence, with mother's mental illness in 1910, there is a frantic recapture of her image in marriage to an older woman. In his first marriage, the primal incestuous tie finally impelled him to abandon the older woman; in the second, he abandoned his wife "fearing harm would come to her" at the outset of his flight from his voices, and later, when the prospects became good that he might be commuted and set free, he made a final turn away from her and chose perpetual immolation.

It is of interest that William attempted to withhold all information of the content of the voices which pursued him. Only once did he make a tacit acknowledgment of their sexual content, of unspecified sexual perversions and "hands touching him." From this, one can make a safe inference that William's development and adaptation (the obverse of his identification with the mother image) would conceal a more profound homosexual orientation towards men. William always doubted his essential maleness and it remained for him to kill a bully whose own doubt motivated his own "bulliness." William saw in the bully the image of a powerful father and, in his attack upon him, William denied his own passivity; what the bully saw in William was the image of the feminine part he would deny in himself.

From our view of this case we can align our thinking into two categories; one legal and the other psychiatric. In the latter reflection we can draw several general conclusions. Our prisoner was mentally ill for some time before his crime. There seems to be little question that his crime was a symptomatic climax of his illness, that the crime occurred when it did out of the chance circumstance of mutual readiness for it in William and in his victim; that his mental illness has existed without complete remission, having its beginning in early life. William tells us that the causes behind his crime remain matters of speculation. We have offered some speculations which purport to communicate the "how" of his crime, but we yet do not know the "why" of it, the purposeful causality of it. And, it would seem that there was little point in bringing the speculations of determination causality into the process of legal guilt finding. Causes were matters to be determined and studied after the legal disposition and were matters oriented towards his therapy. The function of psychiatry in William's case was the determination of his mental illness either before or at the time of his trial.

In the legal view it is clear that, in the light of our psychiatric findings, William was improperly tried as a sane man when in fact he was surely insane by medical criteria. His confession, of itself, was an unmistakable psychotic rationalization that passed unnoticed. Yet there are mitigations of this error. In the appearance of things, William seemed to be a man who had willfully slain a man and who took refuge from justice eventually to be brought to it. His fugitive status alone would imply his sanity. Again, at the time of his trial, he did not manifest sufficient oddity to attract notice to the psychotic process within him and it is probable that he made a conscious effort to conceal it. Neither William nor his victim had the appeal of the theater. William was psychotic but it does not follow that he could have been certified as insane. Under the circumstances, there would have been a presumption of his sanity and, in all probability, an alertness to possible malingering. Yet malingering does not enter in the case, if for no other reason than he himself made no effort to erect the defense of insanity. In civil life are many persons suffering with a psychosis. To move against them by legal means is another matter and one cannot think of them as insane unless such a legal move is made. The concept of insanity is the property of the law. It has no place in medicine.[201] A further extenuation of this legal "error" was acknowledged in the after action of the law in certifying him twice as insane after sentence. But, in a legal view, there may remain a correctable error which imposed upon William a double hazard. As a lunatic, his "sentence" is indeterminate; as a criminal, it is a sentence for life. If he is entitled to return to society, it would be in virtue of his recovery from a mental illness; not as a committed criminal.

In a period of about four years, he had established himself at the hospital for the criminal insane. He was returned to the penitentiary in February of 1939 and it was after this that an effort was made to engage legal attention to his case. He was recommitted to the hospital at Farview as insane in March 1943. The circumstances of his second commitment are worth our attention. The following is a stenotype of a conversation between William and the psychiatrist who initiated his second commitment:

Q. Well, it occurred to me after our meeting the other day that you might like to discuss your situation.
A. Well, I had expected—rather, I was in hopes that I would be sent up there (Farview State Hospital) last Saturday. They usually take the subjects up there on Saturday, and when I didn't go then I supposed that there was a possibility that it might be some time later; that I was perhaps in too much of a hurry. I don't know that anything can be gained by discussion. I still think I belong up there rather than here. I don't think that I was ever a subject for a penitentiary in any case, and there is no question that I was a subject for up there.
Q. I am interested in hearing your reasons; I mean, I have a personal reason for wanting to hear them.
A. Well, it might be summed up in hopelessness. I have no hopes in this institution; that is, any hope of ever receiving the same treatment—not that you're not willing to give me the same treatment that they do others—but my condition and circumstances. I think it's the circumstances rather than my condition—having been up there and things which I did when I was here before, have made it desirable for me to stay away from most of the prisoners. Not all of them. I have known some of them that were quite reasonable. They treat me the same as I have been accustomed to being treated by others, so naturally I feel that I'd like to be able to have the same consideration, the same opportunity that other prisoners have, and I don't have it here. And I do have it at Farview. I consider that because of my condition. I don't consider that there is any great difference either in the patients or in the prisons or in the people—the aims of the people who conduct the institutions. But, I fit in Farview and I don't

fit in here. I got along well in Farview and I don't get along well here, and it's natural that a man should want to be where he fits, where his past experience tells him that he gets along all right.

Q. Tell me, what is it that makes you fit up there and not here?
A. At Farview I'm only one of the crazy people; they're all over the place. Here I am *the* nut, and I don't appreciate the distinction.

Q. Now, up there you're officially regarded as a crazy person. Here you are unofficially regarded as a crazy person, and your companions insist on regarding you as such.
A. And the companionship is far more important than the official consideration, because I have to live with those people, if I'm with them at all, and I don't have to live with the officials—fortunately perhaps, with the officials—but it's equally fortunate for me that I could stay away from men who take the attitude which they have. Of course—I've given up hope years ago of ever having anything desirable in this institution, or even tolerable. But I know that I get along all right in Farview. I feel that I did belong in Farview, and I regard it only as a possibility—not as desirable, but as a possibility.

You see, doctor, since I've been in that trouble—it's been sixteen years now, and I spent four years in Farview. Now, when I was in Farview I had gained for myself certain consideration: ground parole, I could go out all over the place anywhere. I could come and go under practically the same conditions as the guards did, I didn't have to explain where I was going or when I was coming back. I could go out in the morning, and if I felt like coming back for dinner, I could. If I didn't, I could take my lunch. I was trusted. I had a room which was clean, comfortable bed, nice dresser, radio, pin-up bedspreads, my own laundry bag. I had everything that a guard who made his home in the institution could hope to have. I could have my own books and electric safety razor. I could get anything; the very best that they had in the institution.

I'm not a worse person now than I was then. I am not less willing to conduct myself properly than I did then. But I have lost that. Instead of being able to build myself up from the time that I came from Farview, it's just been a waste, a drop, and a very miserable situation.

I naturally would like to be able to return to a place before I am too old so that I might eventually be able to regain, by my own efforts, those same circumstances and the same consideration and comforts which I had before in prison.

It's a strange thing that a man in an asylum can, by his own efforts, gain certain consideration and respect of the guards, and friends among the insane; and yet he can't do it in a penitentiary. That is the condition and I don't think that I am altogether to blame for it, for I am confident that had I been discharged from Farview, the great mass of people, not knowing that I had been in an institution, and not being familiar with all of the things that I did while I was in an insane condition, I wouldn't have been continually condemned and ridiculed for those things for the very reason that people wouldn't have known anything about it.

Here I had to come back to the same thing. Any remark that I made—and I made plenty of any number of remarks—I did what an insane person could be expected to do. But they have never forgotten it. It's amusing. They have no sympathy for the fact that I was in an insane condition. They never will have, and I don't care what they have any more.

The way I have been treated since I came back to this institution has just completely separated me from any desire to ever be around people. I want to stay just as far away from them as I can. My experience in prison, too much prison has made me antisocial. I am thoroughly conscious of it, and that's the existing fact. I still feel I don't belong in prison. I have no hope here. I take the attitude things are just as bad as they possibly can be, and if they get worse, it will be an improvement. So that's that.
Q. Have you had any more thoughts about the matter that we discussed with Mr. Busser (the attorney)?
A. I don't think I understand what you refer to.
Q. Do you recall there was a time several years ago when we developed the idea of having Mr. Busser take some legal action in your behalf? He made inquiries, you recall, of the various people in Ohio and Indiana, and he felt—I thought he felt—fairly clear in his mind that had the facts been known at the time of your trial, you would not have been given a life sentence.
A. Well, doctor, I think that that's possibly true, but it's been so long. That's been so many years ago and I have grown old in prison, and during all that time—it's been sixteen years of nuthouses and penitentiaries, through a thing which, however it's regarded, whatever my fault or whatever my condition—anything in connection with it—I have actually had to suffer more for it than the most hardened criminals are compelled to suffer for

their crimes. I feel that it's largely a matter of neglect. I am at least an ordinary human being. No matter how criminal, or no matter how nutty I may be—if I'm a nut, there's a place in Farview.

I am not worse than all the people in the world, than all the people in Farview, than all the people in the penitentiary, and yet I have had that to go through with, and yet I see no insight.
Q. Well, now I don't know that I'm able to say anything definite about that myself, save that I share your feelings about this thing, and as I have emphasized before, I am not in any position, nor do I possess the power, to remedy things which I believe also to be neglect. I felt all along that you should have been sent to Farview State Hospital at the very outset.
A. I was as insane as a man gets, at the time of the trial. I was, and I even surrendered myself in the first place.
Q. Yes, I am in agreement with you on that.
A. I tried to get some action about that, doctor. I called the Warden's attention when I first came here to the fact, and the only information—or help—that I could get from him on the subject was that I was legally sane.

Well, now, that's absolutely no help to me; that's a technicality such as a criminal might use in trying to escape punishment—but it's absolutely no help to me. I'm no longer interested in the legal aspects of the matter, or the mental aspects of the case. I've told honestly everything I knew about it; the way I felt about it, and all I knew about it—I've been perfectly free to say anything that I felt. And I couldn't have done worse if I had been as deceitful and as untruthful as it's possible for a person to be: for the results were just absolutely nothing in any case.
Q. Well, would you be at all hopeful that perhaps even if there has been a bad handling of your case, that there might yet come a day when the Pardon Board would feel inclined to reduce your sentence, we'll say, from life to something else; so that you know there is a termination to it? And that there would be prospects of being released?
A. Well, I would be—I'm perfectly willing to do anything that I can do to better my condition, but I'm getting old—
Q. How old are you?
A. I'll be fifty-five in August, and my time laying around prison as I have for so long has unfitted me for earning a living. I would have to rehabilitate myself some way. I don't know just what I could do. If I should make any effort to try and have my sentence

reduced or anything: the first thing that people would want to know: what would I do for a living? And I have no reason to believe that I would be met with any more consideration than I have been in the past.

For instance, one of the things which I have been asked: what about your mother? My mother was insane. Dr. Z. told me when I asked him about it. He said: "I'll tell you quite frankly. I think it is quite probable that you are hereditarily (sic) insane." I feel that's not a mistake, and he's a man of authority in the profession. And if I am—if I am hereditarily insane, why should I go ahead and have that up my sleeve?

I'm not in a position to do anything about it, it must be done by others, because I am not going up against that kind of a hopeless proposition. I am not going to hold up hope for myself when I have no reason to believe that there is any hope.

Q. Have you been in recent communication with your wife?
A. No, sir. When I came to the conclusion that there was absolutely no use, I felt better to cut myself off from all outside connections.
Q. How long has it been since you have been in touch with her?
A. Oh, over a year since I even wrote a single letter. But I have received gifts and—she knows where I am. Those things I can't remove; I can't do anything about them. I can't help the condition that my mother suffered, and when I talked to Dr. B. he said: "Well, you might go insane again." (sic) I'm not going to try and go up against that stone wall of prejudice, and those conditions which I can't possibly remedy.

Now, if I had never been insane; if my mother had never been insane, I might possibly have something to go to people with; make some kind of claim. They couldn't say such things to me. I can't remove them and I know how people feel about it, and I have no reason to think that they feel any better about them. I'm less fit to be out today than I was years ago.
Q. You're less fit not because you are insane or because you're charged with a crime, but because you've been here as long as you have, do you mean?
A. Because of the condition, because things being just as they are. As far as my mental condition and my physical ability, if I were under proper conditions, if I was free from prejudice and from the conditions—that is, if I was put on the street—I would be just exactly the same as any other penniless man of my age and physical being. As far as my mental capacity and my willingness and my desire to get along and so on, I would be perfectly

all right. But as long as I am under the conditions which I am, I can't overcome those things at all. I can't even deny them.

If I were to be put into a community, most any community that I couldn't get away from, and everybody knew that my mother was insane, everybody knew that I was a murderer, and everybody knew that I done time in nuthouses and prisons—I was an old jailbird and that sort of thing—I wouldn't get along well in that community, because certain individuals in that community would just make me miserable. But that's a possibility because I can get away from them; but in here I can't get away from it. I'm just as locked in that little cell as I can get in it, and I know nothing better in this institution because of that condition.

You can't change people, and you can't change my circumstances. You can't change the facts concerning me; but if those facts were changed, if those circumstances were changed, I would get along just about as well as anybody else, because I've always have, and I'm the same person as I used to be; I'm no different man than I used to be—a little old—

Q. Do you remember Mrs. A. came in and talked to you on a number of occasions? Do you feel you got anything out of those discussions with her?

A. Well, only that it was nice to talk to a lady. I think aside from that there was no—it was the pleasure, I would say, rather than a benefit. Of course, there's always benefit to be derived from a conversation with good people anytime.

Q. What can I do for you, William?

A. I don't think that there is anything you can do, doctor. There might have been, years ago; but you see, anything that's done now is post mortem.

Q. Well, what could I have done years ago? I've only been here eight years.

A. At that time you couldn't have done anything because of my condition.

Q. All I could do was ask that you be sent to Farview.

A. And I don't think you could have done anything more than you did four years ago. It's just the way things turned out. I didn't have what it took to get out when I should have been out. If I ever was to have been out, I think it was when I came back from Farview. Of course, legally, to be technical, I have only served eight years. But actually I've suffered sixteen years for that business and it's getting awful old—because during the time that I was fugitive I was insane. I was hungry and miserable, and it's a wonder that I ever lived through it. And that was all suffering, I know about it. And you can hardly say that: well, it's the man's own fault—the things that he suffers while he's in an insane condition. I wouldn't have suffered those things if I could have helped it. They were very terrible. Yet it all arose from that *condition.*

You know and I know, everyone knows, that there are any number of murderers, terrible crimes committed, for which men do less than sixteen years of suffering, *both with and without the assistance of the State.* I feel that I have just been in a mill. Things just had to go in a certain way. I have received no more consideration than the other material in the mill. Yet some of them will be ground out in time; but there's no end to my time. I have nothing to look forward to. I have a life sentence, and when a man gets old, he loses his friends. He loses such little influence that he might have—there was a time when I could exert a little influence in my favor.

For instance, when I wanted to get out of the Navy, anytime I could have my folks out West, people that I knew, get a Congressman or Senator to get me out over the opposition of my officers. But when a man gets old, he loses his friends and any little influence that he might have once had. Well, it's past.

Q. I would be interested, sometime, William, in personally sponsoring some action before the Pardon Board for you.

A. Well, I have nothing to offer them, doctor. You know my circumstances, you know that I'm far away from my work. I have no one on the outside to sponsor me; no one to go to, and I'm in a worse condition, much worse, than I was years ago.

Q. Suppose you think it over after you get up at Farview and things seem a little better, and you reflect on it. I mean, it would be good to hear from you occasionally.

A. Doctor, I would be so afraid of coming back here that I wouldn't pass up a sure thing for any uncertainty. If I can ever get ahold of— If I can get as much comfort, and I feel that I can, because I won't be one of the smartest things in Farview; I won't be in excellent condition. I'll be a good patient in Farview.

Q. I'd like to point out something to you; that you were such a good patient they decided you were no longer legally insane, and they sent you back here.

A. Well, I'll try not to be so good that it will happen again.

Q. That's between you and me.

A. I asked for that. I tried my best to get back here because I felt I was helping myself. I wanted to be declared legally sane.

I felt that it would be a great help legally, and otherwise, toward getting me out of the institution altogether. I felt that I deserved consideration, and I hadn't lost hope. I thought that I would receive consideration.
Q. You had faith in our legal institutions?
A. Yes, I did.
Q. And you feel disillusioned now?
A. I have no more faith in people's ability to do the right thing. I understand people desire to do the right thing, but their ability to really understand, know what they are doing—I think that we're all very limited in that respect. You think that I can look forward to being in Farview before long?
Q. Yes. I want you to know that I am taking a large part of the responsibility in sending you back, William.
A. Well, I should be up there instead of here because it's going to be hard up there for some time, and it's going to take a long while to reinstate myself. I can't go up there and start right where I left off.
Q. But I would like to hear from you occasionally. I hear from the other boys once in a while, and know how you are getting along. I can always write to the Superintendent, but after all, I only get his impression of things; whereas, if I hear from you, I know how things are working out for you personally, and that's my interest.
A. Well, of course, doctor, I—I don't feel that I am insane. I didn't when I went up there the other time—no one does. I feel that I am the victim of circumstances, very largely. I think that if I had influential friends on the outside that I wouldn't be here. I think that I would have been released long ago. But—
Q. Well, let me say this: that I'm still interested. I want to redeem myself as well. I want to vindicate myself by proving to you, if I can, that not only do I want to do the right thing, but also I want that opportunity.
A. Well, you're limited to the possibilities. And there are sixteen years of my life that's been spent in institutions in an insane condition, and that is past. I should never have seen so much time in prison, and the only reason I did is not because I was so much worse than others; or because I was less competent mentally to get along or less social, just—I just had nobody to move, to set the machinery in motion and keep it going. I simply couldn't command the force that was necessary.
Q. Well, you understand that you are again legally regarded as insane, you understand that?

A. Certainly.
Q. I understand it, too, and we'll just have to accept that fiction as something that has to be accepted in order to gain something else.
A. Yes, but I think your choice of words is very good; but it will not be a fiction that I have to return to Farview a second time, which is going to be—well, of course it's only less of an evil than remaining here.
Q. Yes, I agree with you, and I don't want to be remiss in not availing myself of any means of alleviating your situation. After all, I have a record, and that record is something that is useful. In fact, I'm giving you an opportunity this morning to say these things because they are going into my record. I want them in the record.
A. I appreciate that you have given me a chance to try and take some action, some legal action, to try and help myself. But I don't think that there is any possibility of my doing anything. I have only a few dollars and I wouldn't—
Q. I'm not thinking of that aspect so much. When you get up to Farview and after things get sort of lined up for you, you find yourself feeling better, let me know how you feel about it. Express yourself, anyway.
A. But, of course, after I get up there I'll feel like all my energies will be bent to trying to make for myself as much of a home out of the place as I can.

William's return as officially "sane" from the "bughouse" to the penitentiary marked his apparent recovery from his official "insanity." His restoration to sanity had been duly entered and certified in the records of the court. But was William himself changed? Yes, he had changed in the hospital to the extent that it provided some means for reaching a level of apparent sanity. A real change did take place but not in William; only in his environment; from one in the hospital in which he had achieved an "adjustment" and a place for himself in a community of persons who were bound to each other in the tie of a common affliction called insanity, to another in which the affliction had neither official recognition nor binding. In the prison community of officially "sane" inmates, once having been found insane, William could not shake off the taboo of avoidance nor control his inner response to it. He was a marked man. His reluctance to accept our offers of the meager comforts and opportunities for "rehabilitation" provided by the prison would at first appear captious, yet in his restoration to a legal status of sanity William had indeed made a hard trade. For what was in hospital "treatment" a few meaningful human values, and for what was an indeterminate hospital life as a lunatic, he was restored as sane to a troglodytic existence for life. To the psychiatrist, it became apparent that the answer to William's problem could not be found in William but in ourselves. Some answer might be discovered less in what we were saying about William and more in what we were doing to him. It seemed clear that the only real change in William was in the fact that he was older. We had no assurance that hospitalization had effected a fundamental change in his mental life; that he had really "recovered" from the psychosis. We were beginning to observe a recurrence of it following his return to prison as a sane man. The psychosis did not exist alone in William as some isolated demonological entity; it was in the relationship he had with his environment and we who were judging him were a part of it. There remained only one thing to do; restore William to his status of official "insanity," remove him from a prison, where the irrational behavior of "sane" criminals made existence miserable, to a place that provided the solace of an "insanity" shared in common.

It has been suggested that in our climate of doubt and certainty a means of attaining a unified theory of behavior is envisioned in a model of communication. In such a model, the entire range of mental activity can be considered as communication. The fact that certain behavior is inimical to social values, and condemned, does not exclude it as a kind of communication. Thus, criminality is reducible to such analysis as is any form of conventional psychopathology. In this view, the criminal act ceases to be an event isolated from its social context, separated from antecedent and future events. By theoretical necessity, the law cannot take this view of the criminal act; the deed is committed and the doer must reckon with justice. But in practical actions, the law, expressive of mass behavior, is itself likewise a multidimensional communication containing the same contradictory and irrational elements found in the criminal act. Latent in both the behavior of the criminal and of his triers are unconscious black threads of magical operation. Such unconscious elements impel us to confine the criminal behavior within the person of the accused and to ignore its connections with other persons either in the past or present. Crime is explained as something actuated in isolation within the individual. In older times, these actuators exerted themselves in obsession and possession and they explained psychopathology beautifully. Today the same actuators are called intent (mens rea), premeditation, malice, etc. These are the old demons who were once personal and intimate; today they dwell in verbal cocoons between covers of law books. In their metamorphosis, they are yet viable and we will note that mentally disturbed people have implicit belief in them, as witness the case of our William, who for some time found himself pursued by fiends which he feared would drive him mad. Some may point a finger at psychiatry for its own kind of demonology, it's amoral id. But, in defense, we can say that at least our psychoanalytic id is purely metaphor for the child in us and for that part of us close to our original nature. It may be that we can never get away from a demonological orientation to accept not well understood and unpredictable events. It may be that so far as our self-knowledge is concerned, William James spoke a disquieting truth when he maintained that "scientific theories and postulates are mere fashions and the ancient fashion of postulating natural forces as persons—the demon theory—is . . . certain to return in the long run." [202]

Our case of William, the murderer, began sometime in his own beginnings as a person; in middle life there developed signs of disturbance of communication with his surrounding reality. This disturbance broke through in the killing. He was a fugitive for seven years. He was tried and sentenced to life imprisonment, a term which had hardly begun when by chance his disturbance of communication attracted others and he was removed to a hospital. In four years, he was returned to the penitentiary as "recovered" only to find himself again with a return of his mental illness. He was removed a second time to the hospital. William was behind locked doors for twenty-two years—which is some few years beyond the average period of incarceration for homicide in Pennsylvania. The probable average is near fifteen. About eighteen years of a life imprisonment was spent in a hospital for the criminal insane. In the example of William's case, we come upon some yet unanswered questions. I have already alluded to the circumstances of his trial in which the question of his mental condition was overlooked. It remained for psychiatry to initiate the correction of this oversight. His commitment to a hospital, after conviction, was tantamount to setting aside his legal commitment to a penitentiary, but in this move a vital element was left out. Although now adjudged a lunatic, he still remained a criminal. William was faced with a dilemma. If he recovered from his insanity, he faced return to a penal institution and its barbaric rigors; if he continued to be insane, he would, indeed, face a life imprisonment. At the time of the trial, the law was preoccupied with material evidence of a crime, not with its agent. If the law had been so concerned with the person of the accused, it would have discovered, by its own criteria, that no crime had been committed since the accused was an insane actor. William would have been judged either incapable of standing trial at all or, if tried, would have been judged not guilty by reason of insanity and sent to a hospital. Now, under these circumstances, his chances of a restored life in the community would have been possible. If he had not stood trial, upon recovery, he would have had to face it, but the facts would have brought him to an acquittal. Actually his circumstances are such that he has been doubly cursed. He is both a criminal and a lunatic and there is no avenue of escape. William's psychosis was "unsuccessful" in the real sense that psychosis is the price the law abiding pay in order to escape crime. "Our hospitals are filled with people whose latent 'crimes' are lived out in the disguise of symbols and allegory. In them criminal drives lie behind a bizarre façade of social incapacity," [203] but they have been "successful" in avoiding crime as defined by the legal institutes of the community. "From a social standpoint mental illness has a higher premium in the sense that it spares the group at the expense of the individual. It would appear that the mentally ill person who commits a crime is cursed by a double failure of adaptation. His mental disintegration does not go far enough to nullify the remaining ego which on its own becomes a compliant accessory to his latent unlawful drives." [204] If we return to the time of William's second removal to a hospital as an insane criminal and review the communication between him and the pyschiatrist, we can clearly see that he had a clearer perception of his problem than we did. He was entitled to speak of his "insane" condition since the law had formally said he was. He also clearly perceived that it was better for him to remain "insane" than to remain "sane" in a penitentiary for a crime which in theory by law he had never committed.

One could not dispute William's logic here since only he alone experienced it in real life. William's own experiences as an inmate in both a prison and a mental hospital brought him to an operational approach to criminal justice. To him, incarceration was the same even if the places were called by different names. His observation called our attention to the power of words. In the mental hospital, everyone was in the same boat called "insanity"; in the penitentiary he found himself called a "nut" by his fellow inmates who enjoyed the dubious status of official sanity. But the disturbing fact remains that there is not a single inmate in the penitentiary who does not suffer with a disturbance of communication with his surrounding reality, which is to say, that the distinction between a mental hospital and the penitentiary is largely a matter of terminology. From an operational point of view, they are places where socially disabled people are confined. William became impatient with us. He could see through our bureaucratic ritual of attaching a name to him in order that he would get a better bed to sleep in, have greater freedom of movement, and have the consolation of others who had been likewise stamped. The two occasions of his change of legal status from sane to insane required Sanity Commissions each comprised of one lawyer and two physicians, none of whom had more than a nodding acquaintance with psychiatry.

If the law should find a way to abandon its untenable concept of criminal responsibility as it pertains to the subjective element in crime and come to the view that all felons are mental cases, there could be a reformation in penology. Criminals would at last be forced to a confrontation with themselves and with self-awareness, and, after a fair trial with it, those who could not change or refused to do so would automatically segregate themselves. I can think of no more deterrent "punishment" for those who regard term sentences as merely equivalent values played in a game. As matters now stand, the law conjoins with the criminal in a resistance to the idea that a crime is a disturbance of communication, hence a form of mental illness.

Many law-abiding people cherish the belief that punishment by term imprisonment alone will change antisocial character for the better and by example deter others. In fact, the criminal himself clings tenaciously to this article of faith, that by submitting to dependent isolation for an interval of time he is "paying" for his crime. Such payment is determined by the court and is not uncommonly a term that comes out of a kind of bargaining. The offender behaves as if he were a voluntary party to a contract, which imposes on him no performance beyond being conscious of the passage of time, beyond sitting and waiting and vegetating.

This is his "payment," and he is resistant to other terms, to any measure calculated to make him come to grips with himself and thereby affect a real change.[205]

But one can account for the apparent difference between a mental hospital and a penitentiary. Each has its own symbols. The same William was a "con" in one—a "patient" in the other. The penitentiary reflects the symbols of the external tribunal which exist in the paragraphs of law executed by those who know little about child rearing. The mental hospital reflects the symbols and language of the internal tribunal of conscience in a setting of parental figures who are individual-centered. In a penitentiary the cases are mental, but one looks for moral causes rather than mental causes.

The prison symbolizes two principal ideas. It is a place where wicked persons are kept to protect society and it is a place for wicked people to be rehabilitated. The protection of society by imprisonment is ideal but in practice the measure of protection is determined by the crime and not by the personality of the criminal. Thus, some persons who commit a specific felony are relatively not dangerous to society while others are, and likewise some persons who commit only misdemeanors may be, and sometimes are, very dangerous. The idea of protection is an exponent of an idea that precedes it, namely, the severity of punishment, already specified in the law books. The measure of sentence imposed gives an illusory measure of security. Now, the system of term sentencing in time establishes a kind of balance of intake and outgo. In this movement, the index of crime tends to remain more or less constant. Recidivists, added to the never ending supply of new recruits, maintain a fair balance with those being released. Law enforcement continues as a going concern. In 1948, J. Edgar Hoover reported that in the United States three major crimes were committed every minute. Since then there has been a noticeable increase of crime in this country. Imprisonment affords community security only temporarily, but the importance of the symbol lies in its use for the public display of criminal justice. When the public reads in the news that a certain criminal was sentenced to a term of imprisonment, it has an illusory reassurance that society is being protected.[206]

The prison is a symbol of rehabilitation. This is an ideal which, in operation, comes into conflict with the notion of punishment as a reformative and deterrent device. The government of a prison is an authoritarian system which can operate only in terms of arbitrary force. The principles of government in a prison are those which are despised in a democratic system wherein the individual is valued, is regarded as competent and is entitled to share in its privileges and responsibilities. If we can regard a prison as a kind of kindergarten for grownups who failed to grow up, operated on authoritarian principle, we can appreciate that rehabilitation under such tutelage does not equip its graduates for democratic adaptation; rather we would expect that such rehabilitation has a large influence in shaping the antisocial potential. Here we have child-rearing at its worst.[207]

Again there is insistence in the question, is there a real difference between a prison and a mental hospital? The distinction exists only in our ideology and in the language we employ in describing and manipulating such groups. In mental hospitals we have an elaborate descriptive vocabulary, typology and flexible therapy; in prisons we are limited to a vocabulary of good-bad moral evaluations and a rigid discipline of repression. We might discover a "sameness" of the people in prisons as in mental hospitals if we applied the same approach to them. We make certain assumptions about criminals but we do not study criminals themselves, only abstractions about them. If we did, with the same enterprise given to the study of people in mental hospitals, we might come to the realization that prisons are in fact places full of mentally disturbed people whose symptoms are better concealed, people who are harder to change, and certainly people who are a luxury as a conscience fund of the community.

VI SUMMARY

> If you have had your attention directed to the novelties in thought in your own lifetime, you will have observed that almost all really new ideas have a certain aspect of foolishness when they are first produced.
> ALFRED NORTH WHITEHEAD [208]

In earliest times, medical psychology and criminal law were nourished by common roots. Only recently has medical psychology attained a separation from its parent stock and thus attained the capacity for mutational growth in the soil of science. The alignments of this separation are visible, which I have had no other way to conceptualize than in terms of language and communication. In these alignments on the one side, behavior is viewed in class theoretical concepts of static, immutable entities that have separate existence in the natural world. The order of the universe can be grasped directly by the mind: reason has the power to know truth and to establish valid rules of human relations. General concepts or universals possess independent reality and the best way to predict a given case is to know what happens in a general category and then determine what modifiers make exceptions to the general rule. All of this is grounded to a two-valued logic. Within the legal view of the subjective element of crime in the issue of mental illness and responsibility is the notion of "knowledge" as some separate entity of the mind which is believed to be measurable by the psychiatrist and is regarded as the only means to exculpate the lunatic from wrong doing. In this approach, there is a persistent demonological concept of behavior.

On the other side, is the reasoning which rejects the idea of general concepts having reality of their own, namely, "mind," "intent," "will," "insanity," regarding them as verbal impediments to sharing experience. Any exercise of reasoning merely erects hypotheses which must be verified by concrete experience in order that reliable predictions may be made. In this field-theoretical view of events true meanings are to be found by observing what man does with his terms, not by what he says about them. In this view the world is a product of the observer and the observed.

When we think of the alignments of thought in law and psychiatry we discover that they both lead to what we do to and with our fellow men. Our goal is a common one, a goal of social unity and growth through justice. But at times these alignments stand in polar opposition as methods of achieving such a goal. The Ballem case is a full demonstration of this opposition of two systems of thought, both of which are tied to the same axis which turns the issue of capital penalty.

In the field of criminal responsibility and mental disease, the concepts and language of law and of psychiatry are at variable distance; in the individual-centered aspect of criminal justice, the pre- and post-trial phases, the separation is small; in the public-centered trial aspect, the separation is large and has today reached its greatest distance. It has been the thesis of these lectures that the criminal trial is an operation having a religious meaning essential as a public exercise in which the prevailing moral ideals are dramatized and reaffirmed. The religious meaning is the adjusting of tensional moral conflict within the law-abiding. The conflict is materialized in the actions of the criminal, and dissipated in the ritual of guilt fastening, condemnation and punishment. The ritual is the homologue of the child-parent interaction containing the same motivational mechanisms and rationalizations. In this view, the criminal trial has the function of public edification rather than that of welfare of the individual wrong-doers who pass over its stage in an endless procession. In fixed formula and procedure, the trial reiterates the moral parables of our child-rearing and, in the person of the judge, brings to the transgressor a power and punitive enforcement once exercised by the parent. Both judge and parent act as agents of an order defined by the prevailing ethical system.

I have pointed out that the ritual of criminal justice is an end in itself, and that religious content tends to give way to form, and form to indurated dogma. Furthermore, any attempt to bring a scientific discipline into ritual has been and will be met with resistance that flows from a sense of profanation. Nevertheless, on the periphery of the public-centered trial, psychiatry finds less of such resistance in the individual-centered pre- and post-trial phases. In these phases, the law invites objectivity and, in it, there is more room for the content of religion, of religious symbolism through which the sentiments of charity, compassion and forgiveness can be mediated.

I have also attempted to show that the criminal trial is more than a formal, objective operation for "adjusting" the individual wrong-doer to his community; it simultaneously provides subjectively a theater for the repetition of crime and the undoing of it in fantasy with mass participation and also provides an arena of conflict on another level on which the triers contend with each other in a highly stylized game within a game. That the criminal trial is portrayed in such figures does not depreciate its utility or imply in the least a negative view of religion; the portrayal is intended to remind us that in our concern for form we may have tended to lose sight of the content of religion. Moreover, the portrayal of the criminal trial as a religious function does not imply an inherent incompatibility with science. Max Otto reminds us that "We might then indeed speak of science and religion . . . as inseparable and complementary endeavors in man's attempt to make himself at home on this planet." [209] The conflict is between methods of viewing our surrounding reality and this conflict can be reduced to the difference in the symbols we employ affecting our fellow men. Once there can be reached some agreement on our symbols, conflict lessens and we find that the essential religious content of criminal justice can be enhanced. Our difficulty in reaching agreement in the use of our symbols comes out of the irrational anxiety of uncertainty. When our symbols become things, they become idols. We experience the anxiety of uncertainty when we discover that the idols are not things but only symbols. I have suggested that we re-examine the symbols we use in both criminal law and psychiatry. In this spirit of re-examination, I have entered into the difficult world of definition posed by the question, what is mental illness?

I have shown that criminal justice is not confined wholly to the external workings of law enforcement, to the rituals of the courtroom and to the penitential sufferings imposed from without. Every person behaves as if there existed in him an internal tribunal of justice with its own law enforcement, with its expiatory rites and self-adjudicated suffering. This tribunal works on the less conscious levels of mental life and is closer to the archaic symbols of social conflict in the infantile experience.

The workings of these two tribunals could be outlined in the case of our young clergyman. With our conventional symbols which we too often take as things, we cannot explain this young man's undoing. In this case the language of psychiatry was accepted by the court and in its action affecting the accused, the emphasis on individual-centered justice materialized a religious content of mutual help in corrective therapy.

In the pre- and post-trial phases of criminal justice the psychiatrist is offstage from its public-centered operations and in them with his functions and limitations clearly defined, his communication with the law can be the least ambiguous. I have offered the pre-trial examinations of the college boy and the torso slayer, as examples of not only an anachronistic psychiatry imposed by law, but also of the misuse of it by the court. In both, the psychiatrists and the court were straddled by the incubus of M'Naghten.

The story of William, the fugitive murderer and lunatic, has been related in some length in the hope that from it we can extract a moral. I could find none other than this: When names are regarded as things and applied to human beings, they in turn become things which we manipulate in ways that are passing strange.

I have cited four important murder trials in which partisan psychiatry was introduced; the trial of the postman who killed one woman and wounded another; of Edward Gibbs who murdered the young girl in Lancaster, Pennsylvania; of James Colbert Smith, and the case of the torso slayer, Francis X. Ballem. In these, psychiatry figured in the public-centered phase of criminal justice. In these, a kind of psychiatry did accommodate itself to the psychological model of the law, exemplified in the M'Naghten rule. But this psychiatry was a one dimensional psychiatry, a kind of demonological taxonomy which no longer occupies the front rows of psychiatric thought.

I stated that today, in the public-centered phases of criminal justice, the respective concepts and language of law and of psychiatry have reached their largest separation. Yet, there are indications that this separation has passed its apogee. The first notice of this has come from an increasing voice, contained in forensic literature, of dissatisfaction with the role of partisan psychiatry in criminal cases. Many proposals have come from both lawyers and psychiatrists setting forth remedies. The common idea in such proposals has been the abandonment of partisan testimony and the use of court designated experts either on a permanent or part-time basis or by selection from panels of qualified persons.[210] However, such arrangements do not meet two basic issues which should be approached first. One, the public policy issue as to what extent a system of criminal justice based upon metaphysical concepts of moral responsibility is to be or can be replaced— in part or wholly—by a system based upon the operational philosophy of contemporary science. It is important to make some estimate of the tolerable limits of such a change. How much science is desirable in the criminal justice in action? Secondly, the necessity for psychiatrists to re-examine their own premises and determine to what extent their operations are useful or valid in matters of adjudicating criminal responsibility. In these lectures I have made such an attempt in pointing out that in the criminal trial of today the psychiatrist cannot bring his science to the trial, but must act as a moral inquisitor, a role played in earlier times by the theologian. In his more recent examination of his concepts the psychiatrist has come to discover that no psychopathology can calibrate moral responsibility; that moral responsibility is not a measurable objective medical phenomenon but merely a symbol which mediates a group attitude about deviant behavior. Moreover, the psychiatrist has come to a clearer definition of his ethical position. We are reminded again of Jerome Hall's phrase about keeping the psychiatrist "on tap" and again of Zilboorg's pointed comment that "the problem would suggest that there is something immoral in this forcible conversion of the psychiatrist to formalistic concepts of legal insanity—concepts which certainly have no clinical existence in psychiatry or in life itself and which exist on paper only in our penal codes." [211]

The Durham Decision

In the movement away from M'Naghten and kindred tests, the psychiatrist will in time cease to be a moral inquisitor and become properly a reporter of observations within his competence. Inescapably, the moral issue will be in the picture but the psychiatrist will no longer wear the mantle of the moral inquisitor as he did compliantly in the Smith case in which his psychiatric examination consisted in *"talking with Smith, observing his demeanor and reading his confession to him to discover whether or not he could distinguish right from wrong."*

In the District of Columbia the Durham decision of 1954 marks the first move away from M'Naghten. In this decision, written by Judge David L. Bazelon, the instruction to the jury is that in order to convict they must rule out two matters, (1) that the accused was not suffering with a mental disease or defect and (2) even if he was, the criminal act was not the product of mental disease or defect. For, if the jury finds that the mental disease did not cause the act, it should not influence the question of the defendant's guilt. A further break with M'Naghten has taken place in decisional law in a case in Minnesota having to do with inheritance.[212, 213] The Legislature of the Virgin Islands recently abandoned M'Naghten by Act No. 160, approved May 16, 1957, effective September 1, 1957.[214] The Durham decision commemorates a pioneer collaboration of two remarkable figures in American judicial history, Justice Charles Doe of the New Hampshire Supreme Court and Doctor Isaac Ray, author of *The Medical Jurisprudence of Insanity,* one of the Founding Fellows of the American Psychiatric Association and one in whose name these lectures are offered.[215]

The theory and practice of law involves two problems: those of its concepts and aims of justice, and those of its techniques. The Durham decision does not center itself on the first of these problems, beyond restating the aims of the law in the special issue of criminal responsibility and mental disorder and reaffirming the traditional concepts of justice. The decision does modify the technique of justice in accommodation to the kind of knowledge now available from contemporary science. In this respect, the decision removes from the public-centered aspect of criminal justice an impediment to the fuller exploitation of technical information for the use of those who make moral decisions. Furthermore, the decision achieves a greater insulation of those who supply the technical information from those who make the decisions. The expert is less imposed upon to transpose scientific observation into value judgments, less restricted to an intellectual exercise focused exclusively on a single aspect of the *subjective element* of a crime. He is now free to offer information comprehending all the dimensions of the accused. Comprehensive information has been admissible under M'Naghten but, before Durham, in its transit to the jury in the formal instructions it became invisible in the spotlight centered on *knowledge* of right and wrong. Before Durham, the expert's clinical data were the development of the plot as in the play, leading to but not defining the dénouement.

The passing of M'Naghten in 1954 and the revival of the essentials of the New Hampshire rule, invited a re-examination of our traditional concepts and a reconstruction of our philosophy and communication in the manipulation of mentally disordered law breakers.

I would judge that, from the legal side, the prevailing criticism of the Durham decision is that it has removed from the trial a test which is a matter of law. Durham abandoned something that never existed as a matter of empirical fact. In abandoning M'Naghten, as did Justice Doe in the New Hampshire Pike case, the court abandoned a formula that was a mistake.[216] Durham has left the law without definition of "disease" and "defect," beyond identifying them as conditions respectively changeable and unchangeable. A fear is expressed that without definitions of disease or defect any abnormality having a psychiatric dimension cannot be excluded. Soboloff comments that this fear can be met by counseling the law as follows:

> Judges and lawyers boast that there is no definition of fraud; they think this is in aid of the law's effectiveness and does not weaken it. Its very vagueness is said to be a source of strength, for it renders the law more adaptable to unpredictable conditions. ... What we ought to fear above all is not the absence of a defi-

nition but being saddled with a false definition. We must avoid the rigidity which precludes inquiry, which shuts out light and insists on concepts that are at odds with things known and acknowledged not only by the medical profession but all informed men.[217]

A further uneasiness comes out of what is regarded as an unspecified concept of causality. In Durham, a person is not exculpated for an unlawful act if no causal connection exists between it and the disease or defect. One representative critic insists that the Durham opinion "does not face the question of how extensively capacity must be impaired to call for holding the defendant irresponsible." [218] He fears that a mere causal relationship between disease and act is too permissive. Another legal writer concludes that the decision opens too wide the door to any psychiatric theory.[219] Actually in the past three fiscal years in the District of Columbia, the absence of M'Naghten has witnessed scarcely a stir. Under Durham the number of defendants found not guilty by reason of insanity was 7 in 1953–4; 8 in 1954–5 and 11 in 1955–6. The number of cases in which mental illness was found, decreased from 66 to 22 as did the total number of defendants examined, from 92 to 73 and the number examined and found to be of sound mind rose from 15 to 39.[220]

From the side of psychiatry, there is a general expression of relief from the onus of M'Naghten, but a lingering uneasiness both for the definition of "disease" and "defect," and an uncertainty that troubles the psychiatrist in determining the causal nexus between disease and an unlawful act.

Let us take in turn each of these elements of doubt and certainty. The definition of "disease" and "defect" is already in the decision. The decision reads:

> We use "disease" in the sense of a condition which is considered capable of either improving or deteriorating. We use "defect" in the sense of a condition which is not considered capable of either improving or deteriorating and which may be either congenial, or the result of injury, or the residual effect of a physical or mental disease.[221]

SUMMARY

This statement does not define any syndrome of mental illness as it is academically considered, or any classification of intellectual defect beyond reference to the commonly accepted sources of such defect. The separation of those conditions capable of change from those which are not, leads to a secondary criterion of no more than incidental notice so far as the factual evidence supplied by the expert is concerned. The separation has one important operational meaning centered to the question of disposition of the case; we may be moved to regard differently a condition which is changeable from one which is unchangeable. But the virtue of Durham lies in its avoidance of a definition of what constitutes "disease" or "defect," beyond the qualification provided as a general guiding principle. Quite properly the decision places no limitations on the dimensions of "disease" or "defect" since these are matters of scientific description which are relative and changing and which are to be supplied by the experts to the jury. In so imparting to the concept of mental disease, the qualities of process, of relativity, the criminal law in *action* can be likewise flexible and self correcting apace with the advance of medical psychology. As Doctor Isaac Ray advised, the law need not adopt as law the mistakes doctors make of insanity, but rather use what is currently the best available in our climate of doubt and certainty. We can leave to the courts the task of securing the best available.

The dimensions of mental disease are left to the psychiatrist. As I have stated in an earlier chapter, in the natural world there is no such thing as mental disease or defect, but rather certain patterns of behavior to which, in a given social context, we apply certain names which enable us to talk about and to effect certain changes in the social relationships of those who exhibit them and to effect changes in the individuals themselves. At best, we are left to the imposition of purely arbitrary criteria in selecting such persons. In defining the relationship of the individual to his community, of necessity, such criteria are set at the point of intolerance to disturbing and damaging behavior. The medical considerations guide such criteria in two aspects: one, by providing a special competence for selection; the other, by providing a rationale of treatment for those who are changeable and a humane sequestration for those who are not. I have already cited the functional criteria of mental illness exemplified in the Pennsylvania Mental Health Act which simply states that those persons who, for reasons of any illness, change in their social relationships to such an extent that they need custodial *care,* shall be regarded as "mentally ill" or "insane." The matter of judgment of who needs care has been entrusted to those who are ethically dedicated to provide the community with the best available of competence and judgment. In our quest for some order and certainty, these considerations would lead us to regard *care* or commitment as a workable, operational criterion applicable to "disease" and "defect" and, within the present scope of selection, such a criterion would reach the majority of cases who exhibit conventional symptoms of "mental illness." From this point of reckoning, the expert would support his judgment as to either a changeable or unchangeable mental state. At best, in his reading, he could say that the behavior of the accused immediately anterior to the unlawful act warranted the legal imposition of *care.* This is indeed the case in many if not all instances of mentally disorderd persons who commit unlawful acts. This was the case of James Colbert Smith who personally appealed for *care* lest he kill someone. Unfortunately, not only did he not know the right people but also had no personal means to implement his appeal. In its concern for Smith's personal rights against *unlawful care,* the law impelled his involuntary discharge from a public hospital after the expiration of ten days of security, not only for himself but for others. If we bear in mind the individual-centered aspect of the criminal trial, the criterion of *care* is satisfactory for the psychiatrist to employ and, under the Durham rule, there should be no impediment to him in imparting this criterion of judgment to the jury. In effect the

SUMMARY

psychiatrist says *ex hypothesi* to the jury, that if the accused had not committed an unlawful act and by other circumstance come to the expert's notice the imposition of *care* would have been recommended. However, this criterion will not touch certain cases who are mentally ill but in our time have come to be regarded as fair to good risks for ambulatory treatment. Today the courts do regard certain classes of mentally ill persons as fit for what is designated as "medical probation," or non-custodial "care." But such a disposition would be impossible in cases of serious felonies. In these, the enormity of the offense would place the offender within the reach of custodial *care*. In Isaac Ray's time, mentally ill persons were identified as "crazy" people confined in lunatic asylums. Today ambulatory psychiatric cases bulk large in offices and out-patient clinics, and only those whose sense of reality becomes so distorted are manipulated in an environment of custodial "care." Again the criterion of care could be only inferred in those cases in which the criminal act is the first clinical manifestation of larval mental illness. I think such an inference would be correct.

I mention a case in point, bearing upon the functional operations implicit in the broad criterion of *care*. In this case, the defendant killed an older man with whom the defendant's wife had found an open dalliance. For some weeks before the killing the defendant became visibly changed in his behavior. To his friends and family, this behavior was explicit of a failure to cope with the problem and of a regressive retreat to a more primitive adaptation. In this, others sensed the defendant's narrowing margin of control. He became more or less incapacitated for his usual work, and took to drinking in excess. A mood of depression pervaded his feelings, punctuated with weeping spells, alternating with gestures of suicide, both in speech and in writing. His behavior certainly invoked apprehension in others and, in relief of it, some had made suggestions that the defendant needed *care*. This is to say that some intervention in the defendant's life was advisable. Efforts were made to induce him to seek psychiatric help. Some process was at work in the defendant which was lessening his capacity for control in his affairs and social life warranting intervention even to the point of involuntary commitment. But a psychiatrist never came into sufficient connection with the defendant to exert an influence which might have changed the course of events. I believe that if such had been the case and if the psychiatrist had been in full possession of the facts and a description of the defendant's behavior, there would have been little hesitation on his part to intervene and place the defendant in a controlling environment. Such a move would have implied mental illness as defined within an individual-centered operation. Such intervention within the immediate circle of those about the defendant in question did not take place; and the attendant tensions continued at increasing pitch. In the meantime, the tensions within the defendant mounted and culminated in a killing directed away from himself. He had long brooded in the contemplation of a killing directed to himself.

So far, the moral of this account is two-fold; one, in the setting and dimensions before the killing, no one expressed any doubt of the defendant's real disability, his potential danger to himself and to others—in a word, his mental illness; that without intervention one could predict a probable killing (suicide or homicide) in actuality; and the other, that with intervention (*care*), one could predict a killing confined to fantasy, dissipated in the treatment.

If, in the light of Durham, we view the subjective elements of this defendant's behavior prior to the killing, it would scarcely occur to anyone to deny that there existed a unitary process of mind with its outward visible expression, that the subjective elements and the manifest behavior in words and actions were mutually dependent and complementary. All of this was self evident until an unlawful act did take place as a culminating end point of the same unitary process. At this moment, a sanction of the community was invoked and the same facts now held in a public-centered view were perceived in a different light. The process was no longer unitary, but by the method of inquiry bifurcated into a mental illness on the one hand and a "product" on the other. It was the task of the defense to reunite them. The same objective facts were brought into a larger dimension of social interaction in which the resistance to the acceptance of mental illness in the defendant thrust him into a different context which could be worked out only in terms of a kind of game. The game was to restore the unity of the process. In brief, if before the killing the defendant had been placed in a sanitarium no one would have questioned the existence of his mental illness and his latent destructive potential; the same defendant having done the killing, a resistance to the same fact of mental illness interceded and could not be overcome by rational means but only by a kind of exorcism which is the latent meaning of the trial. This exorcism was centered on the defendant but it had the meaning of a vicarious working through of an immemorial moral problem of his triers, who, like equivocal parents, somehow contrived simultaneously and unconsciously to sanction the acting out of the defendant, find vicarious gratification in it, and morally to condemn it.

The preceding observations point to a way which some fear to tread. The criterion of care, i.e., hospital segregation, does not reach all dimensions of mental illness and criminality. It does not touch those whom we have come to accept as proper subjects for psychiatry—those whom we call "psychopathic personalities," or, as their behavior is officially regarded, those who are said to have a "sociopathic personality disturbance." Psychiatry is yet divided in its concept of psychopathy. Some subscribe to the view that the psychopath in our society imposes a greater threat than the conventionally insane and, from the standpoint of social defense, should be manipulated as insane. Others can easily distinguish between mental disease and "character disorder." Yet others find that such distinction exists more in the words than in the facts of danger to society. In view of the criteria of changeable and unchangeable conditions set forth by Durham, the psychopath would be closer to the unchangeable group. Few psychopaths have been changed. The changing of the psychopath is difficult largely because, unlike the neurotic, he does not have sufficient inner suffering to move him to treatment or to remain in it. On the one hand we have tended to shun the psychopath who occupies a significant place in our criminal world; on the other hand those out of jails and those in high places are inaccessible.[222]

In view of Durham, the psychopath would be relieved of criminal responsibility if his behavior were regarded as a product of mental illness. The model code of the American Law Institute has erected a fence around its modified M'Naghten to exclude the psychopath from being held irresponsible. This exclusion has some but not full justification on the grounds of immediate expedience. It is feared that it would divert a large part of our term sentence prison population to indeterminate commitment to mental hospitals which in turn would become prisons. It is doubtful if the community is ready to underwrite such a change, and to abandon its symbols and such a move would certainly demoralize the underworld. An easier way might be to change prisons into hospitals which could be done if we take Arnold's advice:

> To treat criminals with common sense one must classify them as insane. Only in this way can we adopt genuine therapeutic techniques without appearing to tear down the foundations of our society.[223]

Yet, as a measure of social defense, the problem of the so-called psychopath will have to be met. I sense that in this area of social policy the more liberal trends come from the side of law itself. Weihofen believes that the practical consequences of recognizing the psychopath as having a mental disease would probably not be overwhelming. He states: "If enough psychopaths are found irresponsible, we might find it practical to build separate institutions for them, which is probably the best solution." [224] He believes that even state mental hospitals could make administrative adjustments to them and utilize them for research purposes. The fact remains that there is relatively little known about them, and what is known about them has not had wide dissemination or application. Our failure to come to grips with the psychopath may issue from fear that to exculpate him would be to move in the direction of determinism and away from a moral order founded upon the concept of free choice. A practical move would be to have a moratorium on library research into the nature of psychopathy and on the erection of special institutions and instead undertake a large scale research sampling of our prison population. From such findings our social policy makers could then possess directions in keeping with our avowed principles of justice.

Those who resist the innovation of Durham declare that ambiguity is carried in the term "product." The term "product" denotes separateness and implies a lineal causation. As I have commented above, behavior is a unitary process but with license it is spoken of in terms of either its subjective elements or of its outward appearances. This dualistic distinction is linguistic, and has the same implications contained in our mode of talking about the mind and body as if they had separate existence. Causality has meaning depending upon language structure and upon what levels of abstraction are employed. Our language limits us to a lineal step codification of reality and to a world of single one-to-one causality. In reporting objective events, we do not yet have the language expressive of continuous interactions with multiple or circular causality.

In the language of the law, *cause* is regarded as an event which has direct or proximate connection in sequence with another event. This view of causality does not express the ultimate reality of such connection, but serves as a means of mediating common sense predictions from the appearances of things. This is the causality of everyday life and, by a general extensional agreement, we somehow get the work of justice done. On this level, mental illness "causes" crime in some, but not in others. But there remain questions which the psychiatrist must face. First, does such a view of causality compass the probable relationship of mental illness to crime? Second, if mental illness causes some to commit crimes, and not others, do we have a reliable method of discriminating those crimes which have no causal nexus with mental illness? To the first, the answer depends upon how we choose to regard and treat those who create moral tensions in us. To the second, the answer is that psychiatry has yet to discover a method.

In the common sense view of causality, by the rule of law, variance must be determined within a range of selection limited in M'Naghten to "knowledge," and in Durham, to crime as a "product" of mental illness or defect. In the adversary setting, "knowledge" or "product" emerge, one way or the other, as "matters of fact," out of which a moral decision is made.

The concepts of "knowledge" and "product" rest in common upon two assumptions; first, that behavior and its subjective element are variably separate, and second, that precision of detection of variance is achieved by the facility of psychiatry. That such facility is now provided by psychiatry is questionable. As matters stand, all behavior is better viewed as a unitary phenomenon. However, we can recognize that when viewed within a moral system, out of our own psychological needs and design we are impelled arbitrarily to dichotomize behavior into subjective (motivational) and objective elements. This dichotomy sets and maintains the alignments of the adversary system of resolving moral problems. At the same time, however, the dichotomy opens the door to the realm of infinite differences which may come less out of actual differences in nature, and more out of the differences in the persons who report and evaluate them.

We observe that as long as sufficient numbers of persons believe that such separation of mind and act exists in the natural world, not only will we continue to be ranged in partisan disputes over abstractions whether an accused possesses "knowledge", or whether a mental illness or defect causes crime, but also will we continue to witness the enormous expenditure of our resources in almost endless appellate pleadings as in the Smith case.

The adversary system has a precious utility in the uncovering of facts of crime and its doer, and of the facts of mental illness set within recognized psychiatric criteria, but there may be doubt of its utility when it drags psychiatry through the unchartered metaphysics of "knowledge" and "product."

Seemingly, by an inner psychological necessity we are impelled to abstract the outward act from the hypothetical subjective element and to regard the act as a "product." This partakes of psychic repression which achieves a dissociation of outward actions from their inner animations close to our first nature and to the child within us. Repression holds the deeper, older, emotional impetus to outward acts inaccessible to direct conscious expression and maintains our "sanity." Nevertheless, our social behavior is so unconsciously motivated and a good part of our thinking is a *post facto* explanation of it. Our explanations are shaped by the nature of our language which is by necessity a step linear process which intellectually conveys the idea of separateness and sequential causation. Actions speak louder than words, but words have the last say, and we must make our actions appear rational in words especially to ourselves even when we are mentally ill. How can we fit in repression with the idea that mental illness causes crime or that crime is a product of mental illness? Repression insulates the "insane" and/or "criminal" part of ourselves from ourselves, and we have a comfortable sense of separateness from it. The sense of separateness can be framed only in a logic which reifies abstractions to which in turn are attributed the powers to cause a person to commit a crime. This is the logic we employ when we say that mental illness causes crime. We are not describing objective facts of the "mind" and of "crime" of the accused, but describing a mental process of the triers, who separate the accused from the crime by a device which explains that, although the accused did the deed, it was not he but a "mental illness" that *caused* it. In this logic the mentally ill accused is a spectator, like a dreamer who watches himself carry out forbidden behavior and like St. Augustine, thanks God he is not responsible for what he dreams. The pain saving feature of this process of abstraction is evident. The behavioral products can be dissociated from their motivational source. In turn, one can deny that one's antipathic acts have antipathic intentions; in fact, one can deny that one's antipathic intentions have any connections with one's self. In our present application of cause and product we come upon this saving device. "It was not I, but a mental illness that did the deed." This is close to the Manichean heresy that it is not the person who sins, but rather another nature within him. When the criminal act is regared as the product of mental disease or defect the person so afflicted is a mere instrumentality. Although capable of antipathic acts, the "sick" man is nevertheless incapable of antipathic intentions and thus entitled to exculpation. Many persons exhibit behavior within this formula of special premium upon disability which not only explains away bad behavior but also maintains the innocence if not the non-existence of bad intentions. We do not strike back at "sick" people who strike us. By now it must be evident that we are not dealing with objective observations but with unconscious identifications which merely explain our own attitudes towards those "sick" people (so unlike ourselves) who strike at us.

At best, all we can do is to regard behavior as an expression of the subjective element, a symbolic extension of it into another modality of communication. Our attention is centered on the behavior itself but the causal relationship of it is not to be found in its first proximity to a syndrome of mental illness. Those who insist on finding the casual link in such proximity are not reaching *cause,* structured within the process of living and acting out, but are merely finding an immediate *cause* as it exists in a verbal definition. It would be exceedingly difficult to imagine any behavior without determined antecedents and experience and, in this sense, no act could be conceived as separate from the subjective operations of the actor. When a person commits an unlawful act, his mental operations either normal or pathological at the moment of the act, are indissolubly tied to it. The tie will be intact at some level, at times clearly in conscious awareness visible to the actor and to others, or at other times with lesser degree of awareness reaching into unconscious levels invisible to the actor and to others. The significant "causal" tie between the act and the subjective element need not be co-terminal; it is everyday experience that a crime of today is tied to the past, and that the conscious ego of the doer may have little awareness of the earlier connection.[225, 226] In this frame, one could go a step further and say that the "mind," either in health or disease, causes one to do everything one does; it causes one to conform as well as not to. I believe that in the trial the psychiatrist can, with the good conscience of a scientist, testify that a crime committed during any defined mental state is a symptomatic expression of a unitary process of human existence. If the term "product" or "offspring" is employed to elicit his opinion, he can so answer in the affirmative in compliance with an implied agreement with this conceptual model which regards all behavior as an outward expression of an inner process. The affirmative answers a question that is already answered in the finding of not only a "mental illness" but also of any *unnamed* behavior. To regard any act as not having a link with the subjective element of the actor is to take human behavior out of reach of scientific inquiry, beyond the concept of relative determinism which we believe governs the natural world and upon which we place our confidence. If some human acts have no tie with mental life, we must concede the existence of demons who become visible in the acts of those they possess.

If the question posing the "product" concept is by necessity in the language of science answerable in the affirmative and the mental state and the crime are reunited, we immediately perceive that when put to the psychiarist it is no longer a test because no discreet variables come within its range. We can also perceive that the "product" concept like the "knowledge" concept belongs to a different order of operation which is a reflection of the attitude which treats our fellow men as if they were completely free to choose their behavior and upon which we act affecting them. At best, the "product" question can properly remain only within the realm of moral definitions which have a place in the public-centered phase of criminal justice. It does not have the same meaning in the individual-centered model of psychiatry.

When we return to the application of Durham in the public-centered phase of criminal justice, we meet with the hard question of how a jury can find an answer as to whether a mental illness produces a crime. If the psychiatrist testifies only to the existence of a mental illness, can the jury draw from the medical facts alone its own inferences of causation? There seems to be a fear that without the psychiatric opinion on this score the jury would flounder. Weihofen quotes from an important case in the United States Court of Military Appeals [227] in which the Judge averred:

> In light of the esoteric nomenclature used in the field and the hypertechnical divergence between various schools of psychiatric thought, as well as because of the complexity and sheer uncertainty of the area under exploration, it can readily be imagined that wholesale want of enlightenment would eventuate from *purely* medical testimony from the witness, psychiatrist.[228]

This dictum is an overstatement which implies that enlightenment would otherwise be available to the jury. No enlightenment beyond '*purely* medical testimony' is likely to come from psychiatry. Here the psychiatrist can do no more than say that a causal connection invariably exists, for no other reason than that, in his experience and within his psychological model, he has never encountered a case where outward behavior was unrelated to the inward mental life. Weihofen makes a pertinent comment:

> As a matter of fact the problem of proving a causal connection is essentially different in this disorder—and—crime situation than in others. How can we ever prove causation? We don't; instead we present the raw factual material and then try to induce the state of mind in the judge or jury that will prompt him or them to say that the relationship of cause and effect exists. How can they be convinced? Only by their matching the raw facts presented to them against their own background and experience. We ask them for their estimate—their guess if you please—as to whether on the basis of their established observations a causal connection exists. Their answer must come out of that background. It cannot be derived by logic.[229]

In this comment Weihofen pulls the issue out of theory and speculation and brings it within reach of juries who will continue to express the collective sense of justice with or without enlightenment.

At this juncture it may seem that when the psychiatrist joins in the issue of mental illness and criminal responsibility with the Durham formula, he should give consideration to the "product" concept from the following interrogations: (1) If the inner subjective elements and the outward visible expressions of them are invariably linked within the multidimensional range of conscious-unconscious levels of human behavior, must the psychiatrist ultimately conclude that the "product" question can be answered only in the affirmative? (2) If we assume that the inner and outer elements are variably disjunctive and that a psychiatrist can select the kind of mental illness that "causes" crime, do we have a probative device, but one that attributes some modes of behavior "caused" by "disease" and others caused by "free will?" (3)

If the psychiarist finds himself answering the "product" question in the negative, will he not be doing what he does in M'Naghten? And in Board's figure, what he does in M'Naghten in the modern inquisition, is what his medieval predecessors did to extract responses in order to "brand the accused as 'normal' enough to be morally responsible." [230]

The foregoing reflections suggest a procedural modification of a part of Durham, the probative wing of causation and product, but only in the sense that it sets the boundaries of psychiatric testimony. The basis of Durham is the determination of sufficient *objective* data reported by the psychiatrist to the jury. The "product" test is a *subjective* determination upon which is pivoted the question of moral responsibility, i. e. penalty, which the court or jury can and should resolve. It is not too much to ask the triers to make verdicts in their own terms; it is within the power of the courts to do so. I would submit that if the product question is withheld from the expert and confined to the triers, psychiatry can function properly. The jury can decide the matter under applicable law as instructed by the court, since it is determining a moral (legal) issue in its own terms. In this insulation of the psychiatrist from the "product" question we are keeping our symbols straight and pure.

In the recent Wright decision the Court cautioned that a defense request for explanatory instructions should not be refused when there is latent ambiguity in an instruction that conviction depends on a "causal connection." [231] The Court said:

"When we say that one event causes another, do we mean it is *a* cause of it, or the *principal* cause, or the *exclusive* cause? When a jury is told that it may convict the accused if it finds that, though he was mentally ill when he committed the act, the illness did not cause the act, may it convict if it finds that the illness was *one of the causes* of the act, but not the *exclusive cause?*"

SUMMARY

In this decision the Court further cited in part its previous Carter decision as follows:

"When we say the defense of insanity requires that the act be a 'product of' a disease, we do not mean that it must be a direct emission, or a proximate creation, or an immediate issue of the disease in the sense, for example, of Hadfield's delusion that the Almighty had directed him to shoot George III . . .

. . . There must be a relationship between the disease and the act, and that relationship, whatever it may be in degree, must be, as we have already said, critical in its effect in respect to the act. By 'critical' we mean decisive, determinative, causal; we mean to convey the idea inherent in the phrases 'because of', 'except for', 'without which', 'but for', 'effect of', 'result of', 'causative factor'; the disease made the effective or decisive difference between doing and not doing the act. The short phrases 'product of' and 'causal connection' are not intended to be precise, as though they were chemical formulae. They mean that the facts concerning the disease and the facts concerning the act are such as to justify reasonably the conclusion that 'But for this disease the act would not have been committed.' " [232]

These statements bring causality nearer to the probable relationships between mental illness with wrong-doing, which a jury may more readily develop from the breadth and depth of medical testimony strictly limited to the matter of mental illness. Thus implemented the instruction is sufficient without an expert opinion on the matter of causality. If it is exacted, the jury no longer has an instruction within the compass of factual matters, but one extended beyond factuality to matters of partisan opinions on causality.

I have already indicated my belief that the product question is answerable by psychiatry only in the affirmative. However, as a vehicle for expressing the prevailing moral ideals of the community, it can be a question answerable by the triers either way in the language of a moral issue. There should be no objection to addressing the product question exclusively to a jury. It is a simple concept which the jury can answer probably with better facility than it can the involved charges on the law of homicide and of insanity as exemplified in the case of Ballem. Thus Durham provides a start on the right foot. The question of mental "disease" or "defect" in the accused at the time of his offense is answerable by the psychiatric expert; the question of whether the offense was a "product" of the mental disease or defect is answerable by the court or jury in its own system of reckoning.

Thus realigned, the Durham formula provides the public-centered phase of criminal justice with a rational discipline which clearly separates the function of medical data-finding from the function of verdict rendering; in the former, the defendant's mental condition is made known to the triers in the language of science; in the latter, the moral decision is processed in the language of arbitrary human relations. In this arrangement, the expert is purely advisory to the jury on medical data; the judge is guiding on matters of law. The expert and the judge are thus technical advisors to the jury which knows or understands little of either law or psychiatry, but will find a way. That a jury can determine insanity without test questions put to an expert was demonstrated in a recent Philadelphia trial of a man charged with assault, aggravated robbery, and playfully and wantonly pointing a firearm. The defendant was examined by a Sanity Commission, and in bar of trial committed by the Court to a state mental hospital. Later he was returned to Court as fit to be tried. He raised the defense of insanity. The defense elicited lay opinion of the defendant's "insanity"; the attorney who acted as a member of the Commission was subpoenaed to read the conclusions of the Commission; the records of the receiving hospital and the state mental hospital were also read into the record. A court psychiatrist read her pre-trial report to the jury. No test of "insanity" was put to any medical witness. The Court's instructions to the jury contained the M'Naghten tests of knowledge and the jury alone considered them. A verdict of acquittal was returned. In this case, the jury was instructed to consider both lay opinion and the reports of clinical diagnoses which were a part of the defendant's medical record. No medical opinion evidence was introduced responsive to any legal test of insanity.[233]

In a previous chapter, I suggested that when the psychiatrist enters the criminal trial on either side he acts as a kind of special functionary upon whom guilt can be sympathetically displaced. In this light it becomes clear that his function in the courtroom is tied as much to the needs of the triers as to the defendant. This need is vital in a trial of a capital crime; on one side, the triers need a way out of their guilt for a juridic killing; on the other, the defendant needs a way out of his guilt through his mental illness. These remarks are pertinent to the realignments of Durham, in which the psychiatrist is no longer both doctor and oracle but only the doctor who reports the existence of a pattern of behavior designated as a "disease" or "defect." In keeping with my suggestions, the "product" question can be directed in the charge to the jury or the psychiatrist can answer the question in the affirmative. In either case, the guilt adheres to the triers.

Our analysis of the psychiatric role in Durham merits restatement. The rule of Durham is not new:

> It is not unlike that followed by the New Hampshire courts since 1870. It is simply that an accused is not criminally responsible if his unlawful act was the product of mental disease or defect.[234]

The New Hampshire rule was first laid down in 1866 in a dissenting opinion involving testamentary capacity,[235] and later affirmed by a majority opinion of the Supreme Court of New Hampshire in 1869 in State v. Pike [236] in which it was held that "All symptoms and tests of mental disease were purely matters of fact to be determined by the jury." [237] It was later reaffirmed by the same court in 1871 in State v. Jones.[238]

The New Hampshire rule has not come down to us as the "Pike" or the "Jones" Rule named after the defendant after the fashion of Durham. It became known gratuitously as the "product" rule after Durham and Durham has carried the same appellation. It is regrettable that Durham has become known and viewed as the "product" rule rather than the "medical data" rule which replaced M'Naghten and the irresistible impulse. The "product" concept is an unfortunate accident of metaphor which in 1871 was sired by an apt word calculated to further explicate the concept that mental disease dissipates the capacity to form a criminal intent. In 1871 Judge Ladd stated that if a killing was not produced by an actual mental disease, the defendant should be found guilty; that the jury would consider whether the act was the "offspring" of insanity; ". . . if it was, a criminal intent did not produce it; if it was not, a criminal intent did produce it and it was a crime." [239] No one will have trouble in perceiving that this configuration of *mental disease—intent—cause—offspring,* belongs to the same phylum of invertebrate abstractions as does M'Naghten, which can be put to a jury, but not to a psychiatrist. A rule of medical evidence of the existence of mental illness is substantively the heart of the Durham decision; the "product" idea is an artefact of causality and can be no more than rhetorical to the issue of moral responsibility which is not a medical matter.

I have stated my belief that the "product" question can be answered only affirmatively by the psychiatrist or not at all. The "product" question can and should be answered by the jury in the language of arbitrary relations in the manner that they ponder such concepts as "negligence," "fraud," "hot blood," and other undefined legal concepts, and thus within the formula of a moral inquistion, it has a social meaning and utility.

SUMMARY

In the resurvey of what has been presented here, there emerge several lines of possible development in the communication between psychiatry and the criminal law. The underlying problem in such development is a philosophical one which attempts to reconcile the conceptual conflicts between two systems of viewing our surrounding reality. If the criminal law is a religious institution and psychiatry is in alliance with the conceptual foundations of physical science, we may easily conclude that the two are unreconciled in conflict continued from the beginnings of the struggle between science and religion. Yet, the conceptual models of law and psychiatry are not mutually antagonistic provided neither is imposed upon the other. Psychiatry can provide valuable aid to the criminal law if psychiatry remains on the periphery in a purely advisory capacity on medical matters: If psychiatry remains "on tap." If this be the case, there is every chance that the criminal law will find in time that scientific knowledge will enhance the religious content of its operations replacing much of its rigid form.

At this place we may pause to consider fuller implications of a psychiatry "on tap." Psychiatry has a place in the trial limited to opinions as to the existence of mental illness, expressed in the language of science. When we speak of a peripheral position of psychiatry we specify those individual-centered phases outside of the criminal trial itself, the pre- and post-trial phases out of public view and participation. In these phases, scientific data can be exploited to maximum utility in the following administrative aspects: (1) advisory on the question of triability of the accused, (2) informative and advisory leading to appropriate disposition of the convicted, (3) provision of techniques for changing convicted persons in the direction of self awareness and reform, and (4) advisory on questions of release of convicted persons. These administrative functions are essentially penological, and at present are practically non-existent in the operations of criminal justice.

As matters stand, psychiatry looms in the public-centered phase of criminal justice, the trial, not as a source of scientific information but as an oracle which serves more the deeper psychological needs of the triers than those of the accused. The needs of the triers are activated particularly in the solemn issue of capital punishment. It is held by some that psychiatry would find little if any employment in the criminal trial if capital punishment were not the ultimate issue. A juridic killing reaches to the intestinal levels of moral conflict and cannot be explained away except by the rationalizations which formerly displaced guilt upon some higher supernatural image. Today this displacement cannot go beyond the fallible hand of man himself and his hand reaches for support. Today the psychiatrist as a *knower* of the "inner movement of the wills" stands as a lineal successor of the medieval theologian, the *diviner* of them. The psychiatrist has yet to further disassociate himself from this role of diviner, a role imposed upon him when he is put the "right and wrong" questions which are beyond his competence as a reporter of objective medical data. The psychiatrist will never likely disengage himself entirely from this role of diviner; even his reporting of the existence of mental illness in medical terms will carry in the witness box some oracular effect of a moral judgment.

The withdrawal of the "product" wing of Durham from the expert witness will complete the work of liberating medical testimony from the ghost of M'Naghten, and there will remain the foundations for a rational manipulation of mentally ill persons who commit unlawful acts. Durham points to the time when the defense of insanity will be no longer left to caprice and perhaps to the time when the defense of insanity will be no longer necessary; when the idea of "responsibility" as something divisible, diminished, absent or intact, will be recognized as untenable as a means of maintaining the rights of the mentally ill; when we may come to consider

SUMMARY

"the traditional ritual and vocabulary of guilt fastening and condemnation too much an end in itself at the expense of constructive social actions and human values. We may come to a realization that, like some compulsive neurotics, we have been spending too much time and energy in symptomatic contests over abstractions with little left to apply to real living. We do not need to abandon the idea of responsibility but rather regard all persons irrespective of mental state, as "responsible" in the sense that they are susceptible to legal sanctions in keeping with the aims of deterrence, security, treatment and reformation. This would eliminate all trial issues irrelevant to the questions of fact of the unlawful behavior and would leave open the question of the offender's disposition within the scope of prescribed standards to administrative application of tested, scientific knowledge. It would leave to the courts the public exercise of legal guilt finding and relieve the courts of the entire responsibility for determining appropriate measures to insure community protection and the offender's reformation if possible. The adjudication of insanity is an anachronism at bottom tied to archaic rituals of condemnation and to the retributive death penalty. . . ."[240]

This is not a plea to denature the trial procedures of those emotional elements that complement the therapeutic effect on the law-abiding nor need there be any threat to basic constitutional rights. The idea contemplates an enhancement in the dignity and public respect for law enforcement. The view of universal responsibility cannot be applicable as long as the concept of responsibility is confined to its narrow, medieval meaning, a liability only to punishment. It is applicable if the concept is brought to a broader, social therapeutic meaning, a liability to comprehensive treatment provided by law. In this frame of operation the unlawful act invokes a community sanction separate from the guilt finding ritual and at once disposes of the futile exercise of calibrating responsibility to a chimerical scale of legal guilt. Universal responsibility lays open to the law breaker regardless of mental status, a liability to a rational clinical manipulation which has within its resources imprisonment, hospitalization, probation, psychotherapy, etc. This procedure would eliminate the defense of insanity in the guilt-finding process but not bar the introduction of scientific evidence into a separate procedure of disposition.[241]

This proposal is not new and it comes initially from the side of the law. Sheldon Glueck [242] and others have advocated a separation of guilt-finding from disposition. In 1922 Associate Justice Wilbur of the Supreme Court of California urged:

> That insanity be no longer treated as a defense to a criminal charge, and that evidence on that subject be excluded from the jury trying a criminal case; that after conviction the defendant, upon suggestion of insanity, be examined by a board of alienists with a view to determining whether the defendant should be committed to the state hospital, or prison, or be released under probationary supervision to private hospital or other custody; that the judge be empowered to make such supervisory orders from time to time upon the advice of competent alienists as may be necessary, and that the state retain jurisdiction over the defendant even after an apparently complete cure for at least as long as the maximum term of imprisonment for the offense, resuming custody of the defendant during that period whenever symptoms of a relapse make further custody desirable for the protection of the public.[243, 244, 245]

The protection of the public does not exist in a vacuum, nor does the "criminal." As insight is gained into the psychology of man, as language develops so that the insight may be acquired and communicated, we may hope to diminish the "subjective adherences" from our self-picture and from our projections onto the "criminal." If we could eliminate the demonology inherent in the definitions of most crimes, in the legal definition of insanity, and in some of the terms of psychiatry, we might get down to the quest for a sane society. The struggle to find meaning instead of nonsense will disclose that man is neither the bad animal nor a fallen angel but quite completely important in himself, freed from an unnecessary burden of ignorance, fear and guilt.

NOTES

1. Breasted, James H., *The Dawn of Conscience*, Scribner, New York, 1950.
2. Otto, Max, *Science and the Moral Life*, Mentor Books, New American Library, New York, 1949, 91.
3. *Ibid*, 91.
4. Vaihinger, H., *The Philosophy of "As If,"* International Library of Psychology, Philosophy and Scientific Method, Routledge, London, 1949, 147.
5. Robinson, Edward S., *Law and the Lawyers*, Macmillan, New York, 1937, 8.
6. Berman, Harold J. & Hunt, Donald H., "Criminal Law and Psychiatry": *The Soviet Solution*, Stanford Law Review, 2: 635-663, July 1950, 635.
7. Jones, Ernest, *On the Nightmare*, Hogarth Press, London, 1931, 228.
8. Zilboorg, Gregory, *The Medical Man and the Witch during the Renaissance*, Johns Hopkins Press, Baltimore, 1935, 113.
9. See Russell, Bertrand, *The Impact of Science on Society*, Columbia University Press, New York, 1951, 7; Overholzer, Winfred, *The Psychiatrist and the Law*, Harcourt, Brace, New York, 1953.

    As cited by Overholzer the Witchcraft Act of 1735 is still in force in Great Britain and as recently as 1944 a man was convicted under it on a "pretense to conjuration" (*Rex* v. *Duncan & others*, 2 (1944) All ER 220).
10. See: de Rougemont, Denis, *The Devil's Share*, Meridian Books, New York, 1956; Kenyon, Theda, *Witches Still Live*, Ives Washburn, New York, 1929; and Hale, Christina, *Witchcraft in England*, Scribner, New York, 1947.
11. See the account of the Blymire case in the *Philadelphia Record*, October 31, 1944.
12. Evans, Bergen, *The Natural History of Nonsense*, Knopf, New York, 1953, 6.
13. Stephen, Karin, *Psychoanalysis and Medicine*, Cambridge University Press, New York, 1935, 223.
14. See Jones, Ernest, op. cit., 228; Summers, Montague, *The History of Witchcraft*, University Books, New York, 1956; and Tannen-

baum, Frank, *Crime and the Community,* Columbia University Press, New York, 1951, 3-4.
15. The term "primitive" needs qualification. Reference to the primitive stratum of the mind is to the unmoral aspect of the personality, untouched by education in a given culture. Primitive people in their own way are actually quite moral within their own value systems.
16. Freud, Sigmund, *Psychopathology of Everyday Life,* Macmillan, New York, 1948.
17. Piaget, Jean, *The Child's Conception of Physical Causality,* Kegan, Paul, Trench, Trubner & Co., Ltd., London, 1930, 244-245.
18. *Illustrative Strategies for Research on Psychopathology in Mental Health.* Symposium No. 2, June 1956, Group for the Advancement of Psychiatry, New York.
19. Reider, Norman, "The Demonology of Modern Psychiatry," American Journal of Psychiatry, 111: 851-856, May, 1955.
20. Freud, Sigmund, *An Autobiographical Study,* Hogarth Press, London, 1935.
21. Reider, Norman, op. cit.
22. Russell, Bertrand, *The Impact of Science on Society,* Columbia University Press, New York, 1951, 9.
23. After Taylor, A. E., *Aristotle,* Dover Publications, New York, 1955, 50.
   In passing it is of interest to note that in the Aristotelian doctrine of the four causes or conditions for production of things, the literal meanings of the Greek term *aitia, aition,* which he employed to convey the idea of causation, having a curious pertinence to legal matters. *Aition,* an adjective used substantively, means, "that on which the legal responsibility for a given state of affairs can be laid," *Aitia,* the substantive conveys the meaning of "credit" for good or bad, the legal responsibility for an act.
24. See Rapoport, Anatol, *Operational Philosophy,* Harper, New York, 1953, 64.
25. Young, J. Z., *Doubt and Certainty,* Oxford, 1951, 100.
26. Ruesch, J. & Bateson, G., *Communication—The Social Matrix of Psychiatry,* W. W. Norton, New York, 1951.
27. Russell, Bertrand, *Nightmares of Eminent Persons,* Simon & Schuster, New York, 1955, Introduction.
28. Goodwin, John C., *Insanity and the Criminal Law.,* G. H. Doran, New York, 1924, 259.
29. Bridgman, P. W., *The Logic of Modern Physics,* Macmillan, New York, 1927, 7.
30. *Philadelphia Inquirer,* June 23, 1924: "PUBLISHER IS HELD INSANE AT NIGHT, BUT SANE BY DAY; PHILADELPHIA HAS UNIQUE STATUS DUE TO RULINGS BY COURT; JAMES MACUSKER ALTERNATES EACH TWELVE HOURS IN ASYLUM: Confined in the Friends Asylum at Frankford during

the night hours as an insane patient, James E. Macusker for more than a year has been permitted under a court order to leave the institution during the working days of the week, journey to the central part of the city and there conduct his business of issuing a weekly paper. Literally, he is adjudged sane by day but insane by night, according to the interpretation placed on the unusual ruling by those versed in the law."

31. Johnson, Wendell, *People in Quandaries,* Harper, New York, 1946, 38.
32. Fromm, Erich, *The Sane Society,* Rinehart, New York, 1955, 17.
33. See Eissler, K. R., "The Effect of the Structure of the Ego on Psychoanalytic Technique," Journal of the American Psychoanalytic Assn., Vol. 1, No. 1, January 1953, 104-143.
34. Wilson, David C., "Psychiatric Implications of Jefferson's Attitude Towards Freedom of the Mind," Neuropsychiatry, 3: 31-41, Summer, 1953, Dept. of Neurology and Psychiatry, Univ. of Virginia, 33, 34, 35, 40.
35. Fromm, Erich, op. cit., 72-73.
36. *Ibid,* 69.
37. Money-Kyrle, R., *Psychoanalysis and Politics,* W. W. Norton, New York, 44-45.
38. See Rogers, Carl, "Toward a Theory of Creativity," ETC., XI, No. 4, 1954; Hayakawa, S. I., "The Fully Functioning Personality," ETC., XIII, No. 3, 1956; Maslow, A. H., *Motivation and Personality,* Harper, New York, 1954; and Lindner, Robert, *Must You Conform?* Rinehart, New York, 1956.
39. See Bowman, Karl M., & Rose, Milton, "A Criticism of the Terms 'Psychosis,' 'Psychoneurosis,' and 'Neurosis,'" American Journal of Psychiatry, 108: 161-166, Sept. 1951.
    The authors comment: "Our present fund of demonstrable knowledge and well-grounded, generally accepted theory about mental illness is very meager, indeed, and the limitations of our scientific understanding in the field of psychiatry are nowhere more evident than in our use of diagnostic labels that are vague and ambiguous in meaning and have little reference to the actual clinical conditions that they purport to describe." (166)
40. Freud, Sigmund, "Analysis Terminable and Interminable," International Journal of Psychoanalysis, 18: 373-405, Oct. 1937.
    ". . . . every normal person is only approximately normal; his ego resembles that of the psychotic in one point or another, in a greater or lesser degree, and its distance from one end of the scale and proximity to the other may provisionally serve as a measure of what we have indefinitely spoken of as 'modification of the ego.'" (390)
41. Wiener, Norbert, *The Human Use of Human Beings,* Doubleday, New York, 1954, 105.

42. Reik, Theodor, *The Unknown Murderer,* Hogarth, London, 1936.
43. Polsky, Samuel, *The Medico-Legal Reader,* Part II, "Law and the Mind," Oceana, New York, 1956, 32.
44. Biggs, John Jr., "Procedures for Handling the Mentally-Ill Offender in Some European Countries," Temple Law Quarterly, Vol. 29, No. 3, Spring 1956, 254-263.

    "It is apparent from a review of European legal systems that many countries are making use of scientific and humane procedures for handling the mentally-ill criminal; that this is being done without abnegation of the criminal law or chaos resulting therefrom and with no intention of changing these procedures for harsher and antiquated measures. In other words, although recognizing the handicaps of a shortage of forensic psychiatrists, insufficient equipment, and lagging public opinion, the authorities are of the view that these procedures are fundamentally sound and effective."
45. The reader is reminded that these remarks must be by necessity confined to the writer's local experience; in principle they should have some application generally to all jurisdictions.
46. *Commonwealth* v. *Bechtel,* 384 Pa. 184 (1956). Delaware County, Brief for Appellant, 10.
47. Burr, C. A., "Paranoia," Journal American Medical Assn., 45: 1852-1855, June 1907.
48. 16 Corpus Juris, Criminal Law, secs. 71, 72.
49. See Hood, Charles, *Suggestions for the Future Provision of Criminal Lunatics,* John Churchill, London, 1854, 3.

    In 1852 the Earl of Derby, ". . . commented on the anomaly of the expression 'criminal lunatic'" which he affirmed "was a contradiction of terms, inasmuch as the word 'criminal' obviously implies a knowledge of evil, while the word 'lunatic' evidently implies an utter absence of that knowledge."
50. *Leyra* v. *Denno,* 347 U.S. 556. Reversing 208 F. 2d., 605.
51. Philadelphia *Evening Bulletin,* June 8, 1955.
52. Arnold, Thurman, *The Symbols of Government,* Yale Univ. Press, 1948, 130.
53. The word *law* has a common etymological source with the word *religion.*
54. Arnold, Thurman, op. cit., 59-60.

    "A comparison of the law of today and theology of yesterday brings into startling relief the fact that once we take a rational and moral attitude toward any human institution our thinking runs along the same grooves and is complicated by the same logical and moral conflicts. These conflicts are reconciled by the same logical devices in both law and theology. . ."
55. Szasz, Thomas S., "Some Observations on the Relationship Between Psychiatry and the Law," Archives of Neurology & Psychiatry, Vol. 75: 297-315, March 1956.

NOTES   281

> "When physicians first realized that they could assuage the pain of childbirth by the administration of an anaesthetic, they were confused. They still felt that their scientific ideas should not be allowed to contradict their moral ideas and they had told themselves for a long time that the agonies of childbirth had a moral sanction. In medicine, the old philosophy went down before the obvious dictation of the natural facts, because medicine was rapidly reforming its philosophy and setting aside ideas of sin and retribution."

66. Arnold, Thurman, op. cit., 129.
67. *Ibid,* 9.
68. *Ibid,* 10-11.

> "To make clearer how conflicting rational and moral principles condition the behavior of civilized institutions, just as taboos condition the behavior of savage institutions, it may be useful to present some instances to show how rational thinking may lead us in opposite directions at the same time, and how the more elaborately rational institutions, such as our modern courts, can produce completely irrational results.
>
> "Over ten years ago a criminal was convicted of murder in the State of New York. Shortly before he was to hang he got into that state of mind which is commonly called insanity, scientifically described as a psychosis, and legally defined as the inability to determine right from wrong. It was clear that this made it morally, logically, and legally impossible to hang him because he could not know what he was being hanged for. Thus, it could not be a lesson to him. It would be as illogical as hanging an animal—as inhumanitarian as punishing a sick person, a step back to the dark ages when people were punished because they were insane—it would be immoral and contrary to principle. Superficial principles of efficiency might indicate hanging him to get rid of him, but second thought indicates that efficiency which does not promote morality is not really efficient, since morality is always the best policy. Therefore he must not hang."

69. Roche, Philip Q., Chapter 8: "Criminal Responsibility," *Psychiatry and the Law,* edited by Paul H. Hoch & Joseph Zubin, Grune Stratton, New York, 1955, 108.
70. Carroll, Lewis, *Alice's Adventures in Wonderland, etc.,* Modern Library, New York, 83.
71. Murray, Margaret A., *Witchcraft,* Encyclopaedia Britannica (1956), 23: 686.
72. Horace, Sat. 3, Book ii, l. 134 *et seq.* After Hood, W. Charles, *Suggestions for the Future Provision of Criminal Lunatics,* John Churchill, London, 1854, 153.
73. See Burrell, David M., "Willful and Wanton Misconduct—An Essay in Legal Semantics," ETC., vii, No. 4, Summer 1950.

74. Robinson, Edward S., *op. cit.*, 230.
"Among those who are not so naive as to hold that all lawyers are consciously deceptive, the point is often made that the law is at any rate stubbornly conservative. Legal fictions are condemned because they are said to be an aid in holding to the past at times when the past should be frankly left behind. This contention has a degree of justification. The persistence of the word "intent" in complex social problems where conscious intent is either irrelevant or indeterminable probably retards legal progress. The cloudy ethical atmosphere that hovers about this term tends to make difficult the introduction of psychological, psychiatric, economic, and sociological factors which ought to dominate in the composition of social conflicts."

75. After Wechsler, Herbert & Michael, Jerome, "A Rationale of the Law of Homicide," Columbia Law Review, Vol. 37, Nos. 5 & 8, May & Dec. 1937, 711.

76. Cited by Davidson, Henry A., *Forensic Psychiatry*, Ronald Press, New York, 1952, 18-19.

77. Freeman, Lucy, *Before I Kill More*, Crown, New York, 1955.

78. Reiwald, Paul, *op. cit.*, 166-70.

79. Biggs, John, Jr., *The Guilty Mind*, Harcourt, Brace, New York, 1955, 101-102.

80. *Ibid*, 103.

81. Overholser, Winfred, *The Psychiatrist and the Law*, Harcourt, Brace, New York, 1953, 42.

82. Keedy, E. R., "Irresistible Impulse as a Defense in the Criminal Law," University of Pennsylvania Law Review, 100: 956-993, May 1952.

83. GAP Report No. 26, "Criminal Responsibility and Psychiatric Expert Testimony," Topeka, Kansas, May 1954, 3.

84. Biggs, John, Jr., *op. cit.*, 107-108.

85. Weihofen, Henry, *Insanity as a Defense in Criminal Law*, Commonwealth Fund, New York, 1933, 43-44.

86. Weihofen, Henry, *The Urge to Punish*, Farrar, Straus, Cudahy, New York, 1956, 64-65.
Weihofen refers to the ambiguity of the word "wrong" and to the effort of the American Law Institute proposed Model Code to resolve it by substituting the term "criminality." "Strangely enough, although one hundred twelve years have elapsed since the M'Naghten formula was laid down, and although it has been adopted as law in hundreds of cases, there is still no consensus as to just what 'wrong' means, as used in the test. Specifically, does it mean morally wrong or contrary to law?"

87. Szasz, Thomas S., "Malingering: 'Diagnosis' or Social Condemnation?" Archives of Neurology and Psychiatry, 76: 432, No. 4, Oct. 1956.
Szasz comments on the confusion among psychiatrists and psy-

choanalysts who speak of "malingering" (faking) as if it were a diagnosis on equal footing with such concepts as hysteria, neurosis or schizophrenia. He maintains that ". . . this is a logically unsupportable position, for it ignores (or denies) what is probably the most important element in the meaning of this word, namely, that it is applied to a bit of behavior which society, and presumably the psychiatrist himself, regards as morally despicable." "Malingering" is heavy with moral condemnation, and its viability in psychiatry can be accounted for only on the fact that ". . . its implications must be persistently overlooked or ignored, for otherwise this word would long ago have been dropped from the psychiatric 'diagnostic' vocabulary (as have concepts like 'demoniacal possession' or 'falling sickness,' which have now only historical significance) . . . malingering is so heavily impregnated with the moral condemnation of behavior to which it is applied that its usefulness as a scientific diagnostic term is completely vitiated."

88. Diamond, Bernard L., "The Simulation of Sanity," Journal of Social Therapy, Vol. 2, No. 3, Third Quarter, 1956, 158-165.

"Since biblical times people have feared that criminals would escape punishment by malingering of insanity. Yet in actual fact malingered insanity is very uncommon. Much more prevalent is the simulation of sanity—the concealment of delusional systems and other psychopathology even in the face of the death penalty . . ."

89. Roche, Philip Q., "Criminality and Mental Illness—Two Faces of the Same Coin," University of Chicago Law Review, Vol. 22, No. 2, Winter 1955, 322.
90. *United States ex rel. Smith v. Baldi*, 192 F. 2d, 540, 563 (C.A. 3, 1951).
91. *Ibid*, 566.
92. *Ibid*, 566, n. 55.
93. *Ibid*, 563.
94. *Ibid.*, 565.
95. "Habeas Corpus—Due Process in the Determination of an Issue of Insanity in Pennsylvania," Pennsylvania Law Review, 100: 588-594, Jan. 1952.
96. GAP Report No. 26, *op. cit.*, 5.
97. See Ellison and Haas, "A Recent Judicial Interpretation of the M'Naghten Rule," 4 British Journal of Delinquency, 129 (Oct. 1953).
98. See Zilboorg, Gregory, *American Psychiatry 1844–1944*, "Legal Aspects of Psychiatry," The American Psychiatric Association, Columbia University Press, New York, 1944, 567.

Ray, Isaac, *Medical Jurisprudence*, 4th ed., 46-47.

99. *State v. Pike,* 49 N.H. 399, 440 (1869). Reik, Louis E., "The Doe-Ray Correspondence: A Pioneered Collaboration in the Jurisprudence of Mental Disease," Yale Law Journal, Vol. 63, Nov. 1953, 183-192.

"The predicament is one which cannot be prolonged after it is realized. If the tests of insanity are matters of law, the practice of allowing experts to testify what they are, should be discontinued; if they are matters of fact, the judge should no longer testify without being sworn as a witness and showing himself qualified to testify as an expert."

100. Weihofen, Henry, *Insanity as a Defense in Criminal Law*, Commonwealth Fund, New York, 1933, 83.

Weihofen meets the objection to the New Hampshire rule which leaves the question of mental illness as a matter of fact for jury decision: ". . . the present practice, of giving the jury long and involved instructions on the subject of responsibility, in effect often comes to the same thing: the jury unable to understand these long instructions, simply disregard them entirely and settle the question of whether the defendant was 'crazy' or not upon 'horse sense.' "

101. Reik, Louis E., *op. cit.*, 189.
102. MacNiven, Angus, "Psychoses and Criminal Responsibility," edited by Radzinowicz, I. & Turner, J. W. C., *Mental Abnormality and Crime*, Macmillan, London, 1944, 57.
103. Alexander, Leo, "The Commitment and Suicide of King Ludwig II of Bavaria," American Journal of Psychiatry, Vol. 103, 106-7, Aug. 1954.
104. Davidson, Henry A., *op. cit.*, 19.
105. *Ibid*, 19.
106. See Arnold, Thurman, *op. cit.*, 139.
107. Szasz, Thomas S., "Some Observations on the Relationship Between Psychiatry and the Law," Archives of Neurology and Psychiatry, Vol. 75, 1-19, March 1956.
108. Hood, W. Charles, *Suggestions for the Future Provision of Criminal Lunatics*, John Churchill, London, 1854, 124.

". . . and how, when this plea of insanity is raised, can we unveil the mind of the accused, and determine where responsibility ends and irresponsibility begins? There is no physician, however conversant he may be with the phenomena of the disease, that can draw this line of demarcation. We may, it is true, be put into the witness box—but what then?

"May it please your excellency, your thief looks
Exactly like the rest, or rather better;
'Tis only at the bar and in the dungeon
That wise men know your felon by his features."
(Werner, Act II, Scene 1)

"We may appreciate outward and visible signs; but we have no *mentometer* (if I may be allowed to coin a word) which will indicate the thoughts that may be passing through the mind."

109. Holmes, Oliver Wendell, ". . . justice required that each man get his desserts and have his *needs* fulfilled."
110. Gehman, Richard, *A Murder in Paradise*, Signet, New York, 1956.

111. *Ibid*, 94.
112. *Ibid*, 95.
113. *Ibid*, 90.
114. *Ibid*, 149-50. Testimony of Dr. Eleanor Ross quoted by Gehman.
115. *Ibid*, 137-38.
116. *Ibid*, 138.
117. *Ibid*, 155-56.
118. *Ibid*, 158.
119. *Ibid*, 90-1.
120. *Ibid*, 170.
121. *Ibid*, 186.
122. *Ibid*, 185.
123. *Ibid*, 189.
124. *Ibid*, 179.
125. *Ibid*, 179.
126. *Ibid*, 67-69.
127. Menninger, Karl & Mayman, Martin, "Episodic Dyscontrol: A Third Order of Stress Adaptation," Bulletin of the Menninger Clinic, Vol. 20, No. 4, July 1956, 153-165.
128. *Ibid*, 156-57.
129. Gehman, Richard, *op. cit.*, 179.
130. Philadelphia *Evening Bulletin*, November 21, 1956: "SLAYER DIES AFTER TAKING RAT POISON; Realty Man's Killer Also Had Slashed Wrists After Holdup; Rat poison and slashed wrists last night ended the brief criminal career of robber-slayer, Edward H. Maddox, 21. Maddox, confessed murderer of 75-year-old Joseph Langman, took the poison and cut his wrists while hiding from police in a factory building at 3300 Frankford Ave. He died at 9:45 p.m. in the Philadelphia General Hospital . . . He was taken to Hahnemann Hospital, but police said it was too late for a stomach pump to help, and he was transferred to Philadelphia General Hospital, where every effort was made to *keep him alive to stand trial.*"
131. Robinson, Edward S., *op. cit.*, 15.
132. Butterfield, H. after De Santillana, G., *The Crime of Galileo,* University of Chicago Press, Chicago, Illinois, 1955, 2.
133. *Commonwealth of Pennsylvania* v. *Francis X. Ballem*, Ct. Oyer & Term. & Q. S. of Delaware County, June Sessions, 1954, No. 482.
134. *Ibid*, N. T., 1560-1.
135. *Ibid*, N. T., 1562-3.
136. *Ibid*, N. T., 1564.
137. *Sayres* v. *Commonwealth,* 88 Pa. 291 (1879).
138. Personal communication of Albert M. Biele, M.D.
139. Penna. Mental Health Act of 1951, 50 Purdon, Sec. 1072 (11), as amended 1952, P.L. (1951) 2053, Sec. 102 (11).
140. *Commonwealth* v. *Ballem, op. cit.,* N. T., 2264.

141. After Zilboorg, Gregory, *op. cit.*, 567.
142. *Commonwealth* v. *Ballem, op. cit.*, N. T., 2269.
143. *Ibid*, N. T., 2439.
144. *Ibid*, N. T., 2478.
145. *Ibid*, N. T., 2489.
146. *Sayres* v. *Commonwealth*, 88 Pa. 291 (1879).
147. *Commonwealth* v. *Ballem, op. cit.*, N. T., 2498.
148. *Ibid*, N. T., 2500.
149. *Ibid*, N. T., 2501.
150. Penna. Mental Health Act of 1951. 50 Purdon, Sec. 1224, as amended 1956, P.L. (1955), 1897, Sec. 1.
151. *Commonwealth* v. *Patskin*, 375 Pa. 368, 375-376 (1953). *Commonwealth* v. *Gossard*, 385 Pa. 312, 321 (1956).
152. *Commonwealth* v. *Moon*, 383 Pa. 18 (1955).
153. *Commonwealth* v. *Moon*, 386 Pa. 205 (1956). Dissenting opinion of Mr. Justice Musmanno.
154. Otto, Max, *Science and the Moral Life*, Mentor Books, New American Library, New York, 1949, 181.
155. Bacon, Francis, *Novum Organum*, Book I, xli. *Selected Writings of Francis Bacon*, Modern Library, New York, 1955.
156. *Ibid*, I, xlii.
157. *Ibid*, I, xliii.
158. *Ibid*, I, xliv.
159. Menninger, Karl, *The Human Mind*, Knopf, New York, 1953, 7-8.
160. *Ibid*, 9.

    Menninger refers to these Idols as the evolution of the devil. The devil's metamorphosis in still more recent times has appeared in the name of *feeble mindedness* and also of *human nature*, and currently is cloaked in the fallacy under the label of *insanity*. Menninger concludes: "Calling people witches, or devils or psychopathic personalities doesn't help. To do so doesn't indicate any real understanding of why they are and what they are, why they do what they do or what can be done to help matters. If any names are to be called they ought to be names which imply something as to treatment."

161. White, William A., *Insanity and Criminal Law*, Macmillan, New York, 1923, 89.

    "In the law responsibility is dealt with just like crime and insanity, as having some kind of a nebulous, separate existence. The criminal is either supposed to have it or not to have it, much as if he might or might not be possessed of certain real estate, or some other equally tangible asset . . . To conceive that an individual is either absolutely responsible or absolutely irresponsible is to fly in the face of perfectly patent facts that are in everybody's individual experience and is only comparable to such beliefs of

NOTES

the Middle Ages that a person is possessed of a devil . . . and therefore is or is not a free moral agent."
162. Mercier, Charles, *Criminal Responsibility*, Physicians & Surgeons, New York, 1926, 41.
163. MacDonald, J. E., "The Concept of Responsibility," Journal of Mental Science, 101: 704-717, July 1955.
164. Report of Royal Commission on Capital Punishment, 1949-53, 285-87.
165. Weihofen, Henry, *The Urge to Punish*, 34.
166. *Ibid*, 34.
167. *Ibid*, 35.
". . . Unfortunately, when we try to lay down a pat and simple rule to cover complex and varying situations, we wind up with either (1) a rule that is too rigid and which we find we have to circumvent by fictions, by spurious interpretations, by administrative dodges or by open or covert violation; or (2) a rule that is so general and indefinite that it actually says nothing—like 'a person is not negligent if he exercises due care.' "
168. *Ibid*, 35, 37, 38.
169. Gasset, José Ortega y, *The Revolt of the Masses*, New American Library, New York, 1950, 96.
170. Weihofen, Henry, *op. cit.*, 54-55.
171. The Report of the Royal Commission on Capital Punishment, *op. cit.*, 116.
172. American Law Institute, Proceeding of the 32nd Annual Meeting, May 18-21, 1955, 206.
173. Circular Letter No. 225, Group for the Advancement of Psychiatry reports the tabulation and preliminary impressions gained from a questionnaire on capital punishment, distributed to the membership of GAP, comprising 150 members of whom 86 made returns. From this sampling of North American psychiatry the Committee on Psychiatry and Law was able to develop general conclusions of which several follow: (1) Only a few psychiatrists have an established competence in dealing with criminal matters; (2) American Courts assume that any psychiatrist is qualified to testify affecting the disposition of an offender. A clearly defined and accepted standard of expertness is wanting; (3) Psychiatrists avoid giving testimony in criminal cases; (4) The psychiatric profession is in need of better definition of the actual role of the psychiatrist in the trial. (GAP Report No. 26, May 1954, 6.)
See Manfred S. Guttmacher, "The Quest for a Test of Criminal Responsibility," American Journal of Psychiatry, Vol. 111, No. 6, 430, in which only 12% of psychiatrists polled expressed satisfaction with the M'Naghten Rule: Also his article, "Why Psychiatrists Do Not Like to Testify in Court," The Practical Lawyer, Vol. 1, No. 5, 51, in which he states that 10% of psychiatrists

refuse all courtroom employment and 20% testify only if appointed by the Court; also his article, "The Psychiatrist vs. Expert Witness," University of Chicago Law Review, Vol. 22, No. 2, 325, in which he cites from polls the overwhelming rejection of the M'Naghten Rule by the membership of the American Psychiatric Association.
174. Wertham, Fredric, *Social Meaning of Legal Concepts, Criminal Guilt*, No. 2, N. Y. U. School of Law, 1950, 155-156.
175. *Durham v. United States*, 214 F. 2nd 862 (D.C. Cir. 1954).
176. Biggs, John, Jr., *op. cit.*, 160.
177. *Ibid*, 160.
178. Weihofen, Henry, op. cit., 63.
179. Roche, Philip Q., *op. cit.*, 112.
180. Weihofen, Henry, *op. cit.*, 64.
181. *Ibid*, 65.
182. *Ibid*, 85.
183. *Ibid*, 67.
184. See French, Thomas M., *The Integration of Behavior*, University of Chicago Press, 1952, Vol. I, 55.
185. Keedy, Edwin R., op. cit.
186. Locard, Edmond, "La défense contre le crime," Medicine 50, numéro spécial, supplément au numéro 13, Lyon, 1950, 77-8.
 "As one can commit a slip of the tongue or a pen slip, one can commit a criminal act in a completely involuntary manner."
187. See Wolfgang, Marvin E., "Husband-Wife Homicide," Journal of Social Therapy, 2: 263-271, No. 4, 1956.
188. Barnes, "A Century of the M'Naghten Rules," 8 Cambridge Law Journal, 300-321, 1944. After Keedy, Edwin R., op. cit., 965.
189. Wertham, Fredric, "Psychoauthoritarianism and the Law," 22 University of Chicago Law Review, 336-337, 1955.
190. Hall, Jerome, "Psychiatry and Criminal Responsibility," Yale Law Journal, No. 6, Vol. 65, May 1956, 777.
191. Hall, Jerome, "Mental Disease and Criminal Responsibility," Columbia Law Review, 45: 677-718, Sept. 1945.
192. See Guttmacher, M. S. & Weihofen, Henry, *Psychiatry and the Law*, W. W. Norton, New York, 1952, 98-99.
193. Maudsley, Henry, *Responsibility in Mental Disease*, Appleton, New York, 1874, 133.
194. Wertham, Fredric, *Show of Violence*, Doubleday, Doran, Garden City, N. Y., 1949, 13-19.
195. Wertham, Fredric, *Dark Legend: A Study of Murder*, Duell Sloane & Pearce, New York, 1941, 225.
196. After Hayakawa, S. I., *Language, Meaning and Maturity*, Harper, N. Y., 1954, 198.
197. *Ibid*, 199.
198. *Ibid*, 205.

199. *Durham* v. *United States, op. cit.*, 862.
200. *State* v. *Pike*, 49 N.H. 399.
201. See MacNiven, Angus, *op. cit.*, 50.
202. After Custance, John, *Wisdom, Madness and Folly*, Pellegrini, Cudahy, New York, 1952, 121.
203. Roche, Philip Q., "Criminality and Mental Illness—Two Faces of the Same Coin," Univ. of Chicago Law Review, 22: 320-324, Winter, 1955.
204. *Ibid*, 323.
205. Roche, Philip Q., "The Family Problem of the Convicted Offender," Philadelphia Medicine, 40: 1105, 1945.
206. Deutsch, Albert, *The Trouble with Cops*, Crown Publishers, Inc., N. Y., 1955, 53-54.
 "Only a fraction of the reported crimes are ever solved, even in towns with relatively good police departments . . . it is estimated that more than 3,500,000 known criminals are on the loose in this country. The latest FBI statistics show that more than 2,000,000 major crimes were committed in 1954. . . . The extent of ill-recorded or deliberately faked crime reports in many of our cities and towns is astounding. If all crimes were properly reported to and by the police, the number now officially listed in national statistics undoubtedly would increase greatly in most categories. . . . Further and equally startling, recent FBI figures indicate that of the burglaries and robberies known and reported by the police, *less than one-third* result in arrests—and fewer than half of the suspects are convicted. There's no doubt about it: an enormous number of crimes go unreported, unrecorded, unpunished and unsolved."
207. See Shaw, G. B., *The Crime of Imprisonment*, Philosophical Library, N. Y., 1946, 109.
208. Whitehead, Alfred N., *Science and the Modern World*, New American Library, N. Y., 1949, 48-49.
209. Otto, Max, op. cit., 180.
210. See Weihofen Henry, "Eliminating the Battle of Experts," National Probation and Parole Assn. Jour., 1: 105-112, Oct. 1955; and Guttmacher, M. S. & Weihofen, Henry, op. cit., Chapter 11.
211. Zilboorg, Gregory, "The Reciprocal Responsibilities of Law and Psychiatry," The Shingle, 12: 79-96, April 1949, Philadelphia.
212. *Anderson* v. *Grasberg*, 78 N.W. 2d., 450-463 (1956).
213. See Schiele, Burtrem C. & Paulsen, Monrad, "The Minnesota Supreme Court Employs the Durham Test," (Forensic Notes) American Journal of Psychiatry, 113: 559-60, Dec. 1956.
214. The Virgin Islands Code contains provisions abrogating the M'Naghten Rule, as follows:
 If the defense is the mental illness of the defendant, the jury shall be instructed, if they find him not guilty on that ground,

to state that fact in their verdict, and the court shall thereupon commit the defendant to a suitable public institution for custody, care and treatment from which he shall not be discharged until the court is satisfied that he has regained his capacity for judgment, discretion and control of the conduct of his affairs and social relations. 5 V.I. Code, sec. 3637.

All persons are capable of committing crimes or offenses except— (4) Persons who are mentally ill and who committed the act charged against them in consequence of such mental illness; and . . ." 14 V.I. Code, Sec. 14.

215. Reik, Louis E., *op. cit.*, 181-196.
216. *Ibid*, 191-192. Justice Doe's Letter of July 22, 1868.
217. See Sobeloff, Simon E., "Insanity and the Criminal Law: From Mc-Naghten to Durham, and Beyond," American Bar Assn. Jour., Vol. 41, No. 9, Sept. 1955, 796.
218. Wechsler, Herbert, "Criteria of Criminal Responsibility," University of Chicago Law Review, 22: 367-368, 1955.
219. Cavanaugh, John R., "A Psychiatrist Looks at the Durham Decision," Catholic University of America Law Review, 5: 25-54, Jan. 1955.
220. Statistics furnished by Mr. Marques, Administrative Assistant to Judge Laws, on October 5, 1956, United States District Court (District of Columbia).
221. Monte W. Durham v. United States of America, 214 F. 2nd 862 (1954).
222. Comfort, Alex, *Authority and Delinquency in the Modern State*, Routledge & Kegan Paul, London, 1950, x.

"More important perhaps is the growing awareness that, great as is the nuisance-value of the criminal in urban society, the centralized pattern of government is today dependent for its continued function upon a supply of individuals whose personalities and attitudes in no way differ from those of admitted psychopathic delinquents. Society, so far from penalizing antisocial behavior *per se,* selects the forms, often indistinguishable, which it will punish, and the forms which it must foster by virtue of its pattern. The egocentric psychopath who swindles in the financial field is punishable—if his activities are political, he enjoys immunity and esteem, and may take part in the determination of laws. In spite, therefore, of the extent and seriousness of delinquency as a social problem, its most serious aspect for humanity today is the prevalence of delinquent action by persons immune from censure, and by established governments."

223. Arnold, Thurman, op. cit., 148.
224. Weihofen, Henry, *op. cit.*, 89.
225. See Warren, Paul, *Next Time is for Life*, Dell, New York, 1953, 95.

In the author's own firsthand experience with a large group of felons both sane and insane, he did not come upon a single instance in which a prisoner could supply a rational "explanation" of what *caused* him to commit his crime. The prisoner generally accepted the explanation offered by his prosecutor. A killer killed *because* he was vicious and filled with malice, etc.; he burgled or robbed *because* he wished to obtain money. All of the prisoners admitted that what they had done didn't make sense. Their killings gained them nothing except suffering. Their earnings were trifling in terms of the efforts and risks involved. At best, they admitted they could not supply answers. We were left to the conclusion that something else, some inner element had *caused* them to commit crime. Many expressed the thought that some undefined state of mind gave impetus to their acts. In afterthought many said, "I must have been bugs (crazy) to do what I did."

We get a glimpse of these remote *causes* from Paul Warren's *Next Time is for Life*.

"I had tried in desperation to come up with a reason that would sound logical to counter this plan. I guess I must have been figuring that if I had to go back to prison I might as well have the fun of stealing again. I don't know if that makes any sense to you; it doesn't quite to me. But I understood my feelings even though I didn't quite realize what they meant . . . I felt as I have felt so many times just before breaking into a house, the awful sickening fear and the anticipation of that sudden calm that would come after the deed. Would it come now? How would it come?"

226. *Ibid*, 101.

". . . Sometimes I stood for as long as an hour outside a house, trembling, perspiring, jumping at the slightest noise before daring to step in a window I had pried open. But if the panic was greater, so was the kick. I can't really describe this feeling exactly and everything I have said about it before doesn't really convey it all because it was nothing I had ever experienced before. Playing hide and seek with servants in halls, knowing that one false step would be the end, creeping from room to room in the gloom of night, listening to the sounds of breathing as my victims slept. Those feelings that began where terror left off were of such intensity that for seconds they would leave me limp. They were so satisfying, it was worth all the delirium that had gone before. I had never before, in anything I had done, felt such magnificent control of myself."

227. *United States* v. *Smith*, 5 U.S. C.M.A., 314, 324, 17 C.M.R., 314, 324 (1954).
228. Weihofen, Henry, op. cit., 93.
229. *Ibid*, 94.
230. Board, Richard G., "An Operational Concept of Criminal Re-

sponsibility," American Journal of Psychiatry, Vol. 113, No. 4, Oct. 1956, 333.
231. *Wright v. United States,* 250 F. 2d, 4 (1957).
232. *Ibid.,* p. 14.
233. *Commonwealth v. Madara,* Ct. Oyer & Term. & Q.S. of Philadelphia County, March Term 1956, Nos. 496, 497, 498.
234. Durham v. United States, op. cit.
235. Boardman v. Woodman, 47 N.H. 120 (1866).
236. 49 N.H. 399 (1869).
237. After Weihofen, Henry, *Insanity as a Defense in Criminal Law,* 80.
238. 50 N.H. 369 (1871).
239. Weihofen, Henry, *The Urge to Punish,* Notes, 173.
240. See Roche, Philip Q., *op. cit.,* 113.
241. *Ibid,* 114.
242. Glueck, Sheldon, *Crime and Justice,* Little Brown, Boston, 1936. Chapter VIII, "The Horizon of Justice," 248-280.
243. Weihofen, Henry, *Insanity as a Defense in Criminal Law,* 429-30. After Wilbur, "Should Insanity Defense to Criminal Charge be Abolished?" 8 American Bar Assn. Jour., 631-633, 1922.
244. The idea of abandoning the defense of insanity is not new. The Legislature of the State of Washington passed such a bill in 1909. It was promptly held unconstitutional by the Supreme Court of the State. A similar proposal was offered by the New York State Bar Association in 1910 but withdrawn in 1911. Mississippi enacted such a proposal in 1928 but it was held unconstitutional. It remains to be determined if nearly a half a century will have brought to our highest tribunals a more sympathetic hearing for such proposals.
245. See West's Annotated California Codes, Penal Code, tit. 6 #1026.

INDEX

Acting out: 28
"Adherences subjective": 8
Adjustment: 21, 236
Alexander, Leo: 104
Alloplastic resolutions: 28, 85
American Law Institute: Criminal Law Advisory Committee, 176, 178; Model Penal Code, 177, 180, 195, 258
American Psychiatric Association: ix, 250
Aquinas, Thomas: 84, 139
Aristotle: 10; his criterion of good drama, 104
Arnold, Thurman: 64, 79, 258
Augustine, St.: 262
Autoplastic resolutions: 29, 85

Bacon, Francis: 168
Ballem, Francis X.: 134-68; 245, 248, 268
Bateson, Gregory: 13
Bazelon, Judge David L.: 250
Behavior: infantile genesis of, 28; class and field theoretical concepts of, 13, 75, 244
Biggs, Judge John, Jr.: 90, 91, 96, 178
Blackstone: 160
Board, Richard G.: 266
Bradford, Judge John: 27
Breasted, James H.: 1
Bridgman, P. W.: 15
Burr, Charles A.: 36
Busser, Ralph C.: 230

"Care": as operational meaning of mental illness, 254, 256-57
Cambridge Law Review: 185
Carter Decision: 267
Causality: deterministic, 10-11; purposive, 10-11; in language of psychiatry, 11; systems of, 13; in law, 259-60, 262-63, 266, 270
"Character disorder": 257
Child-rearing: 68, 87-89, 101, 157, 193
Cleric, The: case of, 42-63
Cohen, Felix S.: 194
Coke, Sir Edward: 161
Coleridge, Lord Chief Justice: 114
College Student, The: 33-42
Commonwealth v. James Ernest Monroe: 92
Commonwealth v. Edward Lester Gibbs: 114
Commonwealth v. Francis X. Ballem: 134
Commonwealth v. William Conquest: 196
Communication: as model of psychiatry, 13, 23

Conflict: linked to infantile experience: 26-27; alloplastic resolution, 29; autoplastic resolution, 29
Conquest, William: 196-241
Conscience: as variable, 66
Consciousness: loss of in impulsive acts, 129
"Constitutional Psychopathic Inferior": 147, 158
Crime: "subjective element" in, 251; caused by "disease," 265; caused by free will, 265
Criminal: and purposeful cause, 10-11; in public centered operation, 17; as object of contagion, 67; avoidance and isolation of, 67, 69-70; as abstraction, 68; as symbol of forbidden wish, 69
Criminal Justice: articulates religious meaning, 92; symbols of, 171
Criminal Law: symbiosis with psychiatry, 3; pre-trial phase, 30-63; trial phase, 64-195; post-trial phase, 197-244
"Criminal Tendency": 34, 39; defined, 37
Criminal Trial: 65-67; function of, 67; as public drama, 67; as game, 70-82, 106, 135; as obsessive-compulsive ritual, 70; as symbolic of social unity, 71; as repetition of crime, 71; ludic element in, 72-77; chance and fate in, 72; as *agon*, 73; adversary aspect of, 73; audience of, 74; preferential status of press in, 75; "readers interest" in, 75; as "entertainment," 78; as moral lesson, 79; as secularized religious formula, 79, 101; as ritual ordeal, 80; as "adjustment" of law abiding, 245; as exorcism, 257
Criminality: as mental illness, 20, 29; separation from mental illness, 29; in commercial fantasy, 71; in folklore and fairy tales, 71; "subjective element" in, 82-91, 251; "emotionally satisfactory," 89; rationalization similar to dream work, 109; as communication, 237

Dark Legend: 191-92
Davidson, Henry A.: 105
Definition: circular, 11; operational, 15-16; of "similarity," 17; of mental illness, 19; of normality, 22; verbal, 263
Demoniacal possession: 10, 38, 68, 84, 149
Demons: 238
Descartes, René: 12
Deterministic necessity: 10
Devil: creation and exorcism of, 5; and the unconscious, 6
"Disease and defect": 251-53
District of Columbia: 177
Doe, Justice Charles: 113, 250-51
Durham Decision: 109, 177, 186, 195, 249, 251, 256, 258, 260, 264-66, 268, 270; "disease and defect," 251-53; psychopath in, 258; "product" concept of, 259
"Dyscontrol, episodic": 129

Eastern State Penitentiary: x, 198
Ego: of neonate, 26; as internal "feedback," 26; in "episodic dyscontrol," 129

"Elbow Test": 183-84
Entropy: 8
Erskine, Lord John: 86
Evans, Bergen: 6
Exhibitionism: 183

Farview State Hospital: 199, 213, 229, 231, 236
Field-Theoretical Concept of Behavior: 75, 245
Fire setters: 183
Fisher, Charles: 76
Fraud: 251, 270
Frazer, Sir James G.: 1
Free Will: 12, 23, 84, 193
Freud, Sigmund: 8-9, 109
Fromm, Erich: 21-22

Galeanthropy: 7
Gasset, José Ortega y: 175
Gehman, Richard: 114, 118, 125
Gibbs, Edward Lester: 114-34, 180, 192, 248
Glueck, Sheldon: 175, 274
Goodwin, John C.: 14
Group for the Advancement of Psychiatry: 91
Guilt: 139, 193, 223; legal, 31, 111; unconscious, 111; criminal, 177
Guilty Mind, The: 91, 96

Hadfield, James: 89, 109, 267
Hall, Jerome: 96, 186, 249
Heirens, William: 88
"Homicidal Mania": 155, 158
Hoover, J. Edgar: 242

Horace: 82
"Hot Blood": 270
Huizinga, J.: 72, 157
Hypnosis: in pre-trial examination, 40-41

Identification: of triers with accused, 105-6; unconscious, 105-6; with criminal, 149
Idols: 169-70; of justice, 192
Incapacity: 38
"Insaniens": 14
Insanity: meaning of, 14-16; moral, 152; tests of in Pennsylvania, 152, 156; "general," 152, 158; "partial," 153-54, 156, 158; feigning of, 162, 166-67; impulsive, 168
Instruction: 173
Intent: 11, 80, 82-91, 138, 187, 193, 245, 270
"Irresistible Impulse": 179, 182-92, 195; allied with slips and mistakes, 183; as transaction, 184
Isaac Ray Award: ix, 171

Jack the Giant Killer: 71
James, William: 238
Johnson, Wendell: 17
Judges of England: 102
Jurisprudence: as "science of arbitrary human relations," 4; as extension of child-rearing, 66; similarity to unconscious operations, 66; as "transcendental nonsense," 194
Justice: internal tribunal of, 247

Keedy, Edwin R.: 91, 182
Keyes, Baldwin L.: 122
"Knowledge": 167, 187, 193, 250, 260, 261; and unlawful conduct, 12; method of acquiring, 12, 81, 86, 89; legal concept no criterion of normality, 22; determination by psychiatrist, 109-11; inductive and deductive, 111, 193

Ladd, Judge William Spencer: 270
Language: archaic, 138
Lerner, Max: 176
Leyra v. Denno: 40
"Living Out": 28
Llewellyn, Karl N.: 157
Ludic Element: 72, 141

MacDonald, J. E.: 170
M'Naghten, Daniel: 90, 102
M'Naghten Rule: 38, 39, 75, 89, 90, 91, 97, 99, 101-3, 107-8, 112-13, 117, 120-21, 143-44, 167, 172-81, 185-86, 195, 248-52, 258, 260, 266, 269-70; English and Scottish procedures in, 175; abandoned in Virgin Islands, 250; break with in Minnesota, 250; abandoned in District of Columbia, 250; directed only to jury, 269
MacNiven, Angus: 104
Magic: persistence in modern times, 6; in psychotherapy, 9; in ancestral projection system, 20; unconscious dominance of, 24; in mental life of wrongdoers, 54; in projection onto criminals, 67-68
Malice: 11, 80, 138, 187, 193, 238

Mana: 169
Mania: homicidal, 155, 158
Mass Communication: effect on mental health, 20
Maudsley, Henry: 188-89
Mayman, Martin: 128-29
Medical insanity: 15
Medical Jurisprudence of Insanity, The: 90, 250
Mens rea: 82-91, 238
Menninger, Karl: 128-29, 170
Mental Health Act of Pennsylvania (1951): 19, 37, 62, 145, 149, 159-60, 163, 165, 167, 254; hospital commitment of persons convicted of crime, 62
Mental Hospitals: 240-43
Mental Disorder and the Criminal Law: 175
Mental Illness: among Greeks and Romans, 4-5; meaning of, 14, 16; defined, 19-20, 145, 160; as disease of culture, 21; and capacity to stand trial, 32, 61; feigned, 96, 100, 112, 270
Mercy, Prerogative of: 175
Mind: 245
Model Penal Code: 177, 180-81
Moliere: 11
Money-Kryle, R.: 23
Monroe, James Ernest: 92
Moral Instruction: 173-74
Moral Order: as obsessive compulsive warfare, 77; as undermined by psychiatry, 78
Mother Goose: 71
Murder in Paradise, A: 114

Necrophilia: 148
"Negligence": 270

New Hampshire Rule: 177-78, 269
Nomenclature: 24-25
Normality: concept of, 17; defined as "adjustment," 19; defined by Fromm, 22; psychiatric concept of, 22-23; defined by Money-Kryle, 23; defined as self-awareness, 23; explicit in "free will," 23; not defined as "knowledge," 26

"Official mistrust": 157
"Offspring": 270
Operations: public centered, 17, 32; individual centered, 17
Opinion evidence: law status in Pennsylvania, 150-51
"Original sin": 170
Otto, Max: 2, 168, 246
Overholser, Winfred: 90
Oxford Case: 90

"Product": 259-64, 270, 272; and psychic repression, 261
Psychiatric examination: as informal trial, 141
Psychiatrist: as hypnotist, 41; as object of displaced guilt, 106-7; as oracle, 269; as "diviner," 272
Psychiatry: mid 20th century setting of, 1-13; symbiosis with criminal law, 3; mistrust of, 78, 135; "on tap," 96; as advocacy, 149; administrative functions of, 271
Psychoneurosis (neurosis): 24
Psychopathic Personality: 147, 251, 259; sexual psychopath, 25; exclusion from Model Penal Code, 180; in Durham decision, 258
Psychopathology of Everyday Life: 8
Psychopathology: as disturbance of communication, 13
Psychosis: 8, 24; "unsuccessful," 240
Purposive causality: 10

Pardoning power: 175
Pavlov, Ivan P.: 192
Peel: Sir Robert: 89
Pennsylvania Law Review: 101
Pennsylvania Supreme Court: 124, 137
Phrenology: 90, 186
Piaget, Jean: 8
Plato: 88
Plea in bar of trial: 32
Premeditation: 11, 80
Pre-trial Phase: 30-63; Scottish procedure, 32; psychiatric examination as "informal trial," 33
Prison: as mental hospital, 240-43

Ray, Isaac: 90, 102, 149, 171, 250, 253, 255
Reality: magical orientation to, 59
Regression: 21
Reider, Norman: 9
Reik, Theodor: 31
Reiwald, Paul: 70
Religion: symbolism in, 246; conflict with science, 246-47, 271
Repression: 261
Responsibility: 42; in control of antisocial behavior, 4; as Idol of Theater, 169-71; as mystical essence, 170; universal, 273
Robinson, Edward S.: 4
Romans: mental illness among, 14

INDEX

Rorschach Test: 116, 133, 148
Royal Commission on Capital Punishment: 172, 174, 176
Ruesch, Jurgen: 13
Russell, Bertrand: 10, 14, 106

Sanity: feigning of, 165
Sanity Commission: 140, 166-67, 198, 268; adversary setting of examination, 33-42, 42-63, 140-41, 159-65, 166
Science: mid 20th century setting, 2; worship of, 2; doubt and certainty in, 12
Scientific instruction: 173
Self-awareness: 23, 65, 78, 113, 135, 168, 172; as scientific projection system, 2-3; as criterion of normality, 23
Self-incrimination: 112
Sex perversions: 183
Sex psychopath: as demon in modern guise, 25
Show of Violence: 190
Smith, James Colbert: 96, 111, 168, 189, 248, 254
Sobeloff, Simon E.: 251-52
"Sociopathic personality disturbance": 257
State v. Jones: 270
State v. Pike: 103, 251, 269
Stephen, Sir James: 86, 91
Stephen, Karin: 6-7
Strecker, Edward A.: 122-23
"Subjective adherences": 168, 193
"Subjective element": framed in two languages, 138-39; of crime, 251
Supreme Court of California: 274

Supreme Court of Pennsylvania: 124, 137, 152, 159, 161
Symbol: as linkage to early conflict, 62; in inner side of crime, 64
Szasz, Thomas S.: 107

Thematic Apperception Test: 147
Tindal, Judge Nicholas C.: 90
"Transcendental nonsense": 194

Unconscious: 27, 65; and concept of Devil, 5; primitive thinking, 7; and self-awareness, 24; and "free will," 24
United States Court of Military Appeals: 264
United States of America ex rel. James Colbert Smith v. Baldi: 96
Urge to Punish, The: 174

Vaihinger, H.: 4
Victoria, Queen: 90

Weihofen, Henry: 174, 176, 178, 180-81, 258, 264-65
Wertham, Fredric: 177, 186, 190-92
Weyer, Johann: 5
White, William A.: 111
Whitehead, Alfred N.: 244
Wiener, Norbert: 30, 121

Wilbur, Associate Justice: 274
Willfullness: 138
Will: 187, 193, 245
Wilson, David C.: 21
Wright Decision: 266

Young, J. Z.: 12

Zilboorg, Gregory: 5, 249